THE INSTANT ETHNIC COOK

An Herb and Spice Blend Cookbook

*Best-Loved Italian, Chinese, Mexican
and Greek recipes — and more*

MARA REID ROGERS

ILLUSTRATIONS BY MERLE NACHT

LAKE ISLE PRESS • NEW YORK

OTHER BOOKS BY MARA REID ROGERS:
Contemporary One-Dish Meals
Creative Garnishing
The International Spud

ACKNOWLEDGEMENTS
My heartfelt thanks to: Hiroko Kiiffner, who has a knack for "titles"
and for being behind this book 110%!; Jane Ross, for her "brainstorming";
Barbara Koster and Merle Nacht who made this book, art; Karen Reid,
for her meticulous assistance; Evie Righter, for her way with words;
Angela Miller, for her support — who has gone beyond the "line of duty" —
and (I can already tell) will be much more than a well-respected and fabulous
agent, but a friend; Rona L. Gindin and Kathryn A. Clark, for their research;
Samara Farber and Lisa Haft, for their help in the kitchen; and Kim Hertlein,
for her rare dedication and the passion she holds for her career.

THE INSTANT ETHNIC COOK

Published by Lake Isle Press, Inc.
2095 Broadway, New York, NY 10023
Distributed by Publishers Group West,
Emeryville, CA
1 (800) 788-3123

Book design: Barbara Koster
Illustrations : Merle Nacht

Library of Congress Catalog Card Number: 93-78928
ISBN: 0-9627403-4-9

Printed in the United States of America
First printing October 1993
10 9 8 7 6 5 4 3 2 1

This book is dedicated to forging an alliance between good food and good health.

CONTENTS

INTRODUCTION ◆ VII
About the Recipes ◆ 9
Stocking the Shortcut Pantry ◆ 10
About the Seasoning Blends and How to Use Them ◆ 11

CHAPTER 1
Crazy for Creole ◆ 13
Creole Seasoning Mix and Recipes

CHAPTER 2
Paprika, Paprika ◆ 27
Hungarian Seasoning Mix and Recipes

CHAPTER 3
Guten Appetit ◆ 39
German Seasoning Mix and Recipes

CHAPTER 4
Greece: Food for the Gods ◆ 53
Greek Seasoning Mix and Recipes

CHAPTER 5
Sunny Provence ◆ 67
Provençal Seasoning Mix and Recipes

CHAPTER 6
Mangia Bene! ◆ 83
Italian Seasoning Mix and Recipes

CHAPTER 7

Mexican Magic • 97

Mexican Seasoning Mix and Recipes

CHAPTER 8

The Spirit of Spain • 111

Spanish Seasoning Mix and Recipes

CHAPTER 9

Scandinavian Smörgåsbord • 125

Scandinavian Seasoning Mix and Recipes

CHAPTER 10

India Aromatica • 139

Indian Seasoning Mix and Recipes

CHAPTER 11

The Caribbean Beat • 153

Caribbean Seasoning Mix and Recipes

CHAPTER 12

China: Harmony in the Kitchen • 165

Chinese Seasoning Mix and Recipes

APPENDIX

*Glossary of International
Ingredients, Herbs and Spices* • 181

Source List • 186

The Kitchen Bookshelf: A Select Bibliography • 189

INDEX • 190

INTRODUCTION

MY PASSION FOR ETHNIC FOOD and my romance with herbs and spices began when I moved to New York City. My weekends were spent taking mini-journeys on foot through the different neighborhoods of Manhattan, only to discover that each area was its own little world. As I took the few steps from sleepy Little Italy into Chinatown the atmosphere abruptly changed — here, suddenly, was a place full of bright colors, noises, exotic foods and jostling crowds everywhere.

What I recall the most, though, was a tiny, dark and dusty shop I wandered into. It was cloaked in mystery: every wall was lined with minuscule wooden drawers — hundreds of them — and each held herbs and spices, some used for cookery, some for medicine and a few for both. This was the one place in Chinatown that was quiet. The mood was solemn, quite serious, as customers made their purchases and the items were carefully weighed out on a brass scale that looked centuries old, but had been polished to a brilliant sheen. Since I don't speak Chinese, I pointed and gestured my way to purchasing a few handfuls of oddly shaped aromatics, trying to look as if I knew what I was ordering.

I meandered my way back home with my treasures in little brown bags, each holding an intoxicating substance that held the promise of turning ordinary food into a culinary masterpiece. And when I put them to use I was never disappointed, whether it was "grains of paradise" from Ghana, "epazote" from Mexico, or even a few cracked black peppercorns.

I began experimenting with many different herbs and spices. I would take the seasonings most commonly used in a particular country and then try to duplicate the "flavor" of the cuisine by blending them, each in a carefully balanced amount, to make an ethnic seasoning mix. Having selected the herbs and spices to be mixed, I had to consider also their variations in strength, degrees of sweetness, hot versus cooling properties, and physical characteristics such as color, form and texture. And of course I had to anticipate how they would work when variously cooked in the presence of other ingredients, too.

Seasoning blends, comprised entirely of herbs and spices, were developed to make the art of seasoning a quick and easy task. They have been around for centuries, from the Chinese Five-Spice powder to the French *fine herbes*, to the Italian seasoning blends now found on your grocer's shelf. You'll find that the blends that I've developed for *The Instant Ethnic Cook* will extend your culinary expertise to twelve international cuisines just as easily.

These seasoning blends are the key to making some of the most popular ethnic dishes at home. They offer incredible convenience and freedom to the home chef by helping to reduce the time it takes to prepare a meal. Each seasoning blend takes just minutes to make and can be done in advance and stored for later use. In general, by using the blends, along with the shortcut cooking methods and accessible ingredients, you will be able to significantly reduce the time it would normally take to make a fabulous ethnic dish. Now a complete meal — an ethnic meal — can be on the table in less than thirty minutes, and even the more elaborate dishes in an hour — every home chef's dream.

The Instant Ethnic Cook demystifies exotic international cuisines. Ethnic food can be delicious and quickly and economically prepared, but its preparation is often intimidating to home cooks. The blends assure a tasty result, and at the same time, offer a healthy alternative to the salty, high-fat convenience foodstuffs and fast-foods many home cooks rely on today.

Of the twelve chapters in the book, each devoted to a particular region or country, including Provence, Italy, Mexico and Greece, among others, I have selected dishes that are recognized as ethnic favorites and truly representative of the cuisine, regional variations notwithstanding. Of course, regional specialties such as Bourride flavored with Aïoli (Provençal Fish Stew with Garlic-Mayonnaise) are included, too.

Imagine: You are in the mood for Italian food. Just reach for the Italian Seasoning Mix, turn to Chapter 6, "Mangia Bene!," and choose a recipe from the ten selections. You can choose from main dishes, side dishes, and a few one-dish meals. Also, many of the recipes for side dishes can do double-duty as appetizers, and when the yield is increased can serve as entrées. It is possible to make an entire ethnic meal from one ethnic mix: While the recipes share the same flavor base, each dish will vary, according to the ingredients and cooking methods used. In a few recipes, guacamole, and Spaghetti alla Carbonara, for example, I've taken the liberty of adding seasonings not called for in traditional recipes, just to add a delicious new twist.

There are also recipes for Quickies, which allow you to internationalize everyday foods, such as macaroni and cheese. These one-line recipes — adaptations — use the twelve seasoning blends and pantry staples to create dishes with instant ethnic flavor. Your macaroni and cheese can now become Creole-Roni with a shake of Creole Seasoning Mix (See page 14).

And for an even more well-rounded selection of recipes, I have included a few for those occasions when you have a bit more time to make a more elaborate dish. These recipes have been marked with a clock symbol for easy identification.

Also included are thirty international menus (one for each day of the month), complete with recommendations for beverages and desserts. Look for a list of staples to have on hand, a glossary of international ingredients and where to get them, and finally, suggestions for further reading.

Obviously, this collection of recipes is merely a sampling of what there is still to explore among the ethnic cuisines represented. In essence, I have tried to extend the home chef's repertoire by making ethnic food more "universal." I have reinterpreted international recipes by adding seasoning blends, but these improvisations can never exactly duplicate the experience of being and eating in Provence or Madrid or the Greek Isles, for that matter. However, they do capture the essence of a cuisine, albeit with a degree of culinary license, and they will inspire you to try a delectable Provençal artichoke omelette or a Mexican pork-filled burrito, just for a delicious change of pace.

I've always believed that food is much more than nourishment. It should be celebrated! To me, food is entertainment. For extra fun, play music to match the particular international theme of your menu, and set the table accordingly in style. Afterwards, linger over dessert and coffee, savoring the moment and the satisfying meal . . . what could be better!

— Mara Reid Rogers
Atlanta, GA

About the Recipes

THE RECIPES HERE respect today's nutritional guidelines. In fact, many of the traditional ethnic foods are already naturally healthful. For example, Mediterranean cuisine is mostly a high-fiber, low-cholesterol diet. And some Asian cuisines, including Chinese, steam and stir-fry foods, which help preserve the natural vitamins and minerals.

In many cases, I have used smaller amounts of meat and increased vegetables and grains, and in those cases where meat is called for, I recommend a leaner cut. Also, when appropriate, low-fat yogurt is recommended as a substitute for sour cream; skim milk for whole milk; and salt and butter have been kept to a minimum whenever possible. Though I often employ the "season to taste" rule for salt, the use of my flavorful seasoning blends replaces the need for unhealthy flavor enhancers like excess salt.

My aim in creating this collection was to keep the recipes as authentic as possible, but to make them doable for the American home cook in terms of the availability of ingredients and the consideration of time. My style of cooking is always to use ingredients that can be found in the neighborhood supermarket. I much prefer to use fresh ingredients, but I also draw on staple pantry items that bring ease without forsaking nutrition. High-quality ingredients, such as canned low-sodium broths, canned plum tomatoes and frozen vegetables like peas and spinach are excellent substitutions when time is limited.

A dividend to this ethnic mix system is that you are not limited to the recipes contained here, but can add an ethnic accent to an ordinary dish or create an altogether new one with the seasoning blends. All you have to do is substitute the herbs and spices needed in your favorite dish with a little of the blend of your choice — just season to taste!

Most of the recipes serve four (the size of the average family) comfortably. In an effort to help you plan your time, I have given you *approximate* preparation and cooking times and information on whether an entire dish or part of it can be made ahead. (NOTE: When a pre-cooked "leftover" ingredient or accompaniment is called for, it is presumed ready to use and not tallied in the preparation and cooking times specified.) Also included are serving recommendations ("Tabasco sauce to serve," for example, means it must be added for the best possible result) and garnishes, as well as cooking Tips and Hints to save additional time.

My wish is that this book will be liberating and time saving to all home cooks. No longer will you have to choose between convenience and quality when preparing your favorite ethnic foods.

Stocking the Shortcut Pantry

I SUGGEST HAVING ON HAND the following staples for many of the recipes in this book. Once you have your basic ingredients, your pantry will become a "shortcut pantry" so that you can enjoy shopping for additional fresh ingredients as you need them.

THE CUPBOARD

Baking powder

Bottled clam juice

Canned low-sodium broth: beef and chicken

Canned vegetable broth or vegetable boullion cubes

Canned crushed tomatoes

Canned peeled whole tomatoes

Canned stewed tomatoes

Canned tomato paste

Canned tomato purée

Cornstarch

Dry unseasoned bread crumbs

Honey

Oil: corn, olive, peanut, safflower and vegetable

Rice: white and brown

Salt: kosher

Sugar: dark brown, light brown and white

Unbleached white flour

Vinegar: apple-cider, red-wine and white-wine

THE REFRIGERATOR AND FREEZER

Grade A large eggs

Milk: regular (whole) and skim

Unsalted butter and/or unsalted margarine

THE SPICE RACK

(The dried herbs and spices you need to make all 12 of my international blends.)

Allspice, ground

Basil

Caraway seed

Cardamom seeds

Celery seed

Cinnamon, sticks and ground

Coriander seeds

Chile powder

Cloves, ground and whole

Cumin, ground and seeds

Dillweed

Dried French lavender flowers (organic — edible)

Fennel seeds

Ginger, ground

Mace, ground

Marjoram

Mint

Nutmeg, ground

Oregano

Paprika

Peppercorns, black and white

Poppy seed

Red (cayenne) pepper, ground

Red pepper flakes (also called "crushed red pepper")

Rosemary

Saffron threads

Sage, ground

Savory

Thyme

Turmeric, ground

THE VEGETABLE AND FRUIT BIN

Garlic

Lemons

Onions: white and yellow

Potatoes: baking and boiling

About the Seasoning Blends
and How to Use Them

THESE VERSATILE SEASONING BLENDS are easy to use and a foolproof way to make everything you cook taste wonderful. When you open a jar of these international blends, you open up a world of culinary possibilities for every day of the year. The following is a list of tips for making and using the blends.

◆ All the herbs and spices needed for my blends are available in any large, well-stocked supermarket. The only exceptions (which are available at gourmet shops or through mail order) are: edible French lavender flowers (for Provençal seasoning blend); Mexican and Greek oregano (for Mexican and Greek seasoning blends, respectively), though regular oregano from a supermarket can be used; cardamom seeds (for the Indian seasoning blend); and chile powder (ground chiles for Mexican seasoning blend) but commercial blended chili powder can be used. However, if you want to make all twelve blends at one time, it would be more economical to purchase the herbs and spices in bulk. Please see the source list.

◆ The seasoning blend recipes yield about 1/2-cup quantities that should be stored in an airtight glass jar of the same size. Only use clean, dry, airtight glass spice jars — I prefer spice jars with screw-on caps as they preserve the blends the best. Glass stoppers are the second choice and cork is the last resort. When you make a blend, label the jar with its name and the date you made it. Store the spice jars for 3 months away from heat, light or moisture.

◆ When measuring dried herbs and spices for the seasoning blends, always use a dry measuring cup — not a liquid measuring cup — and measuring spoons. Pile the herb or spice lightly into the measuring cup or dip the measuring spoon, then level it (do not pack the herb or spice down) with the dull edge of a dinner knife.

◆ To mix the herbs and spices for the blends: Combine the dried herbs and spices in a small self-sealing plastic bag. Close the seal on the plastic bag and shake the contents until well blended. Alternatively: Gently stir the contents in a small bowl until well combined.

◆ Caution: Only mix the blends in a well-ventilated area of the kitchen in 1/2-cup quantities as suggested. Inhaled dust from larger quantities of herbs and spices can act as an irritant and be harmful. The best method of making the blends is in a self-sealed bag, since the ingredients are contained.

◆ When mixing a blend that contains spices from peppers like cayenne, paprika, chile or chili powder, and red pepper flakes (also called "crushed red pepper"), avoid touching your nose and eyes. When finished making the mix, immediately wash your hands thoroughly with soap and water to get rid of irritating oils.

◆ It is best to make the blends with the freshest dried herbs and spices available. Make each as a single recipe and avoid halving or doubling the recipes. In this way, the mixes will always be at their optimal freshness and the flavor balance of the blend will not be thrown off. These ½-cup amounts will last you a while, because you only need small amounts for the recipes. Always season to taste.

◆ Check your seasoning blends periodically for freshness by smelling them. When dried herbs and spices have lost their aromas, they have also lost their flavor.

◆ When a recipe for a seasoning blend suggests a particular variety of herb or spice like "2 tablespoons paprika, preferably Hungarian sweet," the recipe means just that — preferably. The Hungarian sweet paprika would give you the most authentic flavor, but it is not essential. Regular paprika would be a fine substitute.

◆ When cooking with the blends, "crumble" the mixture between your fingers to crush the herb leaves. This helps release their flavor.

◆ To grind dried rosemary (for *Italian Seasoning Mix* recipe), I find the best piece of equipment is an electric spice grinder. Grind only what you need to help keep the seasoning fresh. When finished grinding the herb or spice, unplug the spice grinder and then wipe it clean with a dry paper towel.

◆ Before cooking with a seasoning mix, make sure that it is well blended. Shake it well to recombine the contents evenly before measuring.

◆ While a few ethnic seasoning blends are available commercially, you'll find that those you make yourself are tastier by far and will allow you more control when cooking because you know the exact contents. Most commercial blends contain salt, not to mention preservatives and MSG.

CHAPTER I

CRAZY FOR CREOLE

Creole Seasoning Mix

Shrimp Creole

Southern Dirty Rice

Stewed Okra
with Hominy

Green Beans and
Tomato with Creole
Mustard Dressing

Louisiana's Red Beans
and Rice
with Ham

Creole Corn Pudding

Stuffed Whole Crab

Chicken Gumbo

Plantation-Style
Seafood-Stuffed
Artichokes

Veal Grillades
with Grits

WELCOME TO NEW ORLEANS, the home of Creole cooking, a cuisine now rightfully called an American classic. Making full use of a wide variety of ingredients native to Louisiana — crawfish, crab, shrimp and oysters, wild game and meats, vegetables like bell peppers, scallions and sweet potatoes, sugarcane and rice — Creole cooks have created a brilliant cuisine of mixed cultural ancestry.

Much is derived from the original French settlers, however, including white *roux,* a mixture of flour and butter that is cooked, then used to thicken sauces and soups. White *roux* was modified by the Creoles to brown *roux,* made from flour and lard (I substitute vegetable oil) and cooked until light brown in color and nutty in taste. Brown *roux* is the base for some of the most famous of Creole dishes, such as Shrimp Creole (page 14). This classic also uses onion, celery and green bell pepper "the holy trinity" of Creole cooking, according to Louisiana chef Paul Prudhomme.

Using such accessible ingredients, in combination with paprika, thyme, celery seed, cayenne, cloves, mace and cinnamon, found in my seasoning blend, you can now create the flavors of other New Orleans favorites at home. Stewed Okra with Hominy (page 16), for example, is a bewitching dish that literally bathes in the flavor of tomatoes and is animated by the celery seed and cayenne of the blend.

I have also included the famous Chicken Gumbo (page 21). Classically, this soup is thickened with okra or filé powder (dried ground sassafras leaves). I chose okra for this end-all Creole dish.

Louisiana's Red Beans and Rice with Ham (page 18) is spicy and slightly hot from both the seasoning blend and Tabasco sauce. The seasoning blend adds a nice overtone of thyme that complements the starchy qualities of the beans and rice. Not only a cinch to make, but very versatile and nutritious too. Omit the ham and you have a great vegetarian main course!

QUICKIES: EVERYDAY FOODS MADE INTERNATIONAL

Creole-Roni
Season your favorite frozen macaroni and cheese entrée with *Creole Seasoning Mix* just before serving.

Deviled Chicken Salad
Add *Creole Seasoning Mix* to your favorite chicken salad whether homemade or from the deli, and add

a dash of Worcestershire sauce to taste.

Potato Skins with a Punch

Cut freshly baked potatoes in half, lengthwise. Remove the pulp (reserving it for another use), leaving potato shells about $\frac{1}{16}$-inch-thick. Brush the shells inside and out with melted butter or margarine and sprinkle the inside with some *Creole Seasoning Mix,* salt and pepper. Bake in a preheated 450° F. oven for 15 to 20 minutes, or until toasted and crisp.

Grateful for Grits

Cook packaged grits until thick and smooth, according to package directions. Stir in some shredded Cheddar cheese until melted and season to taste with *Creole Seasoning Mix.*

Workday Bliss

(Fast Menu for 4 to 6)
Shrimp Creole with Rice
Green Beans and Tomato
  with Creole Mustard
  Dressing (page 17)
Pecan Pie (bakery
  or supermarket freezer)
Café Brûlot (coffee with
  brandy and orange peel)

Creole Seasoning Mix

Makes about $\frac{1}{2}$ cup

$\frac{1}{4}$ cup paprika
2 tablespoons dried thyme leaves
2 teaspoons celery seed (available at supermarket or gourmet store)
$1\frac{1}{2}$ teaspoons ground red (cayenne) pepper
1 teaspoon ground cloves
1 teaspoon ground mace
$\frac{1}{2}$ teaspoon ground cinnamon

In a small bag or bowl (page 11), combine the paprika, thyme, celery seed, cayenne, cloves, mace and cinnamon. Shake or stir until well blended. Transfer to a clean, dry, airtight glass container. Store up to 3 months away from heat, light or moisture. Shake well before using.

Shrimp Creole

Servings: 4 to 6
Preparation Time: About 15 minutes
Cooking Time: 15 to 20 minutes

3 tablespoons vegetable oil
3 tablespoons unbleached white flour
3 cloves garlic, crushed
1 large yellow onion, finely chopped
1 medium red bell pepper, cut into $\frac{1}{4}$-inch dice
3 ribs celery, thinly sliced
1 28-ounce can crushed tomatoes
1 teaspoon *Creole Seasoning Mix*
1 pound medium-large shrimp (36 to 42 to the pound), shelled and deveined
Salt and freshly ground pepper to serve

5 cups hot cooked white or brown rice (follow package directions), to serve
Tabasco sauce, to serve

1. Heat the vegetable oil in a nonreactive deep heavy 10-inch skillet over medium heat until hot but not smoking. Stir in the flour and

cook, stirring vigorously, about 5 minutes or until the *roux* has thickened and turned an orangy-brown (similar in color to peanut butter). Be careful not to let the *roux* burn; if it does you will see tiny black specks.

2. Stir in the garlic, onion, red bell pepper, celery, crushed tomatoes and seasoning mix. Raise the heat to medium-high and bring to a boil. Reduce the heat to low, and cook, stirring occasionally, about 10 minutes or until the vegetables are tender. Stir in the shrimp, making sure that they are completely submerged, and simmer, stirring occasionally, about 5 minutes or until the shrimp turn pink and are opaque throughout. Season with salt and pepper.

3. Serve at once as a main course with hot cooked rice and pass with Tabasco sauce.

Southern Dirty Rice

Servings: 4 to 6
Preparation Time: About 5 minutes
Cooking Time: 10 to 13 minutes

The name dirty rice was given to this dish because of its dark color, resulting from the addition of chicken livers and giblets. A more modern, but still authentic, rendition uses ground meats in place of the livers and giblets for a truly unique Creole dish.

1 teaspoon vegetable oil
1 medium yellow onion, finely chopped
3 ribs celery, very thinly sliced
4 ounces extra-lean ground beef
4 ounces lean ground pork
1 teaspoon *Creole Seasoning Mix* (page 14)
2½ cups cooked white rice (follow package directions)
3 scallions, green part only, thinly sliced
Salt and freshly ground pepper to taste

1. Heat the vegetable oil in a deep heavy 12-inch skillet over medium heat. Add the onion and celery and cook for 3 minutes, stirring, or until the onion is soft and the celery crisp-tender. Add the ground

HOW TO CLEAN RAW OR COOKED HEADLESS SHRIMP

1. To peel raw or cooked headless shrimp: Pull off the legs, then starting from underneath, peel off the shell. You have the option of leaving the "fan" of the tail-shell intact, for fancier presentations like shrimp cocktail, or removing it.

2. To devein raw or cooked headless shrimp: Using a paring knife make a shallow cut along the back of the shrimp and remove and discard the black vein underneath. (NOTE: Deveining is especially important for medium-sized shrimp and larger since the vein is most noticeable in the larger sizes and is visually unappetizing.)

HINT: To save time: If you do not have any leftover cooked rice stored in your refrigerator, just start cooking the rice 10 minutes before you begin step #1. The rice should be done in time to begin step #2 so this marvelous dish can be prepared from start to finish in less than 15 minutes!

beef, ground pork and seasoning mix and cook, stirring often to break up the clumps, for 6 minutes or until the meat has browned.

2. Add the rice and scallions to the skillet. Using a fork, gently toss the rice and meat mixture together until well combined. Cook for 1 to 3 minutes, tossing constantly until the rice is heated through. Season with salt and pepper and serve at once as a side dish.

Stewed Okra with Hominy

Servings: 4
Preparation Time: About 10 minutes
Cooking Time: 25 to 30 minutes
(can be made up to 4 days ahead)

2 teaspoons vegetable oil
1 medium yellow onion, coarsely chopped
1 large red or green bell pepper, finely chopped
1 pound fresh okra, stemmed (Tip, page 142) and cut into ½-inch-thick slices or frozen chopped okra, thawed
1 16-ounce can stewed tomatoes
2 teaspoons *Creole Seasoning Mix* (page 14)
1 bay leaf
1 14½-ounce can whole golden hominy, drained (available at supermarket)
Salt and freshly ground pepper to taste
8 strips lean bacon, fried until crisp and crumbled, to garnish (optional)

1. Heat the vegetable oil in a 4- to 6-quart nonreactive pot over medium-high heat. Add the onion and bell pepper and cook, stirring often, for 5 minutes or until the vegetables are tender but not brown.

2. Stir in the okra, stewed tomatoes, seasoning mix and bay leaf and bring to a boil. Reduce the heat to low, stir in the hominy and cover. Simmer, stirring occasionally, for 20 to 25 minutes or until the okra is tender and the mixture has a stew-like consistency.

3. Remove and discard the bay leaf and season with salt and pepper. Transfer the mixture to a heated serving platter and sprinkle evenly with the crumbled bacon if desired. Serve hot as a side dish.

Green Beans and Tomato
with Creole Mustard Dressing

Servings: 4
Preparation Time: About 15 minutes
Cooking Time: 5 minutes
(dressing can be made up to 2 days ahead)

DRESSING: (Makes about 1 cup)
¼ cup white wine vinegar
½ cup coarsely chopped red onion
¼ teaspoon *Creole Seasoning Mix* (page 14)
2 teaspoons Creole mustard (available at supermarket or see
    Source List page 186) or other strong brown mustard
⅔ cup vegetable oil or olive oil
Salt and freshly ground pepper to taste

SALAD:
4 large ripe tomatoes, thinly sliced
1 pound fresh green beans, trimmed and cooked until tender

1. To prepare the dressing: Combine the vinegar, onion, seasoning
mix and mustard in the bowl of a food processor fitted with a metal
blade or in a blender. Process the mixture briefly, just until well
blended and the onion is finely chopped. With the machine running,
gradually pour the vegetable oil through the feed tube in a slow,
steady stream until well blended. Season with salt and pepper.

2. To make the salad: Dividing the tomatoes evenly among 4 salad
plates, arrange them in a decorative pattern along the outside rim of
each plate. Divide the green beans evenly, and place in the center of
each tomato "ring."

3. To serve, whisk the dressing to recombine and drizzle over each
salad. Serve the salads at room temperature as an appetizer or side
dish.

**HINT: To save time:
Cook the green beans
up to 2 days ahead,
cover and refrigerate.
Also, the dressing can
be prepared ahead, just
cover and refrigerate
separately.**

Louisiana's Red Beans and Rice with Ham

Servings: 4
Preparation Time: About 15 minutes
Cooking Time: 10 minutes
(can be made up to 3 days ahead)

HINT: To save time: Start cooking the rice 10 minutes before you begin step #1. This way the rice will be done and hot in time to serve.

2 teaspoons vegetable oil
3 cloves garlic, crushed
1 6-ounce slice of smoked ham (available at supermarket deli or from leftover baked smoked ham), cut into ½-inch dice
2 teaspoons *Creole Seasoning Mix* (page 14)
1 large ripe tomato, coarsely chopped
1 15-ounce can red kidney beans, drained and rinsed
Salt and freshly ground pepper to taste
4 cups hot cooked white rice (follow package directions), to serve
3 scallions, green part only, thinly sliced, to garnish
Tabasco sauce, to serve

1. Heat the vegetable oil in a heavy 12-inch skillet over medium-high heat. Add the garlic, ham, seasoning mix, tomato and beans. Cook, stirring often, for 10 minutes or until the mixture is heated through and the flavors are well blended. Season with salt and pepper.

2. To serve, mound the hot rice in the center of a warm shallow serving bowl, surround with the bean mixture and sprinkle with the scallions. Serve hot as a main course and pass with Tabasco sauce.

Creole Corn Pudding

Servings: 4 to 6
Preparation Time: About 5 minutes
Cooking Time: 50 to 56 minutes

This Southern staple is as colorful as it is delicious. I have replaced the classic cream and egg yolk combination with a more modern, healthier version that uses mostly egg whites and skim milk, which still produces a rich, flavorful custard. The use of fresh-cut kernels is scrumptious but my "speed-cooking" adaptation of thawed frozen corn kernels is listed for the busy home cook.

1 teaspoon vegetable oil, plus more to grease pan
5 cups fresh corn kernels (about 10 ears) or 2 10-ounce packages frozen
     corn kernels (5 cups), thawed
1 medium white onion, finely chopped
1 medium red bell pepper, cut into ¼-inch dice
½ teaspoon *Creole Seasoning Mix* (page 14)
½ teaspoon salt
¼ teaspoon freshly ground pepper
1 large egg
3 large egg whites
2 cups skim milk
4 to 6 cups boiling water

1. Heat the vegetable oil in a deep 12-inch skillet over medium-high heat. Add the corn, onion, red bell pepper, seasoning mix, salt and pepper. Cook about 6 minutes, stirring occasionally, or until the vegetables are tender. Transfer the corn mixture to a large bowl and let cool to room temperature, stirring occasionally.

2. Preheat the oven to 350° F. Lightly grease the bottom and sides of an 8-inch-square baking dish.

3. Meanwhile, in a medium bowl, beat together the egg, egg whites and skim milk until well blended.

4. When the corn-mixture is cool, stir in the egg mixture until well blended. Pour the egg-corn mixture into the prepared baking dish and place in a roasting pan large enough to accommodate it. Pour

HOW TO CLEAN COOKED CRAB

Crabs (with the exception of soft-shelled ones) are usually cooked whole, then cleaned of their succulent meat. The following directions are for cooked crab and can be applied to any species, depending on where the meat is located. NOTE: To clean four 1½-pound crabs, allow up to 1 hour.

1. Grasp the top shell (at the underside) and pull it up and away from the crab body and reserve. Turn the crab over and remove the triangle-shaped "apron"; at the same time remove the soft spines underneath the apron and discard.

2. Turn the crab over and remove the "dead man's fingers" (the finger-like, white, spongy gills) and the intestines on the top and discard. Remove and discard the mouth parts. Using a dull dinner knife, scrape out the greenish viscera from the body and reserve for another use or discard. Rinse the crab and the reserved top shell thoroughly under cold, running water.

3. Hold the crab legs and claws close to the body and twist them off. Using the back of a sharp knife, gently crack each leg shell

enough hot water into the roasting pan to reach halfway up the sides of the baking dish.

5. Bake the pudding on the center rack of the oven for 45 to 50 minutes or until the pudding is set and a knife inserted near the center comes out clean. Be careful not to overcook. Remove the baking dish from the roasting pan and let the pudding stand for 10 minutes before serving. Serve hot directly from the baking dish as a side dish.

Stuffed Whole Crab

Servings: 4 (1 stuffed crab each)
Preparation Time: About 1½ hours
Cooking Time: 30 to 35 minutes
(crabs can be cooked and cleaned
[step #1] up to 1 day ahead)

This is one of the more adventurous recipes in my cookbook, but you'll find the spectacular result well worth your effort. Each crab shell performs as a creative and pretty serving vessel for individual portions — a great way to "wow" your next dinner guests!

4　1½ pound fresh whole hard-shell crabs, preferably Dungeness
　　blue crab from the Northwest
1　medium yellow onion, cut into eighths
2　ribs celery, cut into eighths
1　medium green bell pepper, cut into eighths
¼　cup fresh lemon juice (2 to 3 small lemons)
1　teaspoon *Creole Seasoning Mix* (page 14)
1　cup dry unseasoned bread crumbs
2　tablespoons finely chopped fresh parsley
¼　cup skim milk
1　large egg
½　teaspoon salt
¼　teaspoon freshly ground pepper
1　medium lemon, cut lengthwise into eighths, to serve

1. Add the crabs to a 10- to 12-quart stockpot of boiling water, return to a boil, then boil the crabs for 20 minutes. When cool

enough to handle, remove the meat from each of the crabs; see side note for directions. Using the dull edge of a dinner knife, scrape the hair off each top shell. Rinse and pat dry the top shells and reserve.

2. Meanwhile, combine the onion, celery, bell pepper, lemon juice and seasoning mix in the bowl of a food processor fitted with a metal blade. Process the mixture about 1 minute or until finely chopped, scraping down the sides of the bowl. Add the bread crumbs, parsley, milk, egg, salt and pepper and pulse the mixture 2 to 3 times or until well blended. Transfer the mixture to a medium bowl and stir in the reserved cooked crabmeat until well blended.

3. Preheat the oven to 400° F.

4. Divide the crabmeat mixture evenly among the four reserved top crab shells, firmly packing the mixture into each shell and smoothing the surface. Transfer the stuffed shells (stuffing-side-up) to a baking sheet.

5. Bake for 30 to 35 minutes or until the stuffing is set and golden brown. Serve each crab hot, placing each shell stuffing-side-down, with 2 lemon wedges on an individual dinner plate as a main course.

Chicken Gumbo

Servings: 4 to 6
Preparation Time: About 10 minutes
Cooking Time: 20 to 25 minutes
(can be made up to 2 days ahead)

An old Louisiana folktale says that when a Louisianan dies and goes to heaven and finds there is no gumbo there, he comes right back.

3 tablespoons vegetable oil
3 tablespoons unbleached white flour
1 medium yellow onion, coarsely chopped
3 cloves garlic, crushed
1 medium red or green bell pepper, cut into ¼-inch wide strips
8 ounces fresh okra, stemmed (Tip, page 142) and cut crosswise into
    ½-inch pieces or 1 10-ounce package frozen chopped okra, thawed

so that the crab meat is exposed and can be removed with a lobster or shellfish fork.

4. Hold the crab body and snap it in half (you may need to cut it with a heavy knife or cleaver). Remove the meat from the shell by carefully picking it out. Pick over the crab meat to remove any cartilage and remaining pieces of shell.

Shades of the South
(One-Dish Meal or Make-Ahead Menu for 4 to 6)
Front Porch Mint Juleps or Iced Tea
Chicken Gumbo with Rice
Bread Pudding with Whiskey Sauce

HINT: To beat the clock: Cook the rice while the gumbo is simmering. Also, use frozen okra and corn kernels in place of fresh; the substitution eliminates the time needed for chopping and cutting the vegetables. I call for skinless, boneless chicken breasts because no extra time is needed to prepare them for serving and the reduced fat content is so much better for you.

5 cups canned low-sodium chicken broth
2½ teaspoons *Creole Seasoning Mix* (page 14)
1½ pounds skinless, boneless chicken breasts, cut into 1-inch cubes
1½ cups fresh (about 2 ears) or thawed frozen corn kernels
Salt and freshly ground pepper to taste

5 cups hot cooked white rice (follow package directions), to serve

1. Heat the vegetable oil in a nonreactive 4-quart pot over medium heat until hot but not smoking. Stir in the flour until well blended and smooth. Cook, stirring vigorously, for 5 minutes or until the *roux* has thickened and turned an orangy-brown (similar in color to peanut butter).

2. Stir in the onion, garlic and bell pepper. Then stir in the okra, chicken broth and seasoning mix. Raise the heat to high and bring to a boil.

3. Reduce the heat to medium-low and stir in the chicken and corn kernels. Simmer for 15 to 20 minutes, stirring occasionally, or until the chicken is cooked, the okra is tender and the soup has thickened slightly. Season with salt and pepper to taste.

4. To serve, mound a cupful of hot rice in the center of a heated shallow soup bowl, spoon some gumbo around it and serve hot as a main course.

Plantation-Style
Seafood-Stuffed Artichokes

Servings: 4 (1 stuffed artichoke each)
Preparation Time: About 20 minutes
Cooking Time: 45 minutes (artichokes can be cooked
[steps #1 and #2] up to 2 days ahead;
dressing can be made up to 2 days ahead)

Historically, this impressive dish was served at formal plantation dinners; it is still wonderful for entertaining. The assertiveness of the Creole Mustard Dressing is a splendid contrast to the richness of the shrimp-based stuffing. I have streamlined the original recipe by offering solutions to some of the traditional time-consuming steps. For example, instead of packing the stuffing in between each individual artichoke leaf, I suggest filling the artichoke cavity. To save even more time: Ready and cook the artichokes and make the dressing up to 2 days ahead. Cover and refrigerate separately.

ARTICHOKES:
4 medium artichokes, 3 to 4 inches in diameter at base (about 8 ounces each)
½ lemon

STUFFING:
8 ounces small shrimp (51 to 60 to the pound), shelled and deveined
    (page 15), finely chopped
4 ounces short-stemmed mushrooms, coarsely chopped
4 scallions, green part only, thinly sliced
¼ cup dry unseasoned bread crumbs
¼ cup freshly grated Parmesan cheese (1-ounce piece)
¼ teaspoon *Creole Seasoning Mix* (page 14)
Salt and freshly ground pepper to taste
1 large egg, lightly beaten
1 tablespoon plus 1 teaspoon olive oil or vegetable oil, to coat
3 cups boiling water

1 recipe *Creole Mustard Dressing* (page 17), at room temperature, to serve

1. To prepare the artichokes: Place each artichoke on its side, and using a small sharp nonreactive knife, slice about 1 inch from the

top. Cut the stem off each artichoke so it sits upright. Remove and discard any bruised outer leaves, and using nonreactive scissors trim ¼ inch off the points of the remaining leaves.

2. Bring 6 quarts of water to a boil in a 10- to 12-quart nonreactive stockpot over high heat. Add the artichokes and the lemon half. Place a heavy 8-inch-wide nonreactive lid on top of the artichokes to act as a weight to keep them submerged in the water. Bring to a second boil over high heat and boil for 10 to 15 minutes, or until a leaf can be pulled from near the artichoke base with only slight resistance. (NOTE: Be careful not to overcook, as artichokes will be cooked again later in the recipe. Here they must be cooked enough to be able to remove the chokes.) Using tongs, invert the artichokes into a colander to drain, and refresh under cold running water.

3. Meanwhile, prepare the stuffing: Combine the shrimp, mush-

rooms, scallions, bread crumbs, Parmesan cheese and seasoning mix in a medium bowl. Season the mixture with salt and pepper and stir in the beaten egg until well blended.

4. Preheat the oven to 400° F.

5. Gently spread open each cooked artichoke, grab hold of the central small leaf-cluster at the tip, twist and pull it out in one movement and discard it. Using a spoon, scrape off and discard the fuzzy choke from the cavity of each artichoke, being careful not to damage the tender heart just beneath it. Divide the filling evenly among the artichokes and firmly pack into each artichoke cavity. Press the artichoke leaves back into a more closed position, to re-form each artichoke. Using your palms, rub the outside of each artichoke with 1 teaspoon olive oil until coated evenly.

6. Stand the artichokes upright in the bottom of a 3-quart baking dish and pour the 3 cups boiling water around the base of the artichokes. Bake in the bottom third of the oven for 45 minutes or until the filling is set and the artichokes are completely tender.

7. Serve the artichokes hot as a main course with the Creole Mustard Dressing passed separately as an accompaniment.

Veal Grillades with Grits

Servings: 4
Preparation Time: About 10 minutes
Cooking Time: About 25 minutes

This is a Louisiana breakfast dish that I love for dinner!

4 4-ounce boneless veal round steaks (from veal tenderloin), trimmed
    (have butcher pound to ¼-inch thickness or see page 35)
1 tablespoon vegetable oil
1 medium yellow onion, finely chopped
2 medium green bell peppers, cut into ¼-inch strips
4 medium-sized ripe tomatoes, coarsely chopped
1 teaspoon *Creole Seasoning Mix* (page 14)
Salt and freshly ground pepper to taste

Quick-cooking grits (available at supermarket; follow package directions
    for 4 servings), to serve

1. Heat the vegetable oil in a heavy 12-inch skillet over medium-high heat. Add the veal steaks and cook for 3 to 4 minutes on each side, or until a rich golden brown on the outside but still slightly pink within. Transfer the veal to a plate and reserve.

2. Carefully pour off the fat from the skillet, and add the onion, green peppers, tomatoes and seasoning mix. Cover and cook, stirring once, for 5 to 6 minutes or until the vegetables are tender. Season with salt and pepper.

3. Meanwhile, prepare 4 servings of the grits, following package directions.

4. Add the reserved veal steaks to the skillet with the sauce and cook for 2 minutes more, or until the veal is heated through. Divide the grits evenly among 4 warmed dinner plates, spreading it to make a "bed" of grits. Top each bed of grits with a veal steak, then ladle some sauce over the top. Serve at once as a main course.

CHAPTER 2

PAPRIKA, PAPRIKA

Hungarian Seasoning Mix

Chicken Paprikás

Beet-Horseradish Salad

Paprika Potatoes

Caraway Soup with Noodles

Spiced and Breaded Cauliflower

Stuffed Kohlrabi

Sweet and Sour Cabbage with Bacon

Hungarian Goulash

Marhatekercs

Gypsies' Sausage with Peppers

Csipetke

HUNGARIAN CUISINE is unique in its prodigious use of paprika, a spice ground from the dried pods of the red capsicum that adds true homespun flavor and color to a wide range of Hungarian dishes. Even though paprika is not indigenous to Hungary, the country is still known for its use and paprika is its national spice. Both the rose (sweet) and cherry (hot) varieties are enjoyed fully in the cuisine. My seasoning blend is a combination of herbs and spices favored by Hungarians, namely, caraway seed, poppy seed and dillweed, all supported by a paprika base.

As you see from the selection of recipes, there is much to be enjoyed in the delightful cuisine of this country at the heart of a new Europe. Pork is much used in Hungarian cooking, especially in the form of ham, bacon and sausage. It is also minced or ground and used to stuff other foods, such as vegetables. In Stuffed Kohlrabi (page 32), the slightly crunchy and peppery vegetable is filled with ground pork and veal and heightened with onion and the seasoning mix to create a memorable dish.

Hungary is renowned for its vegetable gardens, whose bounties are featured in the cuisine, too. Cabbage, cauliflower, beets and potatoes, and in the summer, vegetables such as string beans, carrots and peas are often used. Try the piquant Beet-Horseradish Salad (page 29) and homey Paprika Potatoes (page 30) or, for more substantial fare, I suggest Sweet and Sour Cabbage with Hungarian Bacon (page 33), which reveals the Hungarian affinity for a sweet and sour play to food, especially when preparing vegetables.

Beef, bell peppers, onion, tomatoes and potatoes are simmered slowly and the rich flavors of the paprika and caraway of the seasoning blend contribute to a thick broth to create the signature Hungarian dish, Goulash (page 34).

QUICKIES: EVERYDAY FOODS MADE INTERNATIONAL

Better-Than-Ever B.L.T.
Season a little mayonnaise with some *Hungarian Seasoning Mix* and spread on bacon, lettuce and tomato sandwich.

Hungarian Hash
Combine homemade or canned corned-beef hash with *Hungarian Seasoning Mix* to taste.

Super-Spuds

Mix a touch of *Hungarian Seasoning Mix* and salt and pepper with sour cream or plain lowfat yogurt as a topping for baked potatoes.

Tomato Soup with a Twist

To add a quick flavor boost: Stir some *Hungarian Seasoning Mix* into canned tomato soup before heating and sprinkle with croutons before serving, if desired.

Hungarian Sojourn
(One-Dish Meal or Make-Ahead Menu for 4)
Chicken Paprikás
Csipetke (pinched dumplings, page 38)
Dóbos Torte (seven-layer torte with chocolate or mocha buttercream filling, glazed with caramel, bakery)
Wine: Hungarian Riesling

Noodles and dumplings often accompany or garnish meats, poultry and soups. One such example is the ethereal, small soup garnish *Csipetke* (pinched dumplings) on page 38, which when added to Goulash creates a final dish just brimming with goodness.

The outstanding Chicken Paprikás (below), one of the pillars of Hungarian cooking, is similar to Goulash, but distinguished by the addition of sour cream, one of Hungary's most adored ingredients.

Both cold and hot soups also play an important role in the Hungarian menu. The deceptively delicate Caraway Soup with Noodles (page 31), which gets an extra flavor boost from the seasoning blend, illustrates the broad range of Hungarian cookery. Enjoy these popular, soul-satisfying dishes!

Hungarian Seasoning Mix

Makes about 1/2 cup

6 tablespoons paprika, preferably Hungarian sweet
   (available at supermarket or see Source List page 186)
1 tablespoon caraway seed
2 teaspoons poppy seed (available at supermarket or gourmet store)
1 teaspoon dried dillweed

In a small bag or bowl (How-To, page 11), combine the paprika, caraway seed, poppy seed and dillweed. Shake or stir until well blended. Transfer to a clean, dry, airtight glass container. Store up to 3 months away from heat, light or moisture. Shake well before using.

Chicken Paprikás

(Hungarian Paprika Chicken)
Servings: 4 (1 1/2 cups each)
Preparation Time: About 10 minutes
Cooking Time: About 25 minutes (can be made up to 2 days ahead)

1 teaspoon vegetable oil
1 large white onion, finely chopped
1 large green bell pepper, cut into 1/2-inch dice

2 large ripe tomatoes, coarsely chopped
1 cup canned low-sodium chicken broth
2 tablespoons *Hungarian Seasoning Mix* (page 28)
1½ pounds skinless, boneless chicken breasts, cut into ½-inch-wide strips
1 cup sour cream or plain lowfat yogurt, at room temperature,
   mixed with 2 tablespoons cornstarch until well blended and smooth
Salt and freshly ground pepper to taste
3 tablespoons finely chopped fresh parsley, to garnish (optional)

1 recipe *Csipetke* (pinched dumplings) page 38, to serve

1. Heat the vegetable oil in a nonreactive 4- to 6-quart pot over medium-high heat. Add the onion, bell pepper and tomatoes. Cook, stirring occasionally, about 7 minutes or until the vegetables are tender but not brown. Stir in the chicken broth, seasoning mix and chicken and bring to a boil. Reduce the heat to medium and cook, stirring occasionally, for 10 minutes or until the chicken is done.

2. Remove the pot from the heat. Stir 1 cup of the hot liquid into a bowl with the sour cream until well blended. Then stir this mixture back into the pot. Set the pot over very low heat, and heat gently for 5 minutes, stirring constantly until the mixture has thickened slightly. Do not let boil. Season with salt and pepper to taste. Serve hot in shallow soup bowls and garnish with parsley. Serve with *Csipetke*, as a main course.

Beet-Horseradish Salad

Servings: 4
Preparation Time: About 15 minutes
Cooking Time: None
Chilling Time: 2 hours
(can be made up to 2 days ahead)

3 tablespoons apple-cider or white-wine vinegar
1 tablespoon sugar
2 teaspoons prepared horseradish
2 teaspoons *Hungarian Seasoning Mix* (page 28)
1 cup minced white onion

PAPRIKA WITH PANACHE

Paprika is Hungary's national spice. Nowhere else in Europe, not even in Spain, has paprika gained such national popularity. Paprika adds distinctive flavor and color to a great variety of Hungarian dishes. Paprika is a powder ground from dried pods of the red capsicum pepper. The word *paprika* is used to describe all the varieties of Capsicum annuum, which can range from sweet to hot peppers. The best paprika is said to be grown in the region surrounding the southern Hungarian town of Szeged.
(cont'd on page 30)

HINT: To save time: Boil 4 medium-sized beets in their jackets (with 1 inch of stem left on) until tender. Peel, cover and refrigerate until ready to continue with the recipe. Can be done up to 3 days ahead. I am thrilled to find that most canned beets taste nearly as good as fresh, and can be successfully used as a substitute in this recipe.

Vitamin-C-rich paprika (3 to 5 times as much vitamin C as citrus fruits) can transform dishes with flavors from mild to ferocious! How much heat a paprika carries is due to how much of the fiery chemical compound "capsaicin" the pepper's seeds hold. Even the seeds from sweet peppers that certain paprikas have been made from are hot. Most Hungarian dishes call for "noble-sweet" paprika, and Hungarians just vary the heat of the dish according to their own individual taste.

Hungarian paprika is available in six different strengths, varying in color and hotness.

◆ Exquisite delicate: Very mild.

◆ Delicatessen: Slightly warmer than exquisite delicate and very red; used mostly for sauces.

◆ Noble-sweet: Red and sweet, the most widely used type in Hungary.

◆ Semi-sweet: Stronger than noble-sweet but yet not hot.

◆ Rose: Paler red than semi-sweet and quite hot.

◆ Hot: Brown in color and very hot, used in small quantities to add heat to Hungarian dishes already seasoned with noble-sweet or delicatessen paprika.

4 medium cooked beets, thinly sliced, or 2 16-ounce cans sliced beets, drained
1 hard-cooked large egg, finely chopped, to garnish (optional)

1. Combine the vinegar, sugar, horseradish and seasoning mix in a medium-sized glass salad bowl and whisk together until well blended and the sugar is dissolved. Gently stir in the onion and sliced beets until well combined. Cover and refrigerate until well chilled. (NOTE: This salad is best when marinated in the refrigerator overnight, but it can be served the day it is prepared.)

2. Divide the salad evenly among 4 chilled salad plates, using a slotted spoon so as not to serve the marinade. Garnish each salad with some hard-cooked egg, if desired, and serve as an appetizer or side dish.

Paprika Potatoes

Servings: 4
Preparation Time: About 15 minutes
Cooking Time: None
(can be made up to 3 days ahead)

1¼ pounds boiling potatoes, cut into ⅛-inch-thick slices
⅓ cup sour cream or plain lowfat yogurt, at room temperature
2 teaspoons *Hungarian Seasoning Mix* (page 28)
Salt and freshly ground pepper to taste

1. Add 2 cups water to a deep 12-inch skillet and bring to a boil over high heat. Add the potatoes. (NOTE: Add more water if necessary; the potatoes should be completely submerged.) Boil the potatoes for 5 to 10 minutes or until tender but not falling apart.

2. Meanwhile, in a medium bowl, combine the sour cream and seasoning mix and stir until well blended. When the potatoes are done, using a slotted spoon, transfer them to the bowl with the seasoned sour cream and gently toss together until the potatoes are well coated. Season with salt and pepper. Serve at once as a side dish.

Caraway Soup with Noodles

Servings: 4 (1 cup each)
Preparation Time: About 5 minutes
Cooking Time: About 20 minutes

1 quart canned low-sodium beef broth
1 tablespoon *Hungarian Seasoning Mix* (page 28)
3 teaspoons caraway seed
1½ cups broad egg noodles
Salt and freshly ground pepper to taste

Combine the beef broth, seasoning mix and caraway seed in a 6-quart pot over high heat and bring to a boil. Reduce the heat to low and simmer for 10 minutes, stirring occasionally. Strain the soup through a fine-meshed strainer back into the pot, discarding the solids, and return the soup to a boil over high heat. Add the noodles and return to a boil. Cook for 5 to 7 minutes, stirring occasionally, or until the noodles are just *al dente* (slightly firm to the bite). Season with salt and pepper and serve hot as a main course.

Spiced and Breaded Cauliflower

Servings: 4
Preparation Time: About 10 minutes
Cooking Time: About 30 minutes

1 2-pound head cauliflower, separated into evenly sized florets
Vegetable oil, to grease pan
2 large eggs
2 tablespoons skim milk
1 cup dry unseasoned bread crumbs
1 tablespoon *Hungarian Seasoning Mix* (page 28)
½ teaspoon salt, plus more for water
1 teaspoon freshly ground pepper

1. Bring 2 quarts of lightly salted water to a boil in a 4- to 6-quart pot over high heat. Add the cauliflower and boil for 6 minutes or until the florets are tender. Drain well, refresh under cold running water and pat dry on paper towels.

2. Preheat the oven to 400° F. Lightly grease a baking sheet.

3. Whisk together the eggs and milk in a medium bowl until well blended. In another medium bowl combine the bread crumbs, seasoning mix, salt and pepper and stir together until well blended.

4. Dip each cauliflower floret into the egg mixture until evenly coated, allowing excess mixture to drip off. Then dip into the bread-crumb mixture until coated evenly, shaking off the excess. Carefully transfer the cauliflower to the prepared baking sheet and place 1 inch apart.

5. Bake in the upper third of the oven for 15 to 20 minutes until the cauliflower coating is crisp and a delicate brown in color. Serve at once as a side dish.

Stuffed Kohlrabi

Servings: 4 (2 stuffed kohlrabi each)
Preparation Time: About 45 minutes
Cooking Time: 30 to 35 minutes
(can be made up to 2 days ahead)

The flavor of kohlrabi is outstanding — that of peppery broccoli — and it should not be missed. Standard fare in Hungary, kohlrabi is a member of the cabbage family and it resembles a turnip in appearance. In fact it is sometimes called "cabbage turnip." Fresh kohlrabi is available in supermarkets and specialty stores: Its peak months are June and July, but it is available from May to December as well.

8 medium kohlrabi (about 3 pounds), leaves and stems trimmed
    and small tender leaves reserved and finely chopped, and bulbs peeled
Vegetable oil, to grease pan
8 ounces extra-lean ground veal
8 ounces lean ground pork
1 small yellow onion, finely chopped
1 tablespoon *Hungarian Seasoning Mix* (page 28)
Salt and freshly ground pepper to taste

1. Bring 3 quarts of water to a boil in a 6- to 8-quart pot over high heat. Add the kohlrabi bulbs and reduce the heat to medium. Simmer

for 30 to 35 minutes or until the kohlrabi is tender when pierced with a fork. Drain well, refresh under cold running water and reserve.

2. Preheat the oven to 375° F. Lightly grease a baking sheet.

3. Scoop out the centers of the kohlrabi bulbs, using a melon baller or sturdy teaspoon, leaving a ¼-inch-thick shell. Reserve the pulp. Coarsely chop the pulp and transfer to a medium-sized bowl.

4. Add the veal, pork, onion, seasoning mix and the reserved finely chopped kohlrabi leaves to the bowl with the kohlrabi pulp and season with salt and pepper. Stir until well blended. Divide the mixture among the kohlrabi and firmly pack the mixture into each of the shells, mounding slightly.

5. Arrange the stuffed kohlrabi bulbs on the prepared baking sheet and bake for 30 to 35 minutes or until the tops are a golden brown. Serves 4, two stuffed kohlrabi each as a light main course, or serves 8, one each as an appetizer or side dish.

Sweet and Sour Cabbage with Bacon

Servings: 4
Preparation Time: About 10 minutes
Cooking Time: About 20 minutes
(can be made up to 2 days ahead)

6 strips lean slab bacon, preferably Hungarian double-smoked
   (Source List page 186), cut into ¼-inch dice
1 small white onion, coarsely chopped
1 small head green cabbage (about 1¼ pounds), shredded ¼ inch thick
2½ teaspoons *Hungarian Seasoning Mix* (page 28)
½ cup boiling water
2 tablespoons honey
2 tablespoons apple-cider vinegar or white-wine vinegar
Salt and freshly ground pepper to taste

1. Add the bacon to a nonreactive 3- to 4-quart saucepan with a tight-fitting lid and fry over high heat, uncovered, for 4 minutes or until well browned and crisp.

2. Reduce the heat to medium-low. Add the onion, cabbage, seasoning mix, the ½ cup boiling water, honey and vinegar. Cover and simmer for 15 minutes, stirring occasionally or until the cabbage is tender. Season with salt and pepper and serve hot as a side dish.

Hungarian Goulash

Servings: 4 (2 cups each)
Preparation Time: About 10 minutes
Cooking Time: 50 minutes (can be made up to 2 days ahead)

Hungarian Holiday
*(One-Dish Meal
    or Make-Ahead Menu
    for 4)*
Hungarian Goulash
Garden Salad
Apple or Cheese Strudel
    (bakery)
Wine: Zinfandel

Goulash is one of Hungary's hallmark dishes; a wonderful showcase for the soulful spice, paprika. This dish benefits from being made up to 2 days ahead, which gives the flavors of the dish time to "wake up." Not only do red-skinned potatoes make for a pretty presentation, unpeeled they are more nutritious and easy to fix.

2   teaspoons vegetable oil
1   medium yellow onion, coarsely chopped
2   pounds boneless beef round, trimmed and cut into ½-inch cubes
1   medium green bell pepper, cut into ½-inch dice
1   14.5-ounce can peeled whole tomatoes, drained and crushed
1   cup canned low-sodium beef broth
2   medium red boiling potatoes, unpeeled but cut into ½-inch dice
1   tablespoon *Hungarian Seasoning Mix* (page 28)
Salt and freshly ground pepper to taste

1   recipe *Csipetke* (pinched dumplings), page 38, to garnish (optional)

1. Heat the vegetable oil in a 4- to 6-quart pot over medium-high heat. Add the onion, beef and bell pepper. Cook for 10 minutes, stirring often, or until the beef is browned all over and the bell pepper is tender.

2. Stir in the drained tomatoes, beef broth, potatoes and seasoning mix and bring to a boil. Reduce the heat to medium, cover and cook for 40 minutes, stirring occasionally, or until the beef and potatoes are tender but not falling apart. Season with salt and pepper and serve hot in heated shallow soup bowls as a main course. Garnish with *Csipetke*, if desired.

Marhatekercs

(Hungarian Pork and Onion-Stuffed Beef Rolls)
Servings: 4 (2 stuffed beef rolls each)
Preparation Time: About 15 minutes
Cooking Time: 50 to 60 minutes
(can be made up to 2 days ahead)

Avoid extra work here by having your butcher pound the butterflied beef top round steaks for this dish. This tip will enable you to skip step #2 entirely.

STUFFING:

1 small yellow onion, finely chopped
8 ounces lean ground pork
1 large egg, lightly beaten
¼ cup dry unseasoned bread crumbs
1 tablespoon *Hungarian Seasoning Mix* (page 28)
½ teaspoon salt
½ teaspoon freshly ground pepper

ROLLS:

1¼ pounds boneless trimmed beef top round; have butcher "butterfly"
    into two ¼-inch-thick round steaks

SAUCE: (Makes about 5 cups)

1 28-ounce can crushed tomatoes
1 cup canned low-sodium beef broth
3 tablespoons finely chopped fresh parsley, to garnish

1. To prepare the stuffing: Combine the onion, pork, egg, bread crumbs, seasoning mix, and salt and pepper in a medium-sized bowl and mix until well combined. Reserve.

2. To prepare the beef: On a work surface, place a butterflied beef slice between two sheets of plastic wrap. Using a meat mallet or wooden rolling pin, pound from the center of the beef slice toward the outer edge until the beef is flattened to about a ⅛-inch thickness; rotate 180 degrees every 4 strikes. (NOTE: The beef should not be so thin that you can see through it.) Repeat with the remaining beef slice, reusing plastic wrap if not punctured.

3. Preheat the oven to 400° F.

4. To prepare the sauce: In a small nonreactive bowl mix together the crushed tomatoes and beef broth until well blended and reserve until ready to use.

5. Cut each of the pounded steaks crosswise in half, so you have a total of 4 slices. Divide the stuffing evenly 4 ways and place the filling at the top of the short side of each beef slice. Starting with the short side, roll up each beef slice tightly, leaving the ends open. Cut each roll in half crosswise so you have eight rolls. Place the rolls seam side down in a 13-by-9-by-2-inch baking dish, or a casserole large enough to accommodate all the beef rolls in a single layer. Ladle the sauce evenly over the rolls and cover with aluminum foil. Bake for 50 to 60 minutes or until the beef is tender and the filling is set.

6. To serve, transfer the beef rolls to a warmed serving platter, ladle the sauce over them and garnish with the parsley. Serve hot as a main course.

Gypsies' Sausage with Peppers

Servings: 4 to 6
Preparation Time: About 10 minutes
Cooking Time: 25 to 30 minutes
(can be made up to 2 days ahead)

2 teaspoons vegetable oil
1 large yellow onion, thinly sliced
1 pound fresh mild or hot Hungarian sausage (Source List page 186)
    or fresh Italian hot sausage (available at supermarket), cut
    into ¼-inch-thick slices
1 large red bell pepper, cut into ¼-inch-wide strips
1 large green bell pepper, cut into ¼-inch-wide strips
1 28-ounce can crushed tomatoes
1 tablespoon *Hungarian Seasoning Mix* (page 28)
1 tablespoon sugar
1 cup sour cream or plain lowfat yogurt, at room temperature
Salt and freshly ground pepper to taste

Warm crusty whole-grain bread, to serve

1. Heat the vegetable oil in a heavy, deep 12-inch skillet over high heat. Add the onion and sausage and cook for 10 minutes, stirring, until the onion is soft and the sausage is browned all over.

2. Add the red and green bell peppers, tomatoes, seasoning mix and sugar and bring to a boil. Reduce the heat to medium and cook for 15 to 20 minutes more, covered with aluminum foil or a lid, stirring occasionally, or until the sausage is cooked through. Place the sour cream in a small bowl, and whisk ¼ cup of the hot liquid from the saucepan into the bowl until well blended. Stir this mixture back into the skillet. Season with salt and pepper and serve hot as a main course, accompanied with bread.

Csipetke

(Pinched Dumplings)

Servings: 4 (¹/₄ cup each), enough for 1¹/₂ quarts of soup
Preparation Time: About 15 minutes
Cooking Time: 5 minutes

These dumplings are traditionally used as a garnish for goulash but make a wonderful accompaniment to dishes like Chicken Paprikás.

¹/₂ cup unbleached white flour, plus more to knead
¹/₄ teaspoon salt
1 large egg, well beaten

1. Combine the flour and salt in a small bowl. Make a well in the center and add the well-beaten egg. Using a fork, mix until well blended and a stiff dough is formed. Turn the dough out onto a lightly floured work surface and knead about 10 turns or until smooth. Cover lightly with plastic wrap and reserve at room temperature until ready to use.

2. Bring 2 quarts of water to a boil in a 3- to 4-quart saucepan over high heat.

3. Divide the dough into 2 parts, and between floured palms roll each part to form a long cylinder about ¹/₄ inch in diameter. Using well-floured fingers, pinch off small pieces of dough as long as a dime is wide until all the dough is used. Then add the dumplings all at once to the boiling water. (NOTE: The dumplings should look as if they have been "pinched" on one end; they should neither be flattened completely or entirely cylindrical in shape.) After the dumplings float to the surface of the water, cook about 5 minutes, stirring occasionally, or until they are cooked through (the centers should not be floury).

4. Drain and stir into hot soup or transfer to a bowl and toss with a teaspoon of vegetable oil to prevent them from sticking to one another and keep warm until ready to serve. Serve at once as a garnish for soup or as a side dish.

CHAPTER 3

GUTEN APPETIT

German
Seasoning Mix

German Warm
Potato Salad

Black Forest
Hunter's Stew

Sauerbraten

Stewed Lentils

Oktoberfest
Bratwürst

Krautwickel

Calves' Liver
with Apples
and Onions

Crispy Potato Cakes

Pork with Sauerkraut

Wiener Schnitzel

THE COOKING OF GERMANY is down-to-earth, wholesome and modest. Very rarely is it frivolous. It should not be surprising, then, that German home cooking is called *gut bürgerliche Küche,* or "good plain cooking."

I have summoned the flavors of this cuisine by using such sweet, full-flavored spices as allspice, ginger, nutmeg and cloves in my seasoning blend, which is enhanced by the bold flavor of caraway seeds, and made complete by the sweet herb, marjoram. This may seem unusual to Americans who are not used to pairing foods, particularly meats, with spices that we would typically reserve for sweets. However, you will notice their wonderful flavor and aroma in dishes such as Wiener Schnitzel (breaded veal cutlets) on page 51 and in Stewed Lentils (page 44).

It is this use of familiar ingredients in unexpected ways that sets German cuisine apart. Their fondness for fusing sweet and sour flavors, as in the legendary dish Sauerbrauten (page 43), is another classic example. The buttery slices of beef are cloaked in a sauce made sweet by golden raisins, gingersnap cookies, the seasoning blend, and sour by the addition of red wine and vinegar.

Though German cuisine is going through many changes, meat is still the cornerstone of German cooking. It is not uncommon to see two or sometimes three different ground meats combined in a single dish. I have included one such recipe — Krautwickel (page 46), which uses spiced ground beef and pork to stuff tender cabbage leaves. Germans are partial to organ meats and love fruits; Calves' Liver with Apples and Onions (page 48) — in the style of Berlin — is a perfect example of this affinity.

Though vegetables, unlike fruits, are not as popular as in other

QUICKIES: EVERYDAY FOODS MADE INTERNATIONAL

German-Style Meat Loaf
Prepare a basic meat loaf recipe and heighten the flavor with finely diced cooked potato, onion, a pinch of *German Seasoning Mix,* salt and pepper. Bake according to the recipe.

Righteous Roast-Beef Sandwich
Add a pinch of *German Seasoning Mix* to brown mustard for a sandwich spread that will add pizazz to your next hot or cold roast beef sandwich.

Apple-a-Day
For a fanciful side dish, add a pinch of *German Seasoning Mix* to jarred applesauce.

Extra-ordinary Cauliflower
Combine crumbled blue cheese, a pinch of *German Seasoning Mix* and cooked hot cauliflower florets and stir until the cheese has melted and creates a sauce.

countries, a fondness for cabbage is seen in the celebrated German specialty, Pork with Sauerkraut (page 50), and no German bill of fare would be complete without the beloved potato. This chapter showcases the bacon-studded German Warm Potato Salad (page 41), unique with its warm dressing, and the ever popular Crispy Potato Cakes (page 49). While potato cakes are typically not seasoned other than with salt and pepper, these are authentic and simply delicious; the caraway seed from the seasoning blend adds a bright spark of flavor to the humble potatoes.

No wonder German cuisine is popular in America, as it is chock-full of "comfort" foods, simply prepared foods that soothe and satisfy, bringing back the true meaning of "home."

German Seasoning Mix
Makes about 1/2 cup

3 tablespoons caraway seed
3 tablespoons dried marjoram leaves
1 tablespoon ground allspice
1½ teaspoons ground ginger
1 teaspoon ground nutmeg
½ teaspoon ground cloves

In a small bag or bowl (How-To page 11), combine the caraway seed, marjoram, allspice, ginger, nutmeg and cloves. Shake or stir until well blended. Transfer to a clean, dry, airtight glass container. Store up to 3 months away from heat, light or moisture. Shake well before using.

German Warm Potato Salad

Servings: 4 to 6
Preparation Time: About 20 minutes
Cooking Time: About 10 minutes

2 pounds medium-sized boiling potatoes, unpeeled
6 strips lean bacon, cut into ¼-inch dice
1 medium white onion, finely chopped
⅛ cup apple-cider vinegar or white-wine vinegar
½ teaspoon *German Seasoning Mix* (page 40)
½ cup canned low-sodium beef broth
1 teaspoon firmly packed dark or light brown sugar
½ teaspoon salt
½ teaspoon freshly ground pepper
2 tablespoons finely chopped fresh chives or parsley

1. Bring a 4-quart saucepan of water to a boil over high heat. Add the potatoes and boil about 15 minutes or until just tender. (NOTE: Be careful not to overcook or the potatoes will fall apart when sliced.) Peel the potatoes while still warm and cut them into ¼-inch-thick slices. Transfer the sliced potatoes to a large nonmetal salad bowl and cover tightly to keep warm until ready to serve.

2. Add the diced bacon to a nonreactive heavy 10-inch skillet over medium-high heat and fry about 4 minutes or until browned and crisp. Transfer the bacon to a paper-towel-lined plate to drain, and reserve.

3. Stir the onion, vinegar, seasoning mix, beef broth, brown sugar, salt and pepper into the skillet with the bacon drippings and set the skillet over low heat. Cook the mixture, stirring occasionally, for 5 minutes or until the onion is tender.

4. Remove the skillet from the heat, stir in the reserved cooked diced bacon and the chives and pour over the reserved potatoes. Gently toss the potatoes and dressing together, taking care not to break the potatoes, until the potatoes are evenly coated with the dressing. Serve at once as a side dish. (NOTE: This salad should be served hot or warm, not chilled.)

Black Forest Hunter's Stew

Servings: 4 (2 cups each)
Preparation Time: About 10 minutes
Cooking Time: 50 to 60 minutes
(can be made up to 3 days ahead)

The At-Home German Supper
(One-Dish Meal or Make-Ahead Menu for 4)
Black Forest Hunter's Stew
German Rye Bread (supermarket)
Gingerbread (bakery or supermarket — mix)
German Beer such as Weissbier (Bavarian "white beer" served with a fresh lemon wedge)

When you think of making a stew you may also think of all the work involved, but this recipe is very quick to prepare — just 10 minutes! Let this bracing and satisfying stew simmer on your stove while you enjoy its wonderful aroma.

1½ pounds lean boneless venison or beef, preferably from the rump or loin, trimmed and cut into ½-inch cubes
2 medium-sized yellow onions, coarsely chopped
2 cloves garlic, crushed
½ cup dry red wine
1½ cups canned low-sodium beef broth
¼ teaspoon *German Seasoning Mix* (page 40)
½ cup canned tomato purée
2 medium carrots, cut into ¼-inch-thick slices
3 ribs celery, thinly sliced
8 ounces mushrooms, thinly sliced
Salt and freshly ground pepper to taste

1. Combine the venison, onions, garlic, wine, beef broth, seasoning mix, tomato purée, carrots and celery in a nonreactive 6-to 8-quart pot over medium-high heat and bring to a boil.

2. Reduce the heat to medium-low and stir in the mushrooms. Cook, stirring occasionally, for 50 to 60 minutes or until the venison is tender. Season with salt and pepper and serve hot as a main course.

Sauerbraten

Servings: 4 to 6
Preparation Time: About 10 minutes
Cooking Time: 1 hour and 25 to 35 minutes

Traditionally Sauerbraten is marinated up to 3 days, but in an effort to reduce the time from oven-to-table, I have omitted that step and replaced it with a recipe that still gives the classic sweet and sour play so crucial to this German dish. My solution was to use a quicker cooking, more tender cut of beef than the customary roast beef, trimmed in smaller pieces, along with my German Seasoning Mix, and select measures of red wine and vinegar, golden raisins and gingersnaps to capture the authentic flavor of classic Sauerbraten.

MEAT:
2 tablespoons vegetable oil
1 2-pound boneless London broil, trimmed and cut crosswise
   into 4 large pieces
1 cup dry red wine
¼ cup red-wine vinegar
1 large white onion, coarsely chopped
½ teaspoon *German Seasoning Mix* (page 40)
1 cup boiling water

SAUCE: (Makes 3 cups)
½ cup sour cream or plain lowfat yogurt, at room temperature
½ cup seedless golden raisins
1 cup finely crushed gingersnaps, about 14 (available at supermarket)
Salt and freshly ground pepper to taste

1. To prepare the meat: Heat the vegetable oil in a heavy nonreactive 4-quart flameproof Dutch oven or flameproof casserole over medium-high heat. Add the 4 London broil pieces and sear until browned evenly on both sides, 3 to 4 minutes on each side.

2. Add the red wine, vinegar, onion, seasoning mix and boiling water. *Be careful — it will splatter — so stand back.* Bring the mixture to a boil.

3. Meanwhile, preheat the oven to 400° F.

4. Cover the Dutch oven and transfer to the rack in the lower third of the oven. Bake for 1 hour and 15 minutes or until the meat is very tender but not falling apart, turning the meat over after 1 hour. Using a slotted spoon, remove the meat and slice thinly, arranging the slices on a warmed serving platter. Cover and keep warm until ready to serve.

5. To prepare the sauce: Using potholders, place the Dutch oven with the remaining cooking liquid over low heat. In a small bowl stir ¼ cup of the hot cooking liquid into the sour cream and then stir this mixture back into the Dutch oven. Cook gently, stirring constantly, for 3 minutes, but do not allow to boil. Stir in the raisins and crushed gingersnaps and cook gently for 2 minutes more, stirring constantly, or until the gingersnaps have dissolved and the sauce has thickened. (NOTE: If the sause is too thick, stir in up to 1 cup of hot water until well blended.) Season with salt and pepper, ladle the sauce over the warm meat and serve hot as a main course.

Stewed Lentils

Servings: 6
Preparation Time: About 5 minutes
Cooking Time: 30 to 40 minutes
(can be made up to 2 days ahead)

1⅓ cups dried lentils (8 ounces), picked over and rinsed
2 medium yellow onions, finely chopped
2 cups canned low-sodium beef broth
1 teaspoon *German Seasoning Mix* (page 40)
2 tablespoons unsalted butter or unsalted margarine
Salt and freshly ground pepper to taste

Combine the lentils, onions, beef broth, and seasoning mix in a 3-quart saucepan over medium-high heat and bring to a boil. Reduce the heat to low and simmer, covered, stirring occasionally, for 30 to 40 minutes or until the lentils are tender. Stir in the butter until melted and well combined, season with salt and pepper and serve warm as a side dish.

Oktoberfest Bratwürst

Servings: 4 to 6
Preparation Time: About 5 minutes
Cooking Time: 45 to 50 minutes

1 tablespoon vegetable oil
1 large white onion, thinly sliced
8 ounces mushrooms, thinly sliced
12 fresh German Bratwürst sausage, about 1¾ pounds,
    (available at supermarket or German specialty food shop
    or see Source List page 186), pricked all over with a fork
2 cups beer — do not use dark beer
⅛ teaspoon *German Seasoning Mix* (page 40)
¼ teaspoon salt
½ teaspoon freshly ground pepper
¼ cup finely chopped fresh parsley, preferably Italian flat-leaf

Mashed potatoes, to serve

1. Heat 2 teaspoons of the vegetable oil in a nonreactive heavy deep
10- to 12-inch skillet over medium-high heat. Add the onion and
mushrooms and cook, stirring, for 6 minutes or until the mushrooms are browned. Transfer to a medium bowl, cover and keep
warm until ready to serve.

2. Heat the remaining 1 teaspoon vegetable oil. Add the sausages and
fry in two batches, about 7 to 10 minutes each batch, using tongs to
turn them until browned all over. Transfer the sausages to a paper-
towel-lined plate to drain and reserve.

3. Add the beer to the skillet with the sausage drippings and boil the
mixture for 1 minute, scraping drippings from bottom and sides of the
skillet. Reduce the heat to medium and add the seasoning mix, salt,
pepper and reserved sausages. Cover with aluminum foil or a lid and
cook for 20 to 25 minutes more, turning the sausages occasionally
until they are cooked throughout and no pink remains. Using a slotted spoon, serve the sausages on a platter and top with the onion-
mushroom mixture, leaving the cooking juices behind. Sprinkle with
parsley. Serve hot, accompanied by mashed potatoes, as a main course.

Krautwickel

(German Stuffed Cabbage Rolls)
Servings: 4 (2 stuffed cabbage rolls each)
Preparation Time: About 20 minutes
Cooking Time: 40 to 45 minutes
(rolls can be made up to 2 days ahead)

My quick-to-fix adaptation of one of Germany's most famous one-dish meals is not only easy to assemble but fun and a lot quicker to prepare than a whole stuffed cabbage!

ROLLS:

1   1½ pound-head green cabbage, tough outer leaves discarded;
      the 8 largest leaves removed and reserved; the remaining cabbage
      saved for another use
3   cups canned low-sodium beef broth
8   ounces extra-lean ground beef
8   ounces lean ground pork
1   large egg, lightly beaten
1   small white onion, finely chopped
1½ teaspoons *German Seasoning Mix* (page 40)
2   scallions, green part only, thinly sliced

GRAVY: (Makes 2 cups)
2   tablespoons cornstarch
¼   cup cold water
6   strips lean bacon, cut into ¼-inch dice and fried
2   teaspoons finely chopped fresh chives
Salt and freshly ground pepper to taste

1. To prepare the rolls: Add the 8 cabbage leaves to a 3-quart saucepan of boiling water over high heat. Boil the leaves for 2 to 3 minutes or until just tender. Drain immediately, refresh under cold running water and reserve the leaves.

2. Pour the beef broth into a 2- to 3-quart flameproof casserole (large enough to accommodate the cabbage rolls in a single layer) with a tight-fitting lid.

3. Combine the beef, pork, egg, onion, seasoning mix and scallions

in a medium bowl and stir together gently until well blended. Spread the leaves out, concave side down, on a work surface. Using a small sharp knife, slice off the raised part of the vein, cutting as close as possible to the leaf without cutting through the leaf. Then cut off the tip of the stem and discard. Repeat with the remaining leaves, then flip each leaf over cut side down.

4. Preheat the oven to 375° F.

5. Place a firmly packed ¼ cup filling (for the smaller leaves) and ⅓ cup filling (for the larger leaves) in the shape of a 2½-inch-long log 1 inch above the stem end of the leaf. Fold the stem end of the leaf over the filling, while rolling the leaf upward. Then fold the two sides of the leaf inward and over the stuffing. Roll the leaf up tightly to enclose the filling. Place the cabbage roll seam side down into the casserole with the beef broth. Repeat with the remaining cabbage leaves and filling, arranging them in a single layer in the casserole, so that they are immersed in the beef stock.

6. Bake, covered, for 40 minutes or until cooked through. When the rolls are done, transfer the rolls to a serving dish and keep warm until ready to serve. Reserve 2 cups of the cooking liquid.

7. To prepare the gravy: Place the casserole with the 2 cups reserved cooking liquid over medium heat. In a small bowl whisk together the cornstarch and cold water until well blended, then whisk into the casserole and bring to a boil. Boil for 4 minutes, whisking constantly, or until the gravy has thickened. Stir in the fried bacon and chives. Season with salt and pepper. Ladle the gravy over the reserved warm cabbage rolls and serve at once as a main course.

Calves' Liver
with Apples and Onions

Servings: 4
Preparation Time: About 5 minutes
Cooking Time: 20 to 25 minutes

3 tablespoons vegetable oil

1 medium yellow onion, thinly sliced

1 medium-sized tart apple, preferably Granny Smith apple, peeled
   and cut into ¼-inch-thick slices

2 tablespoons unbleached white flour, to dredge

1 teaspoon *German Seasoning Mix* (page 40)

4 ¼-inch-thick slices of calves' liver (about 1⅓ pounds); ask butcher
   to remove outer membrane and any connective tissue (NOTE: Liver
   is very perishable and should be used the same day it is purchased.)

Salt and freshly ground pepper to taste

1. Heat 1 tablespoon of the vegetable oil in a heavy 12-inch skillet
over medium-high heat. Add the onion and apple and cook, stirring,
about 4 minutes or until the onion and apple are just tender, not
falling apart. Transfer the onion mixture to a medium bowl, cover
and keep warm until ready to serve.

2. Combine the flour and seasoning mix in a medium bowl and stir
together until well blended. Dredge the liver slices with the flour
mixture until they are coated evenly, shaking off excess flour.

3. Add the remaining 2 tablespoons of oil to the skillet. Heat the oil,
then place the liver slices in the center of the skillet. Cook the liver in
batches if necessary, for 2 to 3 minutes each side or until browned all
over, and it just loses its pink interior. (NOTE: Be careful not to overcook the liver; it should be just tender.)

4. To serve, divide the liver slices among 4 heated dinner plates and
season with salt and pepper. Top each with some of the reserved
onion-apple mixture and serve at once as a main course.

Crispy Potato Cakes

Servings: 4 to 6 (makes 15 potato cakes)
Preparation Time: About 10 minutes
Cooking Time: About 35 minutes

3 large eggs, well beaten
1 medium white onion, minced
¼ teaspoon *German Seasoning Mix* (page 40)
3 tablespoons unseasoned bread crumbs
½ teaspoon salt
½ teaspoon freshly ground pepper
2 pounds medium-sized boiling potatoes
½ to ¾ cup vegetable oil, to fry

Applesauce or imported German lingonberry preserves
    (available at supermarket or from gourmet shop), to serve

1. Mix together the eggs, onion, seasoning mix, bread crumbs, salt and pepper in a large bowl until well blended; cover and reserve.

2. Peel the potatoes, then shred them into long, thin strips, using the shredding disk of a food processor or the large holes on a 4-sided box grater. As you shred the potatoes stir them into the bowl with the egg mixture until they are well coated, re-covering with plastic wrap each time.

3. Heat ½ cup of the vegetable oil in a heavy deep 12-inch skillet over medium-high heat, until the oil sputters. Working quickly, drop loosely packed ⅓ cupfuls of the mixture into the skillet and using a spatula flatten each into a cake 4 inches in diameter. Fry the potato cakes in batches, making sure the edges do not overlap, for 3 to 4 minutes each side or until the outside is golden brown and the edges are crispy. Add up to ¼ cup more oil as needed to maintain a depth of ⅛ inch and reheat between batches. Drain the potato cakes on a paper-towel-lined plate between batches, then transfer the cakes to a heated ovenproof serving plate and keep warm in the oven until ready to serve. Serve at once as a side dish with applesauce.

Pork with Sauerkraut

Servings: 4
Preparation Time: About 10 minutes
Cooking Time: 50 to 60 minutes

1 medium yellow onion, coarsely chopped
1 pound bag of sauerkraut (NOTE: Sauerkraut that comes in a plastic bag, available in the meat case of the supermarket works best.)
2 cups canned low-sodium broth
¼ cup white-wine vinegar
¼ cup firmly packed light or dark brown sugar
3 tablespoons red currant jelly (available at supermarket)
1 teaspoon *German Seasoning Mix* (page 40)
1½ teaspoons salt
4 ½-inch-thick pork rib chops (about 2¼ pounds)
4 medium-sized red boiling potatoes, unpeeled but cut into 1-inch-thick slices
4 teaspoons spicy brown mustard, preferably Dusseldorf

1. Preheat the oven to 375° F.

2. Combine the onion, sauerkraut, chicken broth, vinegar, brown sugar, currant jelly, seasoning mix, and salt in a 4-quart nonreactive casserole or Dutch oven and stir until well blended. Place the pork chops and potatoes in the sauerkraut mixture so that they are completely submerged.

3. Bake, covered, for 50 to 60 minutes or until the pork chops test tender and no pink remains; the potatoes should be tender and the sauerkraut moist.

4. To serve, using a slotted spoon, transfer the sauerkraut into the middle of a large heated platter. Lay the pork chops on top and surround with the potatoes. Spread the "eye" of each pork chop with 1 teaspoon mustard. Ladle some of the remaining juices over the sauerkraut and potatoes and serve hot as a main course.

Wiener Schnitzel

(German-Style Veal Cutlets)
Servings: 4 (2 veal cutlets each)
Preparation Time: About 5 minutes
Cooking Time: About 20 minutes

German Respite
(Fast Menu for 4)
Wiener Schnitzel
Braised Baby Carrots
German Warm Potato
  Salad (page 41)
Baked Apples
Wine: German
  Gewürztraminer

8 small veal cutlets (about 1 pound); have butcher pound
    to a ⅛-inch thickness or see step #1 below
1 cup dry unseasoned bread crumbs
1 teaspoon salt
½ teaspoon *German Seasoning Mix* (page 40)
2 large eggs, well beaten
2 to 3 tablespoons vegetable oil
½ cup sour cream or plain lowfat yogurt,
    at room temperature, to garnish
3 gherkin pickles, thinly sliced, to garnish

1. On a work surface, place a veal cutlet
between two sheets of plastic wrap. Using a meat
mallet or wooden rolling pin, pound from the cen-
ter of the cutlet toward the outer edge until the cutlet is flattened to about ⅛ inch thick; rotate 180 degrees every strike.
(NOTE: The veal should not be so thin that you can see
through it.) Repeat the process with the
remaining veal cutlets, reusing the plastic
wrap if not punctured.

2. Combine the bread crumbs, salt, and
seasoning mix in a medium bowl and stir
together until well blended. Add the
beaten eggs to another medium bowl, and
one by one dip each cutlet into the egg, let-
ting excess drip off, then into the crumb
mixture until evenly coated. Shake off any
extra bread crumbs.

3. Heat 1 tablespoon of the vegetable oil in a heavy
deep 12-inch skillet over medium-high heat. Add
the veal in a total of 3 batches to the skillet, cooking for 2 to 3

minutes on each side or until golden brown, adding 1 tablespoon more vegetable oil between batches and heating it. Transfer the veal slices to a warm serving platter, cover and keep warm until ready to serve.

4. To serve, distribute the veal cutlets among 4 warmed dinner plates, garnish each with a dollop of the sour cream, then sprinkle with some of the sliced gherkin pickles. Serve at once as a main course.

CHAPTER 4

GREECE: FOOD FOR THE GODS

Greek Seasoning Mix

Soúpa Avgolémono

Melitzanosaláta

Stuffed Peppers
with Rice and
Kefalotíri Cheese

Greek Summer Salad

Briami

Baked Fish
with Tomato Sauce

Lamb Chops
with Skorthaliá

Keftéthes

Pastítsio

Chicken
with Walnut Sauce

GREEKS LOVE A PARTY and Hellenic social life revolves around a love of food, whether at home or at the boisterous Greek institution, the local *taverna*. When Greeks celebrate, they are celebrating both the food and the people. The Greek quest for the good life, coupled with warm hospitality, is revealed in an exuberant cuisine, and the result is always a bounteous table of food fit for the gods.

These foods are enhanced by the Greeks' favorite herbs and spices — oregano, mint, dill, cinnamon and allspice — which also happen to be some of the most seductive and popular seasonings in the world. I've included these in my seasoning blend. The herbs and spices of the blend work very differently depending on the dish. The cinnamon and allspice of the blend are warm and assertive, and make a delightful marriage with the creamy white sauce in the soothing baked macaroni and meat dish Pastítsio (page 64), for example. Yet, the sweet, cooling mint comes to the fore when you taste the refreshing Greek Summer Salad (page 58). In the presence of white wine and garlic, the sweet mountain-grown herbs of the blend impart a delicate flavor to fish, a favorite food among Greeks, represented here by a wonderful Baked Fish with Tomato Sauce (page 61).

Greek cuisine is known for its wide variety of nourishing dishes made from humble but delectable ingredients. Eggplants, tomatoes, lemons, bell peppers, garlic, olives and their oil are the mainstays of Greek daily life. These principal foodstuffs and the Greek passion for an abundance of these and other fresh vegetables inspires several of the dishes in this chapter. Begin with the ubiquitous eggplant

QUICKIES: EVERYDAY FOODS MADE INTERNATIONAL

Different Strokes
For bread with more flavor: Knead *Greek Seasoning Mix* into your pick of a single-loaf thawed frozen prepared white bread dough mix and bake according to package directions.

Chilled Rice Salad

Toss chilled cooked rice together with some slivered pitted Greek olives and scallions until well blended. Season with a touch of olive oil, *Greek Seasoning Mix,* salt and pepper.

Corn with a Cause

Sprinkle *Greek Seasoning Mix* over hot buttered corn on the cob for corn with spirit.

Double-Duty Dressing

Whisk together 1 part white-wine vinegar and 2 parts olive oil with *Greek Seasoning Mix,* salt and pepper to taste. Use as a dressing or marinade.

which is roasted to make Melitzanosaláta (page 56), a very unusual salad with a relish-like texture. Yogurt and lemon juice give this smoky-flavored salad a tangy quality.

Greece produces beautiful, large, flavorful lemons, and they take full advantage of them, using lemon juice in many dishes. Fragrant lemons and eggs create one of the most popular soups in Greece — and one of the most distinctive in the culinary world — Soúpa Avgolémono (page 55).

Lamb and garlic were made for each other, especially when seasoned with the herbs and spices that epitomize Greek cooking. Lamb Chops with Skorthaliá (page 62) shows us these two popular ingredients. Lamb is the favored meat in this country and garlic is never used sparingly. Skorthaliá is a garlic-laden sauce that is cousin to the French aïoli, and is distinguished by the addition of mashed potatoes, or sometimes even walnuts or almonds.

More glories of the Greek table await you as you try the recipes in this chapter. Now you too will see why the Greeks are always celebrating!

Greek Seasoning Mix

Makes about 1/2 cup

¼ cup dried oregano leaves, preferably Greek (Source List page 186)
2 tablespoons plus 1 teaspoon dried mint leaves
1 tablespoon plus 1 teaspoon dried dillweed
½ teaspoon ground cinnamon
½ teaspoon ground allspice

In a small bag or bowl (How-To page 11), combine the oregano leaves, mint leaves, dillweed, cinnamon and allspice. Shake or stir until well blended. Transfer to a clean, dry, airtight glass container. Store up to 3 months away from heat, light or moisture. Shake well before using.

Soúpa Avgolémono

(Greek Egg- and Lemon-Based Soup)
Servings: 4 (1¾ cups each)
Preparation Time: About 5 minutes
Cooking Time: 10 minutes

3 8-ounce bottles clam juice and 2 cups water
1 medium yellow onion, coarsely chopped
1 tablespoon *Greek Seasoning Mix* (page 54)
3 large eggs
1 cup fresh lemon juice (8 to 10 small lemons)
2 tablespoons finely chopped fresh parsley, to garnish

1. Bring the clam juice and water to a boil in a heavy nonreactive
2- to 3-quart saucepan over high heat. Add the onion and seasoning
mix and stir to blend. Reduce the heat to low and simmer for
7 minutes, stirring occasionally.

2. Meanwhile, in a nonreactive medium bowl, whisk the eggs while
gradually adding the lemon juice until a froth is formed. Gradually
pour in ½ cup of the hot (should *not* be boiling) clam juice mixture
while whisking constantly. Then stir this mixture back into the
saucepan with the remaining clam juice mixture. Stir the soup constantly for about 2 minutes more or until the soup thickens slightly.
Distribute the soup evenly among four soup bowls, sprinkle with
parsley and serve at once. (NOTE: The soup should still be frothy
when served.) Serves 4 as a main course or 6 as an appetizer.

Melitzanosaláta

(Greek Roasted Eggplant Salad)
Servings: 4
Preparation Time: About 15 minutes
Cooking Time: About 55 minutes
(Eggplants can be roasted up to 2 days ahead)

This delightful salad with the consistency of a relish is very refreshing; it has an unusual smoky flavor from the roasted eggplant that is then balanced with the sweet herbs and spices the Greeks are so fond of. This is a simple dish to prepare; to use your time wisely, roast the eggplants (steps #1 and #2) up to 2 days ahead. Let cool and refrigerate. On the day of serving just proceed with steps #3 and #4.

2 1-pound eggplants, unpeeled
1 medium yellow onion, coarsely chopped
2 cloves garlic, crushed
1 tablespoon plus 1 teaspoon *Greek Seasoning Mix* (page 54)
¼ cup fresh lemon juice (2 to 3 small lemons)
3 tablespoons olive oil, preferably Greek (available at supermarket)
2 tablespoons plain lowfat yogurt or skim milk
Salt and freshly ground pepper to taste
2 tablespoons finely chopped fresh parsley
⅓ cup coarsely chopped walnuts, to garnish (optional)
½ cup drained Greek Kalamata olives (available at supermarket)
    or other brine-cured olives, pitted, to garnish (optional)

Whole-wheat pita bread (Middle Eastern flat pocket bread),
    available at supermarket, toasted to serve

1. Preheat the oven to 375° F.

2. Place each whole eggplant directly on the burner or over a medium-low flame on the stove, with the stem pointed away from the flame. Carefully roast for a total of 7 minutes or until the skin becomes evenly charred and begins to blister, using tongs to rotate every few minutes. Remove the eggplants and prick each all over with a fork. Wrap each eggplant in foil and seal tightly. Then transfer the eggplants to the middle rack of the oven and bake for 45 minutes, turning occasionally.

3. Carefully unwrap the eggplants (to avoid steam burn). When cool enough to handle, remove and discard the skin and stems. Transfer the pulp to the bowl of a food processor fitted with a metal blade. Add the onion, garlic, seasoning mix and lemon juice. Process, while adding the olive oil through the feed tube, to prevent the blade from stopping. Continue to process until the mixture is smooth and well blended. Transfer the eggplant mixture to a medium nonreactive bowl and stir in the yogurt until well blended. Season with salt and pepper and stir in the parsley until combined.

4. Garnish the eggplant salad with walnuts and olives if desired. Serve chilled as a side dish or at room temperature as a dip accompanied by toasted whole-wheat pita bread.

 # Stuffed Peppers with Rice and Kefalotíri Cheese

Servings: 4 (2 peppers each)
Preparation Time: About 20 minutes
Cooking Time: 40 to 45 minutes
(can be made up to 2 days ahead)

For a shortcut, pour boiling water over the cored and seeded peppers several times before filling. This will abbreviate the baking time by about 10 minutes, helping to tenderize the peppers more quickly.

8 medium-sized red or green bell peppers (about 3¼ pounds)
   (NOTE: Choose peppers with flat bottoms so that they can stand up easily)
1 28-ounce can crushed tomatoes
3 cups cooked white rice (follow package directions)
1 medium yellow onion, finely chopped
½ cup unseasoned dry bread crumbs
¾ cup freshly grated *kefalotíri* cheese (hard Greek sheeps' milk cheese, available at cheese shop or see Source List page 186) or Parmesan cheese (3-ounce piece)
2 teaspoons *Greek Seasoning Mix* (page 54)
Salt and freshly ground pepper to taste

1. Preheat the oven to 375° F.

HINT: If you do not have any leftover rice stored in your refrigerator, one option is to plan to cook rice up to 2 days ahead. Or, just start cooking the rice 10 minutes before you begin step #1.

2. Slice the top 1 inch off of each pepper, leaving the stem on, and reserve. Core and seed the peppers.

3. Combine 2 cups of the crushed tomatoes, the cooked rice, onion, bread crumbs, ½ cup of the *kefalotíri* cheese and seasoning mix in a large nonreactive bowl. Stir together until well blended and season with salt and pepper.

4. Firmly pack each pepper ¾ full with the stuffing and stand peppers upright in a large baking dish (a 14-by-10½ by 2½-inch dish works well). Replace the reserved bell pepper tops and drizzle with the remaining 1½ cups crushed tomatoes and the remaining ¼ cup cheese.

5. Bake for 40 to 45 minutes or until the peppers are tender. The stuffed peppers may be served hot or at room temperature as a main course.

Greek Summer Salad

Servings: 4
Preparation Time: About 25 minutes
Cooking Time: None

SALAD:
4   medium-sized ripe but firm tomatoes, cut into eighths
1   medium red onion, very thinly sliced
1   medium green bell pepper, cut into ¼ -inch-wide strips
1   medium unpeeled cucumber, thinly sliced
1   4-ounce piece of feta cheese, crumbled
1   cup drained Greek Kalamata olives (available at supermarket)
       or other brine-cured olives, pitted

DRESSING: (Makes about ¾ cup)
½   cup olive oil, preferably Greek (available at supermarket)
¼   cup fresh lemon juice (2 to 3 small lemons)
2   teaspoons *Greek Seasoning Mix* (page 54)
Salt and freshly ground pepper to taste

Whole-wheat pita bread (Middle-Eastern flat pocket bread), available
   from supermarket, to serve

1. To prepare the salad: In a large glass salad bowl toss together the tomatoes, onion, green bell pepper, cucumber, feta cheese and olives.

2. To prepare the dressing: In a small nonreactive bowl whisk together the olive oil, lemon juice and seasoning mix until well blended. Season with salt and pepper and pour over the salad. Gently toss the salad with the dressing until the salad is well coated. This salad can be served as a main course for 4 accompanied with bread or as a side dish for 6.

Greek gods had human characteristics — both vices and virtues — and even their immortality was not guaranteed. The ancient Greeks credited their gods for most occurrences in the world. The roles of gods changed over the centuries, but each had a basic personality that endured through the ages.

♦ Thunderbolt-carrying Zeus was the king and most powerful god of all. When he wasn't overseeing the other gods, he was watching over his home, Olympus — heaven — eating ambrosia and drinking nectar.

♦ Athena was the goddess of wisdom and crafts. She was a warrior, and unseen protectress of heroes, defending them against foes.

♦ Tumultuous Poseidon, the god of the sea, carried a fisherman's trident and had a "stormy" temper.

Briami

(Greek Vegetable Casserole)
Servings: 4
Preparation Time: About 15 minutes
Cooking Time: 30 to 35 minutes
(can be made up to 3 days ahead)

½ pound red boiling potatoes, unpeeled but cut
     into ¼-inch-thick slices
12 ounces green bell peppers, thinly sliced
1½ pounds ripe tomatoes, coarsely chopped
1 cup finely chopped red onion
½ pound medium zucchini, cut lengthwise into ¼-inch-thick slices
½ cup olive oil, preferably Greek (available at supermarket)
2 teaspoons honey
1 tablespoon *Greek Seasoning Mix* (page 54)
3 cloves garlic, crushed
Salt and freshly ground pepper to taste
3 tablespoons finely chopped fresh dillweed or parsley,
     to garnish (optional)

1. Preheat the oven to 450° F.

2. Arrange the potatoes in a single layer on the bottom of a 2-quart baking dish. Top with a layer of the green bell peppers, tomatoes, onion and then zucchini, pressing down on the top.

3. In a small bowl whisk together the olive oil, honey, seasoning mix and garlic and season with salt and pepper. Pour evenly over the vegetables in the baking dish.

4. Bake in the middle third of the oven for 30 to 35 minutes or until the top is a delicate brown and the vegetables are tender. Baste the vegetables with their juices and garnish with the dillweed if desired just before serving. Serve hot as a main course for 4 or as a side dish for 6.

Baked Fish with Tomato Sauce

Servings: 4
Preparation Time: About 5 minutes
Cooking Time: 15 minutes

4 (7-ounce) red snapper fillets or other mild, firm, white-fleshed fish
2 medium-sized ripe tomatoes, coarsely chopped
2 tablespoons tomato paste
¼ cup dry white wine
2 tablespoons olive oil, preferably Greek (available at supermarket)
2 cloves garlic, crushed
2 teaspoons *Greek Seasoning Mix* (page 54)
Salt to taste
2 tablespoons finely chopped fresh parsley, to garnish (optional)

1. Preheat the oven to 350° F.

2. Arrange the fish fillets in a single layer, skin-side-down in the bottom of a 13-by-9-by-2-inch baking dish. In a nonreactive medium bowl combine the tomatoes, tomato paste, white wine, olive oil, garlic and seasoning mix, stirring until well blended, and season with salt. Ladle the tomato mixture over the fillets until covered evenly.

3. Cover the baking dish with aluminum foil and bake for 15 minutes or until the fish filets are opaque throughout. Garnish with parsley if desired and serve at once as a main course.

◆ Apollo was the god of music, poetry, purification, prophecy and healing.

Many other gods played major and minor roles in Greek mythology. Among them were Aphrodite, goddess of physical beauty and love; Ares, the god of war; Demeter, goddess of the grain; and Dionysus, the god of ecstasy, wine and vegetation.

Mediterranean Feast
(*Vegetarian Menu for 4*)
Baked Fish with Tomato
  Sauce
Melitzanosaláta (page 56)
  served with pita bread
  (supermarket)
Rice Pudding (supermarket
  or deli — premade)
Wine: chilled Greek Retsina
  (traditional Greek white
  wine with a distinctive
  pine flavor)

Lamb Chops with Skorthaliá

(Lamb Chops with Greek Garlic Sauce)
Servings: 4
Preparation Time: About 15 minutes
Cooking Time: 25 to 30 minutes
(Skorthaliá *can be made up to 1 day ahead*)

HINT: To save time: If you do not have leftover mashed potatoes, you can prepare 1 cup mashed potatoes up to 2 days ahead. Alternatively, the mashed potatoes can be made while the lamb is cooking by boiling and mashing 2 medium potatoes. In this way, the potatoes will be ready in time to proceed with step #3.

LAMB:

4 boned loin lamb chops, about 1½ inches thick
    (about 6 ounces each, trimmed)
1 tablespoon *Greek Seasoning Mix* (page 54)
⅛ cup finely chopped fresh mint or oregano, to garnish (optional)

SAUCE: (Makes 1¼ cups)
1 small head garlic, cloves peeled
1 cup leftover firmly packed mashed potatoes (or fresh,
    made from 2 medium potatoes)
½ cup olive oil, preferably Greek (available at supermarket)
¼ cup white-wine vinegar
Salt and freshly ground pepper to taste

1. Preheat the oven to 350° F.

2. To prepare the lamb: Using kitchen twine, tie each chop into a neat round. Season both sides of each chop with some of the seasoning mix. Place each chop on a piece of foil, seal the foil packets tightly and transfer to a baking sheet. Bake for 25 to 30 minutes for medium-rare, depending on thickness. (NOTE: Be careful not to overcook the lamb, as it will continue to cook slightly after being removed from oven due to retained heat.)

3. Meanwhile, to make the sauce: Add the peeled garlic cloves to the bowl of a food processor fitted with a metal blade or to a blender and process the garlic about 1 minute or until minced. Add the mashed potatoes, ¼ cup of the olive oil and the vinegar and process just until blended. With the machine running, gradually pour in the remaining ¼ cup olive oil in a slow, steady stream through the feed tube until it is incorporated and the sauce is completely smooth. Season with salt and pepper. (NOTE: The sauce should have a mayonnaise-like consistency.) Whisk to combine just before serving.

4. To serve, open each packet carefully to avoid steam burn. Remove and discard the twine and place each chop on a heated dinner plate. Spoon some of the sauce over each, garnish with fresh mint if desired and serve at once as a main course.

Keftéthes

(Greek Meatballs)
Servings: 6 as an appetizer
Preparation Time: About 15 minutes
Cooking Time: 20 minutes

1 pound extra-lean ground beef or lean ground lamb
½ cup dry unseasoned bread crumbs
1 small white onion, minced
1 tablespoon *Greek Seasoning Mix* (page 54)
3 tablespoons *ouzo* (Greek anise-flavored liqueur) or Sambuca
   (Italian anise-flavored liqueur)
2 tablespoons finely chopped fresh mint or parsley
½ teaspoon salt
¼ teaspoon freshly ground pepper
1 large egg

1. Preheat the oven to 450° F.

2. Combine the beef, bread crumbs, onion, seasoning mix, *ouzo*, 1 tablespoon of the mint, salt, pepper and the egg and mix thoroughly until well blended. Spoon a tablespoon of the mixture and using your hands shape into tightly packed balls about 1 inch in diameter. Repeat the process until you have about 2½ dozen meatballs.

3. Place the meatballs about ½ inch apart on a baking sheet. Bake for 20 minutes or until the meat is cooked and no pink remains, and the meatballs are golden brown all over. Serve hot garnished with the remaining 1 tablespoon of fresh mint for hors d'oeuvres (pass with cocktail picks) or as an appetizer.

HINT: Use this work saver to shape dozens of meatballs in minutes! Roll the meatball mixture into a log 1-inch in diameter. Slice the log into 1-inch-long pieces and round the pieces into balls. If the meat mixture is too sticky, rinse your hands with cold water before starting to shape the meatballs.

Pastítsio

(Baked Macaroni with Meat)
Servings: 4
Preparation Time: About 15 minutes
Cooking Time: About 80 minutes

If you love pasta, then you will adore this elaborate but easy-to-make Greek dish. Heightened by red wine and cloaked with a soothing sauce, this is a meal you will not forget.

FILLING:

8 ounces elbow macaroni
1 pound extra-lean ground beef
1 medium yellow onion, coarsely chopped
¾ cup dry red wine
2 tablespoons tomato paste
1½ tablespoons *Greek Seasoning Mix* (page 54)
¾ cup freshly grated *kefalotíri* cheese (hard Greek sheeps' milk cheese, available at cheese shop or see Source List page 186) or Parmesan cheese
Salt and freshly ground pepper to taste
Vegetable oil, to grease pan

SAUCE:

3 tablespoons unsalted butter or unsalted margarine
3 tablespoons unbleached white flour
4 cups skim milk, at room temperature
3 large eggs, lightly beaten, at room temperature
⅛ teaspoon ground nutmeg, preferably freshly grated
Salt and freshly ground pepper to taste

1. To prepare the filling: Bring a 4- to 6-quart pot of water to a boil. Add the macaroni, return to a boil and cook for 5 to 9 minutes, stirring occasionally, or until just *al dente* (slightly firm to the bite). Drain, refresh under cold running water and reserve.

2. Combine the beef, onion, wine, tomato paste, seasoning mix and *kefalotíri* cheese in a nonreactive medium bowl and stir until well blended. Season with salt and pepper.

3. Lightly grease the bottom and sides of a 3-quart baking dish.

Spread half of the cooked macaroni in the bottom of the dish. Spread evenly with all the meat mixture. Then top with an even layer of the remaining macaroni.

4. Preheat the oven to 350° F.

5. To prepare the sauce: In a 2- to 3-quart saucepan over low heat, melt the butter, then whisk in the flour until large bubbles appear, about 2 minutes. Cook, whisking constantly, for 2 minutes more, but do not let brown. Gradually add the milk, whisking constantly until well blended and smooth. Then cook, whisking constantly for 3 to 4 minutes more or until slightly thickened.

6. Whisk ⅓ of the milk mixture into the beaten eggs, then whisk this mixture back into the saucepan along with the nutmeg. Cook, stirring vigorously for 3 minutes; the sauce should be very thick. Do not let the sauce come to a boil. Season with salt and pepper.

7. Ladle the sauce evenly over the macaroni, smoothing the surface with a spatula, so that none of the macaroni is left exposed. Bake for 50 to 60 minutes or until the filling is cooked, no pink remains and the top is a delicate brown. Let stand 10 minutes before serving. To serve, cut into squares and transfer to heated dinner plates. Serve hot as a main course.

Chicken with Walnut Sauce

Servings: 4
Preparation Time: About 15 minutes
Cooking Time: 25 to 30 minutes

CHICKEN:
4 boneless, skinless chicken breasts (1¼ pounds)

SAUCE: (Makes ¾ cup)
3 ounces walnuts (¾ cup), toasted (procedure page 102)
   and coarsely chopped
1 tablespoon olive oil, preferably Greek (available at supermarket)
½ cup dry white wine
2 teaspoons *Greek Seasoning Mix* (page 54)
1 tablespoon honey

A NUT FOR WALNUTS

There's more to walnuts than the occasional nibble with cocktails; classic dishes from many nations feature walnuts and they have a history rich in flavor. For the Romans, the walnut simulated the human brain: its outer green husk the scalp, the hard shell the protective skull, the paper-like partitions between the nut halves the membrane and the double-lobed nut, the two hemispheres of the brain.

It has been said that at one time in Germany walnuts were so revered that a farmer had to plant a specified number of walnut trees before he was allowed to marry. Ancient Greeks fried their foods in walnut oil, Europeans of the Middle Ages ground walnuts to a paste and then used the paste to thicken sauces — much as the Arabs and Persians did decades before. Fourteenth-century Frenchmen preserved walnuts in spiced honey, and three centuries later, French peasants ground walnuts with acorns and used the paste to make bread. And the English have even made catsup from walnut meats.

The walnut is an excellent food for vegetarians because its protein is closer to animal protein than any vegetable except the soybean.

The Walnut Family Tree

There are at least 17 species of walnuts, with the most common varieties being:

◆ Black Walnuts: They are native to North America and there are both wild and cultivated varieties.

◆ Persian Walnuts: Also called "English Walnuts," they are much easier to crack open than black walnuts and are considered to have superior flavor.

◆ White Walnuts: Also called "Butternuts," they are the nut of the hickory tree (a member of the walnut family). White walnuts grow wild and were popular with American Indians, who used to boil the walnut meats and use the resulting fat as a lubricant, the liquid for baby food and the ground meat for flour.

Salt and freshly ground pepper to taste

⅛ cup finely chopped fresh mint, to garnish

1. Preheat the oven to 350° F.

2. To make the sauce: Combine the walnuts, olive oil, white wine, seasoning mix and honey in the bowl of a food processor fitted with a metal blade or in the container of a blender. Process about 2 minutes or until puréed but not completely smooth. Season with salt and pepper.

3. Arrange the chicken breasts in a nonreactive 3-quart baking dish. Spread the walnut mixture evenly over the surface of the chicken breasts. Cover the dish with aluminum foil and bake for 25 to 30 minutes or until the chicken tests done when pierced in the thickest part and the juices run clear.

4. Using a slotted spoon, transfer the chicken breasts to individual heated plates and ladle some of the sauce over each. Sprinkle with salt and pepper, and garnish with the finely chopped fresh mint. Serve hot as a main course.

CHAPTER 5

SUNNY PROVENCE

Provençal Seasoning Mix

Ratatouille

Artichoke Omelette

Tapenade

Soupe au Pistou

Tomato Gratin

Pissaladière with Black Olives

Daube de Boeuf Provençale

Provençal Shepherds' Lamb Chops with Mint

Bourride Flavored with Aïoli

Papeton d'Aubergines

PROVENCE, IN THE SOUTH of France, is justly famous for its cuisine, different from the cooking of any of the other regions of France. The cuisine of this charming area evokes the French countryside, where wild herbs flourish and abound among the sun-drenched hillsides. Of all the cuisines of the world, none uses the flavor of herbs more memorably than Provence. The classic seasoning blend *herbes de Provence* is used throughout the region and has many variations. The recipe I have given you on page 68 includes thyme, basil, savory, fennel and edible French lavender flowers that Provence is so well known for.

As in many other Mediterranean lands, Provence bases its cuisine on pearly garlic, noble olive oil and pungent, bursting tomatoes, not on excess salt and dairy products as in other areas of France. What draws people to this cuisine is the lavish, but careful, use of fresh, intensely flavored ingredients, which gives Provençal cuisine its characteristic fragrance and explosion of tastes. What the sun, sea, and salt air provide is a highly flavored cuisine with an earthy quality.

The world-famous spread, Tapenade (page 71), made from olives, anchovies, capers and fresh basil, demonstrates how a few ingredients, if combined correctly, can burst with flavor. Simple ingredients like eggplant, zucchini, tomatoes and bell peppers, as used in Ratatouille (page 69) become vibrant when enhanced by the flavor and fragrance of the seasoning blend .

Now you can sample one of Provence's most famous beef dishes, Daube de Boeuf Provençale (page 75), a succulent stew braised in lively red wine. The versatile Pissaladière with Black Olives (page 74), a Provençal onion tart, can be served for a stylish luncheon, as a buffet dish or as finger-food at a picnic. The perfume-like lavender flowers of the seasoning blend contrast nicely with the mellowness

QUICKIES: EVERYDAY FOODS MADE INTERNATIONAL

Tuna Treat
Add *Provençal Seasoning Mix* to homemade or deli tuna salad for tuna salad with style.

Terrific Tomatoes
Halve 2 large ripe but firm tomatoes crosswise. Brush the cut side of each half lightly with olive oil. Sprinkle each half with

Provençal Seasoning Mix, salt and pepper. Arrange cut-side-up on a broiler pan and broil in a preheated broiler about 5 minutes or until the top of the tomatoes are a delicate brown and soft to the touch.

Stuff It!
Combine homemade unseasoned bread stuffing or prepared unseasoned stuffing mix with a small handful of dried currants until well blended. Stir in some *Provençal Seasoning Mix* and salt and pepper to taste.

Fast French Onion Soup
Prepare canned onion soup according to package directions, and divide among 4 ovenproof 2-cup soup bowls, filling each three-quarters full. Sprinkle the top of each with some shredded French or Swiss Gruyère cheese in an even layer, followed by a little *Provençal Seasoning Mix.* Bake in a preheated 375° F. oven for 15 minutes or until the cheese is melted and dappled golden brown.

of the caramelized onions and the boldly flavored anchovies of this tart. And don't overlook the redolent Bourride Flavored with Aïoli (page 79), a fish stew scented with garlic mayonnaise, known as "the butter of Provence."

After you have tasted some of these recipes, I hope you will agree that Provence is the land of some of life's purest culinary pleasures.

Provençal Seasoning Mix
Makes about 1/2 cup

2 tablespoons dried thyme leaves
2 tablespoons dried basil leaves
2 tablespoons dried savory leaves (available at supermarket or gourmet store or see Source List page 186)
1 tablespoon fennel seeds
1 tablespoon dried French lavender flowers* (see Source List page 186)

In a small bag or bowl (How-To, page 11), combine the thyme leaves, basil leaves, savory leaves, fennel seeds and lavender flowers. Shake or stir until well blended. Transfer to a clean, dry, airtight glass container. Store up to 3 months away from heat, light or moisture. Shake well before using.

* NOTE: Only buy edible, organically grown dried French lavender flowers. Do not buy flowers that have been chemically treated, particularly if they are meant for use in potpourri or room scent.

Ratatouille

Servings: 4 (1¼ cups each)
Preparation Time: About 10 minutes
Cooking Time: 20 minutes
(can be made up to 3 days ahead)

1 tablespoon olive oil, preferably French (available at supermarket)
1 large yellow onion, coarsely chopped
3 cloves garlic, crushed
1 small unpeeled eggplant (about ¾ pound), cut into ¼-inch dice
1 small zucchini, cut into ¼-inch dice
4 medium-sized ripe plum tomatoes, seeded and coarsely chopped
1 7-ounce jar roasted red peppers, drained and coarsely chopped
　　(available at supermarket or gourmet store)
1½ teaspoons *Provençal Seasoning Mix* (page 68)
2 tablespoons fresh lemon juice
Salt and freshly ground pepper to taste
2 tablespoons finely chopped fresh basil (optional)

1. Heat the olive oil in a nonreactive heavy 12-inch skillet over medium-high heat. Add the onion and garlic and cook, stirring, about 4 minutes or until the onion is softened. Transfer the onion mixture to a medium bowl.

2. Add the eggplant, zucchini, plum tomatoes, red peppers and seasoning mix. Cover the skillet with aluminum foil or a lid and cook, stirring occasionally, for 15 minutes or just until the eggplant and zucchini is tender.

3. Stir the eggplant mixture into the bowl with the onion mixture along with the lemon juice. Season with salt and pepper and stir in the basil if desired. Serve at room temperature as a side dish.

Artichoke Omelette

Servings: 2
Preparation Time: About 5 minutes
Cooking Time: 20 to 25 minutes

2 large whole eggs
6 large egg whites
2 tablespoons cold water
½ teaspoon *Provençal Seasoning Mix* (page 68)
¼ teaspoon salt
¼ teaspoon freshly ground pepper
1 tablespoon olive oil, preferably French (available at supermarket)
2 6-ounce jars marinated artichoke hearts, drained and quartered
    lengthwise (available at supermarket or gourmet store)

Garden salad, to serve

1. Combine the whole eggs, egg whites, water, seasoning mix and salt and pepper in a medium bowl and whisk until well blended. Heat the olive oil in a heavy 9-inch ovenproof skillet over low heat. Add the artichoke hearts and cook, stirring, for 3 minutes or just until heated through.

2. Preheat the oven to 350° F.

3. Pour the beaten egg mixture over the artichokes in the skillet. Cook for 8 to 12 minutes, or until the edges are set. (NOTE: Do not stir the egg mixture, just shake the skillet gently once after 4 minutes.)

4. Transfer the skillet to the oven and bake in the middle third of the oven, for 7 to 9 minutes or until cooked through and thoroughly set but not dry. To serve, cut the omelette into 4 wedges and serve at once for 2 as a main course with a garden salad or for 4 as a side dish.

Tapenade

(Provençal Olive Spread)
Servings: 4 to 6 (makes about ¾ cup)
Preparation Time: About 15 minutes
Cooking Time: None
(can be made up to 2 weeks ahead)

1 cup drained Nyons olives or other brine-cured black olive,
    such as Greek Kalamata olives (available at supermarket or
    gourmet store), pitted
4 anchovy fillets, rinsed and patted dry with paper towels
3 cloves garlic, crushed
2 tablespoons drained vinegar-packed capers, rinsed
1 teaspoon *Provençal Seasoning Mix* (page 68)
1 tablespoon finely chopped fresh basil or parsley (optional)
3 tablespoons olive oil, preferably French (available at supermarket)
2 tablespoons fresh lemon juice

Toasted thinly sliced bread of choice, to serve

Combine the olives, anchovies, garlic, capers, seasoning mix and
basil if desired in the bowl of a food processor fitted with a metal
blade. Process about 1 minute or until the mixture is very finely
chopped. With the machine running, gradually add the olive oil,
then the lemon juice through the feed tube in a thin, steady stream.
Process about 2 minutes, scraping down the sides of the bowl as
needed, or until the mixture is fairly smooth and paste-like. (NOTE:
Traditionally, this is served at room temperature and spread on toast
for hors d'oeuvres or as an appetizer. But it may also be used as a
dressing for a salad, in soups or tossed with pasta.)

VARIATION: SUN-DRIED TOMATO TAPENADE. Though this is not a traditional Provençal dish, the additional flavor of the tomatoes is very
Provençal. Substitute 1 cup drained marinated sun-dried tomato halves
for the olives. Reserve 3 tablespoons of the oil from the tomatoes and
use it in place of the 3 tablespoons olive oil. Makes about 1 cup.

THE CALL OF THE CAPER

Capers are the small unopened flowers of the *Capparis spinosa* bush that are harvested just as the plants begin to bud. The flowers are then pick-led in vinegar or brine. The piquant capers are either sold vinegar-packed in glass jars or salt-ed and sold loose (in bulk) from wooden vats of brine. Although they are demure in size (the size of a pearl or smaller), each caper packs a bouquet of unique flavor.

Caper Cachet
Of the 170 varieties of capers, the best are said to be the tiny and aromat-ic *nonpareils* from the South of France. Larger varieties are usually from North Africa or Spain.

Storage
◆ For vinegar-packed capers: Store capers in an airtight nonmetal con-tainer submerged in the original vinegar in the refrigerator for up to 9 months.

◆ For salt-packed capers: Store salted, loose capers in an airtight nonmetal container at room tem-perature for up to 5 months.

Soupe au Pistou

(Provençal Vegetable Bean Soup with Basil and Garlic)
Servings: 4 (2¼ cups each) or 6 (1½ cups each)
Preparation Time: About 15 minutes
Cooking Time: About 35 minutes
(Soup can be made up to 3 days ahead;
pistou up to 4 days ahead)

HINT: To save time: Substitute 1 cup prepared pesto available at the supermarket or gourmet store for the *Pistou* sauce. If done in this way, you can speed through this recipe, skipping step #2 altogether.

⟅⟆

Fanciful France
(Make-Ahead Vegetarian Menu for 4 to 6)
Soupe au Pistou
French Baguette
Fresh Fruit Tart (bakery)
Wine: Côtes du Rhône

⟅⟆

SOUP:

1 tablespoon olive oil, preferably French
1 medium white onion, coarsely chopped
4 small leeks, white part only, thinly sliced
2 ribs celery, thinly sliced
½ teaspoon salt
2 quarts canned low-sodium chicken broth
2 medium red boiling potatoes, unpeeled but cut into ¼-inch dice
4 medium-sized ripe tomatoes, seeded and coarsely chopped
4 ounces green beans, ends trimmed and beans cut diagonally into thirds
2 teaspoons *Provençal Seasoning Mix* (page 68)
1 15-ounce can cannellini beans or red kidney beans, drained and rinsed
1 cup *ditalini* or other small pasta such as *rotini* or elbow macaroni
½ teaspoon freshly ground pepper
Freshly grated Parmesan cheese or shredded Gruyère cheese,
    to garnish (optional)

PISTOU: (Makes 1 cup) or 1 cup prepared pesto (available at supermarket
    or gourmet store)
4 cloves garlic
3 cups fresh basil leaves (about 4 bunches), washed thoroughly and dried
¾ cup freshly grated Parmesan cheese
½ cup olive oil, preferably French (available at supermarket)
Salt and freshly ground pepper to taste

1. To prepare the soup: Heat the olive oil in a nonreactive 6- to 8-quart pot over medium-high heat. Add the onion, leeks, celery and salt. Cook for 6 to 8 minutes, stirring often, until the onion is soft and the leeks tender. Stir in the 2 quarts chicken broth, potatoes, tomatoes, green beans and seasoning mix. Bring to a boil, reduce the heat to medium and cover. Cook for 15 minutes, stirring once.

2. Meanwhile, to prepare the *Pistou*: In the container of a blender or in the bowl of a food processor fitted with a metal blade pulse the garlic about 1 minute or until very finely chopped. Add the basil and Parmesan cheese and process until well blended, scraping down the sides of the bowl as necessary. With the machine running, gradually pour in the olive oil through the feed tube in a slow, steady stream until you have a smooth paste. Season with salt and pepper. Reserve the *pistou* until ready to serve.

3. Stir the cannellini beans, pasta and pepper into the soup. Cook, uncovered, for 5 to 9 minutes more or until the pasta is *al dente* (slightly firm to the bite).

4. To serve, ladle the soup into bowls and just before serving stir some *pistou* into each bowl and garnish with Parmesan cheese if desired. Serve at once as a main course and pass the remaining *pistou* in a bowl separately.

Tomato Gratin

Servings: 4
Preparation Time: About 5 minutes
Cooking Time: 15 to 20 minutes

2 tablespoons olive oil, preferably French (available at supermarket)
4 cloves garlic, crushed
⅓ cup finely chopped fresh parsley
½ teaspoon *Provençal Seasoning Mix* (page 68)
Salt and freshly ground pepper to taste
1¼ pounds ripe but firm tomatoes, cut into ¼-inch-thick slices
⅛ cup dry unseasoned bread crumbs

1. Preheat the oven to 450° F.

2. Combine the olive oil, garlic, parsley and seasoning mix in a small bowl. Stir together until well blended and season with salt and pepper.

3. Overlap the tomato slices in a pattern of parallel lines but in a single layer in a nonreactive 1-quart gratin dish or baking dish. Spread the parsley mixture over the tomatoes, then sprinkle evenly with the bread crumbs.

THE LOVE APPLE

In the past, the tomato, along with a few other vegetables such as the potato, was misunderstood and maligned. Now the tomato is revered and loved and is one of the most widely used vegetables worldwide. Centuries ago, it was referred to as the "golden apple" because the first tomatoes to reach Europe were yellow. The French and English nurtured tomatoes in their gardens as an ornamental plant and the tomato earned a reputation as an aphrodisiac — hence the term "love apple."

The Italians could be considered the tomato "pioneers." They were the swiftest in finding a culinary home place for the tomato after its arrival in Europe and their cuisine has made full use of its extraordinary flavors. Now the tomato has become a mainstay of American and European diets.

Tomato Tricks

◆ Always store ripe tomatoes at room temperature, but, if they need ripening, place them in a brown paper bag and close tightly. Keep at room temperature for a day or two. The paper bag captures the ethylene gas emitted from the tomatoes, which helps ripen them.

◆ To peel tomatoes quickly, drop whole tomatoes in a pot of boiling water for 10 to 12 seconds. Refresh immediately under cold running water. When the tomatoes are just cool enough to handle (but still warm) remove the skin carefully with a sharp paring knife.

4. Bake for 15 to 20 minutes in the upper third of the oven or until the top is golden brown and almost all the liquid is gone. Serve hot directly from the gratin dish as a side dish.

Pissaladière with Black Olives

(Provençal Onion Tart)
Servings: 4
Preparation Time: About 15 minutes
Cooking Time: 50 to 55 minutes
(Dough can be made through step #1 up to 2 days ahead;
onion mixture can be made through step #2 up to 2 days ahead)

I love to serve Pissaladière for an informal dinner or Sunday brunch.
I firmly believe in my "make-ahead strategy"— what can't be done tomorrow is done today. In other words, make the dough and filling ahead, so that all you have to do the day of serving is assemble the tart, which takes just 5 minutes.

DOUGH:
1½ cups unbleached white flour, plus more to dust
1 teaspoon salt
½ cup unsalted butter or unsalted margarine (1 stick),
    cut into 8 pieces and chilled
1 large egg yolk beaten with 2 tablespoons cold water
3 to 4 tablespoons ice water

FILLING:
1 tablespoon olive oil, preferably French
2 pounds yellow onions, thinly sliced
1 teaspoon *Provençal Seasoning Mix* (page 68)
10 anchovy fillets, rinsed, dried and cut in half lengthwise
6 Nyons olives or other brine-packed black olive such as
    Greek Kalamata, cut in half lengthwise and pitted

1. To prepare the dough: In a medium bowl sift together the flour and salt. Using a pastry blender or fork, cut in the chilled butter a few pieces at a time, until mixture resembles coarse cornmeal. Stir in the egg yolk beaten with water until well blended. Then stir in the

ice water a tablespoon at a time, as needed to allow the dough to form but not become sticky. Form into a flat disk and wrap in waxed paper and chill until ready to use.

2. Meanwhile, to prepare the filling: Heat the olive oil in a heavy deep 12-inch skillet over medium-low heat. Add the onions, stir in the seasoning mix and cover with aluminum foil or a lid. Cook, stirring occasionally, for 30 minutes or until the onions are light golden brown and just beginning to fall apart. Reserve until ready to use.

3. Preheat the oven to 425° F.

4. Roll out the dough on a lightly floured work surface and trim the edges evenly to form a 14-inch-by-10-inch rectangle. Line a 13-inch-by-9-inch-by-2-inch baking pan with the dough, allowing ½ inch of the dough to come up all 4 sides to form a ridge. Spread the onion mixture in an even layer over the dough and smooth the surface. Arrange the anchovy fillet halves, end-to-end, in a lattice pattern over the onion mixture and place a pitted olive half in the center of each of the lattice-formed diamonds (Figure 1).

5. Bake in the middle third of the oven for 20 to 25 minutes or until the crust edges are crisp and a delicate brown. Serve hot as a main course for 4 or as an appetizer or side dish for 6.

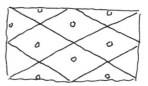

Figure 1

Daube de Boeuf Provençale

(Provençal Beef and Wine Stew)
Servings: 4 (1½ cups each) or 6 (1 cup each)
Preparation Time: About 25 minutes
Cooking Time: About 2 hours and 15 minutes
(can be made up to 3 days ahead)

In the past, French stews of this kind were braised in a daubière, a pot with a saucer-shaped lid from which this recipe derived its name. Historically, this stew was cooked for 6 hours or more, to allow the meat to become full-flavored and tender. Though I have altered the recipe to reduce the braising time by a third, by carefully balancing amounts of certain ingredients and using a faster cooking cut of meat in smaller, bite-size pieces, the hearty taste and tender meat of the classic French stew remains. This stew is best when

The Perfect Provence
(Entertaining Menu for 4 to 6)
Daube de Boeuf Provençale
Macaroni Gratin (page 77)
Tossed Green Salad
Fruit and Cheese Board
Wine: Cabernet Sauvignon

HINT: A work saver: Pit olives ahead of time and return them to their jar with the brine and refrigerate until ready to use.

made ahead up to 3 days, which allows the flavors to blend. Traditionally this dish was served with Macaroni Gratin; see opposite page for a fast and easy recipe.

¼ cup unbleached white flour
Salt and freshly ground pepper to taste
2 pounds lean, boneless beef, preferably chuck, trimmed and cut
    into 1-inch cubes
2 tablespoons olive oil, preferably French (available at supermarket)
1 medium white onion, coarsely chopped
3 cloves garlic, crushed
1 28-ounce can crushed tomatoes
1 cup dry red wine
2 teaspoons *Provençal Seasoning Mix* (page 68)
¼ cup drained Nyons olives or other brine-cured black olive such as
    Greek Kalamata (available at supermarket or gourmet store), pitted
¼ cup drained Picholine olives or other brine-cured green olive such as
    Calabrese (available at supermarket or gourmet store), pitted

1. Preheat the oven to 325° F.

2. Combine the flour, salt and pepper in a large bowl and mix until well blended. Add the beef and dredge with the flour mixture until well coated, shaking off the excess flour; reserve.

3. Heat the olive oil in a heavy nonreactive 6- to 8-quart flameproof casserole over medium-high heat. Add the onion and garlic and cook for 4 minutes, stirring often, or until the onion is soft but not browned. Add the beef and cook for 7 to 9 minutes, turning until browned evenly.

4. Stir in the crushed tomatoes, red wine and seasoning mix and bring the mixture to a gentle simmer, stirring occasionally. Remove the casserole from the heat, cover and transfer to the oven.

5. Bake, covered, for 1 hour. Then uncover the casserole and bake for 1 hour more or until the beef is tender and the stew has thickened. Stir in the black and green olives and serve hot as a main course accompanied by Macaroni Gratin, if desired.

Macaroni Gratin

Servings: 6
Preparation Time: About 10 minutes
Cooking Time: 2 to 3 minutes

1   pound elbow macaroni
1½ cups canned low-sodium beef broth
1¼ cups freshly grated Parmesan cheese

1. Preheat the broiler.

2. Meanwhile, prepare the macaroni: To a 4- to 6-quart pot of boiling water add the macaroni. Return to a boil and boil for 4 to 6 minutes, stirring occasionally, or until *al dente* (slightly firm to the bite). Drain in a colander.

3. Spoon half the cooked macaroni into a 2-quart ovenproof gratin dish, spreading evenly. Ladle the beef broth over all and sprinkle the surface evenly with half the Parmesan cheese. Add the remaining cooked macaroni, smoothing evenly, and top with the remaining Parmesan cheese.

4. Broil 4 inches from the heat source for 2 to 3 minutes or just until the Parmesan cheese is lightly browned. Serve hot as a side dish.

┌─────────────────────────┐

Casual Provence
(Fast Menu for 4)
Provençal Shepherds'
  Lamb Chops
  with Fresh Mint
Ratatouille (page 69)
French Rolls (bakery)
Lemon Sorbet
  (supermarket)
Wine: Chardonnay

└─────────────────────────┘

GOURMET GARLIC

Garlic is an extremely versatile aromatic. Not only can it be served raw, but it can be baked, grilled, stewed or roasted. Depending on whether it's served raw or cooked, garlic can lend a fragrant, intense flavor or a mild, nutty flavor to food. Garlic has infused many dishes worldwide and inspired many more. There is even garlic wine and garlic ice cream!

The Glory of Garlic

According to ancient lore and contemporary scientists, garlic is good for you: It is high in sulfur and an excellent source of potassium, calcium and vitamin C. Garlic is actually an herb and a member of the lily family (along with onions, chives, shallots and leeks). The bulb has been credited with

Provençal Shepherds' Lamb Chops with Mint

Servings: 4 (2 chops each)
Preparation Time: About 5 minutes
Cooking Time: 7 to 10 minutes

8 rib lamb chops, about 1 inch thick (3 to 4 ounces each),
    at room temperature
6 whole medium cloves garlic
1 tablespoon dry white wine
½ teaspoon *Provençal Seasoning Mix* (page 68)
½ teaspoon salt
½ teaspoon freshly ground pepper
2 tablespoons firmly packed finely chopped fresh mint

1. Preheat the broiler.

2. Combine the garlic, wine, seasoning mix, salt, pepper and mint in the bowl of a food processor fitted with a metal blade or the container of a blender. Process about 2 minutes, scraping down the sides of the bowl as necessary, or until the mixture is finely chopped and forms a paste.

3. Arrange the lamb chops on the top half of a broiler pan. Broil 7 inches from the heat source, for 4 to 6 minutes on one side. Remove the broiler pan from the broiler, and flip over the chops and spread the "eye" of each chop with ½ teaspoon of the garlic mixture. Return the chops to the broiler and broil for 3 to 4 minutes more for medium-rare, depending on thickness. Be careful not to overcook. Remember that the chops will continue to cook slightly even after they have been removed from the broiler. Serve at once as a main course.

Bourride Flavored with Aïoli

(Provençal Fish Stew with Garlic Mayonnaise)
Servings: 4 (2 cups each)
Preparation Time: About 20 minutes
Cooking Time: 15 to 20 minutes

AÏOLI: (Makes 1 ¾ cups)
8 cloves garlic
2 large egg yolks, at room temperature
¼ cup fresh lemon juice (2 to 3 small lemons)
1½ cups olive oil, preferably French (available at supermarket)
Freshly ground white pepper to taste

BOURRIDE:
1 tablespoon olive oil, preferably French
2 small leeks, white part only, thinly sliced
1 medium white onion, coarsely chopped
¾ cup dry white wine
2 cups boiling water
8-ounce bottle clam juice
2 teaspoons *Provençal Seasoning Mix* (page 68)
1½ pounds bass fillets, cut into 2-inch pieces
1½ pounds haddock or cod fillets, cut into 2-inch pieces
1 pound halibut steaks, cut into 2-inch pieces
Salt and freshly ground pepper to taste
1 Recipe Aïoli (recipe above), to serve
3 large egg yolks, lightly beaten, at room temperature

1. To prepare the Aïoli: In the container of a blender or the bowl of a food processor fitted with a metal blade pulse the garlic until minced. Add the egg yolks and lemon juice and pulse just until blended. With the machine running, add the olive oil through the feed tube in a slow, steady stream until incorporated and you have a sauce-like consistency. Transfer the mayonnaise to a small nonreactive bowl, season with white pepper, cover and refrigerate until ready to use.

2. To prepare the Bourride: Heat the olive oil in a nonreactive heavy 4- to 6-quart pot over medium-high heat. Add the leeks and onion and cook, stirring, about 4 minutes or until the onion is soft but not

easing many ailments, from the common cold to high blood pressure.

Garlic is a key ingredient in cuisines throughout the world. Italy, Spain, France and Greece are well known for their abundant culinary use of garlic, but a lesser-known fact is that China, Korea and Brazil each use more garlic per capita.

Garlic Gossip
◆ History shares with us the belief that wearing a "necklace" of garlic will scare away vampires and evil spirits. When consumed, garlic is said to be a powerful aphrodisiac.

◆ Even if you are not afraid of demons, you might fear "garlic breath." If so, just munch on a small sprig of fresh parsley and good-bye garlic!

Purchasing
The entire garlic bulb is called a "head" and each section a "clove." Choose plump firm, bulbs with clean, tissue-like skin. Do not buy bulbs that are soft, sprouting or shriveled.

Storage
Store garlic in a cool, dry, well-ventilated place. Do

not wash, refrigerate, or wrap garlic in plastic.

Preparation

Remove the papery skin on garlic by placing the clove under the flat side of a wide, sturdy knife blade. Press down firmly on the flat of the blade with the palm of your hand and the garlic will pop right out of its sheath.

browned. Add the wine, water, clam juice and seasoning mix and bring to a boil. Stir in all the fish, beginning with the densest first. Return to a boil, then reduce the heat to low and simmer, stirring occasionally, for 4 to 6 minutes or until the fish is opaque throughout, being careful not to overcook.

3. Using a slotted spoon, transfer the cooked fish to a deep warm serving dish, cover and keep warm until ready to serve, reserving the fish stock in its pot over low heat. Place 1 cup of the Aïoli in a large bowl (transferring the remaining ¾ cup to a bowl to be passed separately at serving time. Cover and refrigerate until ready to serve.) Whisk the 3 egg yolks into the 1 cup Aïoli until well blended, then whisk in ¼ cup of the hot stock until well blended. Stir this mixture back into the pot with the hot stock. Cook, stirring constantly, for 7 to 10 minutes or until the soup is slightly thickened. Do not let mixture come to a boil or the eggs will curdle.

4. To serve, ladle the soup over the fish in the serving dish and serve at once as a main course. Pass the bowl of chilled Aïoli separately for guests to help themselves.

AïOLI

Papeton d'Aubergines

(Provençal Eggplant Mousse)
Servings: 4 to 6
Preparation Time: About 10 minutes
Cooking Time: About 90 minutes

This delectable creation proves that soufflés are not just meant for cheese or chocolate! A vegetarian soufflé made with an unexpected vegetable — eggplant — might just be the very best type of soufflé. To make the most of your time: While the soufflé is baking, make the simple tomato sauce.

2 tablespoons olive oil, preferably French
   (available at supermarket), plus more to grease pan
1 large yellow onion, finely chopped
3 cloves garlic, crushed
2 pounds eggplant, peeled and coarsely chopped
½ teaspoon *Provençal Seasoning Mix* (page 68)
½ teaspoon salt
¼ teaspoon freshly ground pepper
½ cup minced fresh parsley
6 large eggs, lightly beaten
3 to 4 cups boiling water, to bake

1 cup crushed seeded ripe tomatoes seasoned with salt
   and freshly ground pepper, at room temperature, to serve

HINT: To seed fresh tomatoes: Just cut the tomato in half and using a teaspoon, scoop out and discard the seeds and liquid from the cavities.

1. Preheat the oven to 350° F. Lightly grease a 1 ½-quart soufflé dish.

2. Heat the olive oil in a heavy deep 12-inch skillet over medium heat. Add the onion, garlic, eggplant, seasoning mix, salt and pepper. Cover the skillet with aluminum foil or a lid and cook, stirring often, for 25 to 30 minutes or until the eggplant is very tender and begins to fall apart.

3. In the bowl of a food processor fitted with a metal blade process the eggplant mixture about 2 minutes or until it is a smooth, thick purée. Force the eggplant mixture through a fine-meshed strainer over a medium bowl and discard the eggplant seeds in the strainer. Stir the minced parsley into the eggplant mixture, then whisk in the eggs until well blended.

4. Working quickly, pour the mixture into the prepared soufflé dish and transfer to a baking dish large enough to accommodate the soufflé dish. Add enough boiling water to the baking dish so that it reaches 1½ inches up the sides of the soufflé dish.

5. Bake in the middle third of the oven for 40 to 50 minutes or until puffed and golden brown on top and a knife inserted near the center comes out clean. Serve at once as an appetizer or side dish with the crushed tomatoes seasoned with salt and pepper.

CHAPTER 6

MANGIA BENE!

THE ITALIAN ART of cooking (and eating) is world renowned, with a rich heritage of traditional dishes unchanged for centuries. Nowhere else is eating so applauded: It is an intrinsic part of the culture. Italians have a very direct approach to cooking. They depend on the very best ingredients for freshness of flavor (it is often said that Italian cooking "begins in the marketplace") and their variety is impressive.

While endless kinds of pasta and fish may be the nation's staples, the basics of the Italian pantry include the honored olive oil, a variety of meats (fresh and cured), poultry, game, salami, rice, cornmeal, bread and cheese. However, the greater glories of Italy are its vegetables, leafy greens and fruit, and no Italian kitchen would be complete without garlic and both fresh and dried herbs and spices. Basil, oregano, marjoram, sage and rosemary are featured in my blend. Needless to say, wine is essential, for drinking and in the preparation of many sauces.

It is impossible to imagine modern Italian cooking without the tomato. In fact, it was the Italians who first cultivated a red variety bearing large fruit. At first, tomatoes were only used in salads; it wasn't until later that they were used regularly in cooking. When the ingenious Neapolitans added this latest discovery to the traditional pizza (baked dough dressed with olive oil and sprinkled with herbs), they invented the pizza as we know it today. On page 92 you'll find a recipe for this crisp-crusted Neapolitan Pizza, in which I have added some mozzarella and a few more seasonings for a tastier result.

Turn the pages and you will find some more of the recipes Italy has given the world. Minestrone (page 85), one of the great soups of Italy, draws from the produce of farm kitchens for its satisfying heartiness and can be a meal in itself. Lastly, among Italy's other remarkable dishes, I have included the ineffable Spaghetti alla Carbonara (page 89), delicate strands of pasta spun with an ethereal bacon and egg sauce. These are just some of the tastes of Italy: *"Mangia Bene!"*

Italian Seasoning Mix

Polenta

Minestrone

Chicken Cacciatore with Black and Green Olives

Baked Cheese Manicotti

Zucchini with Parmesan

Spaghetti alla Carbonara

Lasagne

Prawns in Red Sauce

Pizza alla Napoletana

Melanzane alla Parmigiana

Veal Scaloppine with Marsala

QUICKIES: EVERYDAY FOODS MADE INTERNATIONAL

Pizza Pronto
Sprinkle *Italian Seasoning Mix* on frozen pizza just before baking.

Garlic Bread with Gusto
The next time you make garlic bread: Season the crushed garlic and melted

butter (or margarine) mixture with some *Italian Seasoning Mix.*

Bruschetta for the Busy

Toast a small loaf of sliced Italian Bread. Meanwhile, finely chop a few large, ripe but firm, seeded tomatoes. Season the tomatoes with some olive oil, minced garlic, *Italian Seasoning Mix* and salt and pepper. Spoon some of the tomato mixture over the toasted bread. Let stand for 15 minutes to let the juices soak into the bread.

Swift Pasta Sauce

Combine some *Italian Seasoning Mix* with melted butter or margarine or canned crushed tomatoes for a no-fuss pasta sauce.

ALWAYS OLIVE OIL

Olive oil has been enjoyed for over 6,000 years, due to the characteristics and delicious natural flavors that allow it to be used for a range of preparations. A little can go a long way and it can be employed as a "seasoning," and not just for dressings. It is now a popular staple of almost everybody's pantry. Olive oil has been prized for centuries, and there are references to it in four books of the Bible and in the Koran.

Italian Seasoning Mix

Makes about ¹/₂ cup

3 tablespoons dried basil leaves

3 tablespoons dried oregano leaves

1 tablespoon dried marjoram leaves

2 teaspoons ground sage

1 teaspoon dried rosemary leaves, ground (How-To page 12)

In a small bag or bowl (How-To page 11), combine the basil leaves, oregano leaves, marjoram leaves, ground sage, and ground rosemary. Shake or stir until well blended. Transfer to a clean, dry, airtight glass container. Store up to 3 months away from heat, light or moisture. Shake well before using.

Polenta

Servings: 12 pieces
Preparation Time: About 5 minutes
Cooking Time: 5 to 10 minutes
(can be made up to 2 days ahead)

1 13.2-ounce package (2¹/₈ cups) instant polenta (Italian precooked cornmeal), available at supermarket or gourmet shop

1 teaspoon salt (optional)

1. Bring 6 cups water to a boil in a 3-quart pot over high heat. Reduce the heat to low and slowly add the polenta to the boiling water. Stir in the salt if desired.

2. Cook, stirring constantly, for 5 minutes or until the polenta is very thick and begins to pull away from the sides of the pot. Firmly pack the polenta into a shallow baking dish, a 13-by-9-by-2-inch one works well, smoothing the surface with a metal spatula, dipping the spatula into hot water. Cover and if necessary reserve at room temperature until ready to use. The polenta will "set" and become firm enough to cut. Cut the polenta into 12 squares and serve at room temperature as a side dish.

Minestrone

Servings: 4 (2 cups each)
Preparation Time: About 10 minutes
Cooking Time: 15 minutes

2   tablespoons olive oil, preferably Italian
2   leeks, white part only, thinly sliced
1   medium yellow onion, coarsely chopped
3   cloves garlic, crushed
2   carrots, cut into 1/8-inch-thick slices
2   quarts canned low-sodium chicken broth
1   tablespoon tomato paste
1½ cups *conchigliette* (small pasta shells) or elbow macaroni
½   small head red cabbage (about 8 ounces), shredded
2½ teaspoons *Italian Seasoning Mix* (page 84)
1   15-ounce can pinto or cannellini beans, drained and rinsed
1   cup fresh (1 pound in pods) or frozen green peas, thawed
1   tablespoon fresh lemon juice
Freshly ground pepper to taste

Freshly grated Parmesan cheese, to serve

1. Heat the olive oil in a nonreactive 6- to 8-quart pot over medium-high heat. Add the leeks, onion, garlic and carrots and cook, stirring, for 5 minutes or until the carrots are crisp-tender.

2. Raise the heat to high. Stir in the chicken broth, tomato paste, *conchigliette*, red cabbage and seasoning mix and bring to a boil. Boil for 4 minutes. Reduce the heat to medium-low and stir in the pinto beans, green peas and lemon juice. Simmer, stirring occasionally, for 4 to 7 minutes or until the vegetables are tender and the pasta is *al dente* (slightly firm to the bite).

3. To serve, season with pepper, transfer to a warmed soup tureen and serve hot as a main course with a bowl of grated Parmesan cheese.

Autumn in Italy
(Fast Menu for 4)
Minestrone
Garlic Bread
Fresh Figs with
    Gorgonzola Cheese
Aqua Minerale (mineral
    water) such as
    San Pellegrino

A Shake of the Tree

As with wine, the flavor, body, color and aroma of olive oils vary according to many factors: the soil, the climate and other variables. Also, the color of an olive oil does not indicate its flavor. For example, a darker colored olive oil does not insure a more intense flavor. In general, southern Italian, Greek, and Spanish olive oils are heavier than those from Tuscany and Provence.

Olive oil flavors are described by the following categories:

◆ Mild (delicate, light or "buttery").

◆ Semi-fruity (stronger, with more of the fruity taste of the olive).

◆ Fruity (oil with a full-blown olive flavor).

◆ The new "light" olive oils, an American invention, have just a trace of olive flavor, or rather, are "light" in flavor.

Italian Alfresco
(Entertaining One-Dish Menu for 4 to 6)
Antipasto
Chicken Cacciatore with Black and Green Olives
Polenta (page 84)
Tomato, Mozzarella and Fresh Basil Salad
Cannoli (bakery)
Cappuccino

Chicken Cacciatore with Black and Green Olives

Servings: 4 to 6
Preparation Time: About 15 minutes
Cooking Time: 20 to 25 minutes
(can be made up to 2 days ahead)

1 tablespoon olive oil, preferably Italian
1 medium yellow onion, coarsely chopped
1½ pounds skinless, boneless chicken breasts,
    cut into ½-inch cubes
2 cloves garlic, crushed
8 ounces mushrooms, thinly sliced
2 medium green bell peppers, cut into ⅛-inch-wide strips
1 28-ounce can crushed tomatoes, preferably Italian
1 tablespoon *Italian Seasoning Mix* (page 84)
½ cup drained Gaeta olives or other
    brine-packed black olives, pitted
½ cup drained Calabrese olives or other
    brine-packed green olives, pitted
¼ cup dry white vermouth or dry white wine
2 tablespoons finely chopped fresh basil or fresh parsley,
    preferably Italian flat-leaf (optional)
Salt and freshly ground black pepper to taste

Italian bread, cooked pasta or Polenta (page 84), to serve

1. Heat the olive oil in a deep nonreactive 12-inch skillet over high heat. Add the onion, chicken and garlic and sauté about 5 minutes, turning the chicken until lightly browned all over. Reduce the heat to medium-low and stir in the mushrooms, bell peppers and crushed tomatoes. Then stir in the seasoning mix, olives and vermouth and cover with a lid or aluminum foil.

2. Cook for 15 to 20 minutes, stirring occasionally, until the chicken and bell peppers are tender. Stir in the fresh basil if desired and season with salt and pepper. Serve hot as a main course with Italian bread, pasta or polenta.

Baked Cheese Manicotti

Servings: 4 (3½ manicotti each)
Preparation Time: About 10 minutes
Cooking Time: About 45 minutes
(can be made up to 2 days ahead)

The nifty "hassle-free" trick of using a plastic bag in place of a cloth pastry bag saves a lot of time. Not only does it make it easier to pipe filling, but you don't have to wash it afterwards—just throw it away! Also, I have substituted manicotti pasta tubes, readily available from the supermarket, for the time-consuming homemade pasta "crêpes," which can be difficult to work with. This dish freezes well for up to 2 months, or make it ahead, cover and refrigerate it up to 2 days and simply reheat it before serving.

SAUCE: (Makes about 4 cups; or substitute 4 cups prepared
    low-sodium tomato pasta sauce [available at the supermarket]
    mixed with 1 teaspoon *Italian Seasoning Mix* [page 84]).
1 teaspoon olive oil, preferably Italian, plus more to toss pasta
1 medium white onion, finely chopped
2 cloves garlic, crushed
1 28-ounce can crushed tomatoes, preferably Italian
1 tablespoon tomato paste
1 teaspoon *Italian Seasoning Mix* (page 84)
Salt and freshly ground pepper to taste

PASTA:
1 8-ounce package (14 tubes) *manicotti* pasta
    (available at supermarket or gourmet store)

FILLING:
32 ounces part-skim milk ricotta cheese
1 cup freshly grated Parmesan cheese (4-ounce piece)
2 large eggs, lightly beaten
½ teaspoon freshly ground pepper

1. To prepare the sauce: Heat the 1 teaspoon olive oil in a 2-to 3-quart nonreactive saucepan over medium-high heat. Add the onion and garlic and cook for 4 minutes, stirring, until the onions are soft. Stir in the crushed tomatoes, tomato paste and seasoning mix and bring to a boil. Remove the saucepan from the heat, season with salt

◆ Olive Pomace Oil:
Pomace is the part of the olive that is left after mechanical and physical operations remove the oil and water. Additional oil can be extracted from the olive pomace through the use of chemical solvents. The oil is blended with virgin olive oil, and olive pomace oil is the result. This oil has the least flavor of the grades.

Keep the Fruit!
Store olive oil in an airtight glass container, away from light and heat. Refrigeration is not necessary. Stored this way, olive oil can last up to 2 years, longer than any other edible oil.

HINT: You can speed preparation by starting with 1 quart ready-to-use tomato pasta sauce mixed with 1 teaspoon *Italian*

    ◠◡   ◠◡

Italian Romance
(Make-Ahead Menu for 4)
Italian apéritif such as
    Campari
Baked Cheese Manicotti
Zucchini with Parmesan
    (page 88)
Spumone (Italian mousse-
    like ice cream,
    supermarket)

    ◠◡   ◠◡

and pepper, and reserve until ready to use.

2. Meanwhile, prepare the pasta: To a 4- to 6-quart pot of boiling water add the pasta. Return to a boil and boil for 6 to 8 minutes, stirring occasionally, or until *al dente* (slightly firm to the bite). Drain in a colander, then refresh under cold running water. Toss the pasta with some olive oil to prevent it from sticking and reserve at room temperature until ready to use.

3. Preheat the oven to 375° F.

4. Prepare the filling: Combine the ricotta cheese, Parmesan cheese, eggs and pepper in a large bowl and mix until thoroughly blended. Fill a small sturdy plastic bag halfway with some of the filling and snip off a piece from the bottom corner to form a hole to pipe the filling. Using the "pastry bag," fill each cooked pasta tube until firmly packed, piping into both ends if necessary, and refilling the bag with more filling as needed. Arrange the filled manicotti in a baking dish large enough to accommodate them in a single layer; a 13-by-9-by-2-inch baking dish works well.

5. Ladle the tomato sauce over the manicotti, cover with aluminum foil and bake for 30 minutes or until the sauce is bubbling and the manicotti are cooked through. Let stand for 10 minutes. Serve hot as a main course.

Zucchini with Parmesan

Servings: 4
Preparation Time: About 5 minutes
Cooking Time: 5 minutes

2 tablespoons olive oil, preferably Italian
1 pound small zucchini, cut into ¼-inch-thick slices
2 cloves garlic, crushed
½ teaspoon *Italian Seasoning Mix* (page 84)
¼ cup freshly grated Parmesan cheese (1-ounce piece)
Salt and freshly ground pepper to taste

Heat the olive oil in a heavy 12-inch skillet over high heat. Add the zucchini and sauté about 5 minutes or until tender and golden brown. Transfer the zucchini to a warm serving bowl and toss with the garlic, seasoning mix and Parmesan cheese until well coated. Season with salt and pepper and serve at once as a side dish.

Spaghetti alla Carbonara

(Spaghetti with Bacon and Egg Sauce)
Servings: 4 to 6
Preparation Time: About 5 minutes
Cooking Time: About 20 minutes

4 large eggs, at room temperature
2 tablespoons skim milk
½ cup freshly grated Parmesan cheese (2-ounce piece)
¼ teaspoon *Italian Seasoning Mix* (page 84)
½ teaspoon freshly ground pepper
1 pound spaghetti
6 strips lean bacon, cut into ½-inch dice

1. In a medium bowl beat together the eggs, milk, Parmesan cheese, seasoning mix and pepper until well blended. Set aside.

2. Add the pasta to a 6- to 8-quart pot of boiling water set over high heat. Return to a boil and boil for 7 to 9 minutes, stirring occasionally, or until the pasta is *al dente* (slightly firm to the bite.)

3. Meanwhile, in a deep heavy 12-inch skillet over medium-high heat fry the bacon about 6 minutes or until browned and crisp. Drain the bacon on a paper towel-lined plate, reserving the skillet with the bacon drippings.

4. Working quickly, drain the cooked pasta thoroughly and return it to the pot along with the bacon. Cover and keep warm until ready to serve. Heat the skillet with the bacon drippings over very low heat and stir in the beaten egg mixture. Heat gently, stirring constantly, for 2 minutes, but do not let the eggs curdle.

5. Stir the egg mixture into the pasta in the pot and set over very low heat. Gently heat the pasta, tossing vigorously, for 3 minutes or until the pasta is heated through. You will see steam rising. (The egg mix-

Another incentive to buy wedges over grated is that the rind lends a fabulous flavor to sauces or soups such as minestrone! Just scrape off the exterior coating of the rind and drop the rind into the simmering stock. Get ready for the flavor of Italy!

For Parmesan Aficionados
Know Your Parmesan

◆ New Parmesan: Parmesan of the previous season — 12 months old

◆ Vecchio: Parmesan that is well-matured — 12 to 24 months old

◆ Stravecchio: Parmesan that is extra-matured — 4 to 5 years old

ture will create a glossy coating to the pasta, but should not cook so far that it is "scrambled.") Serve at once on heated dinner plates as a main course.

Lasagne

Servings: 6 to 8
Preparation Time: About 10 minutes
Cooking Time: About 1½ hours (meat sauce and tomato sauce can be made up to 2 days ahead)

There are many types of lasagne. This version from Bologna usually has a meat filling topped with a white sauce. I have substituted a tomato sauce for the white sauce for a "lighter" meal.

HINT: Here are a few time savers: Prepare the meat sauce up to 2 days ahead and use 1 quart prepared low-sodium tomato pasta sauce (available from supermarket) mixed with 1 teaspoon *Italian Seasoning Mix* (page 84) instead of homemade tomato sauce.

16 curly-edged lasagne noodles (about one 16-ounce box)
1 teaspoon olive oil, preferably Italian, plus more to toss pasta
3 cloves garlic, crushed
8 ounces extra-lean ground beef
8 ounces extra-lean ground veal
6 ounces lean ground pork
1 28-ounce can crushed tomatoes
⅔ cup dry red wine
1½ teaspoons *Italian Seasoning Mix* (page 84)
½ teaspoon salt
¼ teaspoon freshly ground pepper
1 recipe homemade tomato sauce (from *Baked Cheese Manicotti*, recipe page 87, or 4 cups prepared low-sodium tomato pasta sauce [available at supermarket] mixed with 1 teaspoon *Italian Seasoning Mix* [page 84])
½ cup freshly grated Parmesan cheese (2-ounce piece)

1. Add the lasagne noodles to an 8- to 10-quart stockpot of boiling water over high heat. Return to a boil and boil the noodles for 10 to 14 minutes, stirring occasionally, or until *al dente* (slightly firm to the bite). Drain and rinse briefly under cold running water. Toss lightly with some olive oil. Reserve at room temperature until ready to use.

2. Heat the olive oil in a heavy nonreactive deep 12-inch skillet over medium-high heat. Add the garlic, ground beef, ground veal and

ground pork. Cook, breaking up the ground meats with the back of a wooden spoon, about 5 minutes or just until there is no trace of pink. Carefully pour off the fat. Stir in the tomatoes, red wine, seasoning mix and salt and pepper and bring to a boil. Boil for 20 to 25 minutes, stirring occasionally, or until the sauce has thickened.

3. Preheat the oven to 375° F.

4. Arrange 8 of the cooked lasagne noodles in a double layer to cover the bottom of a 13-by-9-by-2-inch baking dish, cutting the noodles as needed to fit the short side. Then spread evenly with all of the meat sauce. Place the remaining 8 noodles in a double layer over the meat sauce, gently pressing down with your palms to flatten. Ladle the tomato sauce over all and sprinkle the top evenly with the Parmesan cheese.

5. Bake for 30 to 40 minutes or until the Parmesan cheese is a delicate brown and the lasagne heated through. Let stand for 10 minutes before serving, cut into 12 equal portions and serve hot directly from the baking dish as a main course.

Prawns in Red Sauce

Servings: 4
Preparation Time: About 15 minutes
Cooking Time: About 10 minutes

1 tablespoon olive oil, preferably Italian
2 whole cloves garlic, peeled
16 farm-raised (freshwater) prawns (ask your fishmonger to remove heads) shelled (How-To page 15)
¼ cup Cognac
2½ pounds ripe tomatoes, seeded and coarsely chopped
½ teaspoon *Italian Seasoning Mix* (page 84)
Salt and freshly ground pepper to taste
2 teaspoons finely chopped fresh oregano or Italian flat-leaf parsley, to garnish

Italian bread, to serve

1. Heat the olive oil in a nonreactive deep 12-inch skillet over medi-

PASTA PERFECT

There are some 650 different pasta shapes on the Italian market at any given time. It seems that every year one shape is retired and a new one is born. But, surprisingly, as of 1991, the United States manufactured 4.8 billion pounds each year, more than any other country.

The word *pasta* literally means "paste," referring to the paste of durum semolina (a flour made from ground durum wheat) and water from which pasta is made. For the most part, pasta shapes are named after what they look like, such as *agnolotti* (little slippers) or *farfalle* (butterflies).

Who, What and Where?
Where does pasta come from? There are many opinions: some believe Italy, some China, others the Middle East or Germany. Naturally, since pasta is so popular, many countries want to take credit for its invention. It does appear in ancient records of numerous countries. Since pasta is so easy to make, it has been suggested that pasta sprang up simultaneously in several different countries.

um-high heat. Add the whole garlic cloves and the prawns. Cook, stirring, about 5 minutes, just until opaque throughout, being careful not to overcook. Remove and discard the garlic. Sprinkle the prawns with the Cognac and carefully ignite with a match. (*Be careful — the flames will be high, so stand back.*) Shake the skillet gently until the flames subside.

2. Transfer the prawns to a serving plate and reserve. Reduce the heat to medium-low, stir the tomatoes and seasoning mix into the skillet and cook for 5 minutes, stirring occasionally. Season the sauce with salt and pepper. Return the reserved prawns to the skillet, along with the oregano and cook, stirring, for 1 minute more. Serve at once as a main course with Italian bread.

COMMENT: Generally in America, the terms "prawns" and "shrimp" are used interchangeably. In fact, when you think you have ordered prawns from a restaurant menu, 9 out of 10 times you will be served a plate of jumbo shrimp. Prawns are small lobster-like crustaceans, the most famous member being the Italian s*campi.* However, prawns are now being farm-raised in the United States and are more readily available. To prepare *scampi* for cooking, just ask your fishmonger to remove the heads; then at home, shell the prawns as you would shrimp.

A Taste of Italy
(*Entertaining Menu for 4 to 6*)
Prosciutto with Melon (Cantaloupe)
Neapolitan Pizza
Arugula, Radicchio and Romaine Salad
Italian Pine-Nut Cookies (bakery or gourmet store)
Wine: Italian Chianti Classico

Pizza alla Napoletana

Servings: Makes 1 12-inch pizza
Serves: 4 (2 slices each)
Preparation Time: About 1¼ hours
Cooking Time: 20 to 25 minutes

It is loads of fun to prepare your own homemade pizza dough, and kids love to help! Yet if you are short on time, you can prepare the dough up to one day ahead through step #2. Just leave the dough in the bowl but in place of a towel, drape a piece of plastic wrap on top of the dough. Then tightly cover the top of the bowl with another piece of plastic wrap and refrigerate overnight. (The dough will rise in the refrigerator.) The next day, proceed with the recipe, starting with step #3.

(NOTE: If you are still not ready to roll out the dough in the morning,

just pull it away from the sides of the bowl and gently punch down in the center to deflate it. Leave it, covered, to rise again slowly in the refrigerator and it will be ready in at least 4 hours, for rolling out later in the day.)

Instead of homemade pizza dough try out one of the new premade refrigerated pizza doughs available at the supermarket. I prefer Pillsbury's "All-Ready Pizza Crust,"® which you can find in the dairy case. This will reduce preparation time to only 5 minutes, because you can then skip steps #1 and #2. Another time saver: Use preshredded mozzarella cheese, also available at the supermarket.

DOUGH: (or substitute 1 10-ounce tube refrigerated pizza dough
      available at supermarket)
2½ cups unbleached white flour, plus more to knead
1 teaspoon salt
1 package active dry yeast (¼ oz.)
1 cup warm water (110° F)
1 teaspoon sugar
Olive oil, to grease pan

SAUCE:
1½ pounds ripe tomatoes, seeded and finely chopped
2 cloves garlic, crushed
1 teaspoon *Italian Seasoning Mix* (page 84)
Salt and freshly ground pepper to taste
1½ cups shredded part skim-milk mozzarella (6-ounce piece)

1. To prepare the dough: In a medium bowl sift together the flour and salt. In a liquid measuring cup, stir the yeast together with the water. Add the sugar and stir together until the yeast is dissolved. Set aside for 10 minutes or until the surface is frothy. (NOTE: If bubbles do not appear within 10 minutes, discard mixture and repeat process.)

2. Stir the yeast mixture into the flour mixture and mix until a soft dough forms. Transfer the dough to a lightly floured work surface and knead, making about 25 turns, until the dough is smooth and elastic. Lightly grease a medium bowl with some olive oil. Transfer the dough to the bowl and turn the dough once to coat it with the oil. Cover the top of the bowl with a towel and let stand in a warm, draft-free place about 1 hour or until doubled in size.

Pasta's Past
Nevertheless, pasta has a long lineage. Some of the many "pasta memories" include the fact that the Chinese have been eating noodles for over 7,000 years! Pasta, and even a pasta machine, appear in Greek myths. In the 10th century, Arabs (then occupying Sicily) were known to make *ittryia,* a kind of early *fusilli.* In a thirteenth-century Genovese cookbook, there are recipes for several pasta shapes, among them *vermicelli* and *tortelletti.*

Pasta + Tomato Sauce = Delicious
When did tomato sauce come into the equation? The answer is not until the eighteenth century, after the Italians had developed today's meaty red tomatoes from small yellow tomatoes. The yellow tomatoes were introduced into Europe from Mexico by the sixteenth-century explorer, Cortez.

3. Meanwhile, prepare the sauce: In a nonreactive medium bowl combine the tomatoes, garlic and seasoning mix. Stir until well blended and season with salt and pepper.

4. Preheat the oven to 425° F. and lightly grease a 12-inch pizza pan.

5. Transfer the homemade pizza dough to a lightly floured work surface and gently punch dough down once. Then transfer the dough to the prepared pizza pan (if using prepared refrigerated pizza dough unroll it first and do not punch down. Proceed with the recipe). Using your fingers, press the dough so it spreads to the edge to form an even crust. Pinch the edge to form a ½-inch-high rim.

6. Spread the tomato sauce over the dough to the edge. Sprinkle evenly with the shredded mozzarella. Bake in the lower third of oven for 20 to 25 minutes or until the cheese is melted and delicately browned and the crust is crisp and golden. Serve at once as a main course.

Melanzane alla Parmigiana
(Eggplant Parma Style)
Servings: 4
Preparation Time: About 10 minutes
Cooking Time: About 60 minutes
(can be made up to 3 days ahead)

My reduced-fat version of this classic dish is almost as easy to make as take-out is to pick up and has a robust home-cooked flavor that is sure to become a family favorite! To speed your cooking along, take advantage of the pre-grated Parmesan cheese and preshredded mozzarella cheese.

1 28-ounce can crushed tomatoes
3 cloves garlic, crushed
2 teaspoons *Italian Seasoning Mix* (page 84)
Salt and freshly ground pepper to taste
3 tablespoons olive oil, preferably Italian, plus more if needed
1 1-pound eggplant, unpeeled, but cut crosswise into ¼-inch-thick slices
¾ cup freshly grated Parmesan cheese (3-ounce piece)
2 cups shredded part skim-milk mozzarella cheese (8-ounce piece)

1. Combine the crushed tomatoes, garlic and seasoning mix in a nonreactive medium bowl and stir until well blended. Season with salt and pepper.

2. Preheat the oven to 375° F.

3. Heat 1 tablespoon of the olive oil in a heavy 12-inch skillet, preferably nonstick, over medium-high heat. Add the eggplant slices in 3 to 4 batches, and cook for a total of 4 to 5 minutes each batch, or until the eggplant is tender and golden brown on both sides. Add another tablespoon olive oil between batches.

4. Arrange half of the eggplant slices in an overlapping single layer on the bottom of an 8-inch-square baking dish. Pour half of the tomato sauce over all, then sprinkle evenly with half the Parmesan cheese and half the mozzarella cheese. Arrange the remaining eggplant slices over the mozzarella, then cover with the remaining tomato sauce and sprinkle with the remaining Parmesan and mozzarella cheese.

5. Bake for 30 to 40 minutes or until the mozzarella is melted and is a delicate golden brown and bubbling. Let stand 10 minutes before serving, then serve directly from the baking dish as a main course.

Veal Scaloppine with Marsala

Servings: 4 (2 cutlets each)
Preparation Time: About 15 minutes
Cooking Time: About 30 minutes

1 pound (8 pieces) small veal cutlets; have butcher pound to ⅛-inch-thickness or see step #1 below
Salt and freshly ground pepper to taste
¼ cup unbleached white flour, to dredge
2 tablespoons unsalted butter
6 ounces short-stem mushrooms, thinly sliced
1 tablespoon olive oil, preferably Italian
¾ cup Marsala wine
1½ teaspoons *Italian Seasoning Mix* (page 84)
1 medium lemon, cut lengthwise into eighths, to garnish

water — a good rule of thumb is 1 pound pasta to 4 quarts water. The pot should remain uncovered and the pasta stirred occasionally to help prevent the strands or pieces from sticking to one another. How long to cook pasta depends on the type, whether fresh or dried, thin or fat, filled or hollow, so follow your recipe or package instructions for timing (though it is always best just to keep tasting to check for proper doneness).

Always cook pasta to the *al dente* stage (translated, "to the tooth") or when it (cont'd on page 96)

ᕦᕤ

Elegance in a Hurry
(Fast Menu for 4)
Veal Scaloppine
  with Marsala
Steamed Asparagus
  with Lemon
Focaccia (Italian flat-bread,
  gourmet store)
Almond Biscotti (Italian
  almond cookies,
  gourmet store)
Espresso
Choice of Italian liquóres:
  Sambuca (anise-flavored
  liqueur) or Galliano (pale-
  green gold liqueur with
  hint of licorice)

ᕦᕤ

has a slight resistance when bitten into — not crunchy and undercooked or soft and overdone, but just right. When pasta is ready, drain it at once in a colander and shake to remove excess water. Do not rinse it except to serve cold (as a salad).

Pasta's Profile

Pasta is a high complex-carbohydrate food that is low in fat, has a fair amount of protein, and is filled with many nutrients, including many of the B vitamins. Pasta is also relatively low in calories: A 5-ounce cooked portion of plain pasta contains about 210 calories, while a 5-ounce steak has 500 calories.

Pasta Wins the Race

Pasta is the food of choice for people in long-endurance sports such as marathon running since it slowly releases sugar into the bloodstream over several hours. Therefore, not only is your level of energy maintained, but hunger pangs are lessened. Pasta earns even more points: A high complex-carbohydrate food, when eaten, pasta helps your brain release a chemical called "seratonin," which makes you feel happy and safe!

1. On a work surface, place a veal cutlet between two sheets of plastic wrap. Using a meat mallet or wooden rolling pin, pound from the center of the cutlet toward the outer edge until the cutlet is flattened to about ⅛ inch thick; rotate 180 degrees every strike. (NOTE: The veal should not be so thin that you can see through it.) Repeat the pounding with the remaining veal cutlets, reusing plastic wrap if not punctured.

2. Sprinkle both sides of each cutlet with salt and pepper and dredge with the flour until coated evenly, shaking off the excess.

3. Melt 1 tablespoon of the butter in a heavy 12-inch skillet over medium-high heat. Add the mushrooms and cook, stirring, about 3 minutes or until browned. Transfer the mushrooms to a warm serving platter, cover and keep warm until ready to serve.

4. Heat the olive oil in the skillet. Add the veal to the skillet in batches and cook for 2 to 3 minutes on each side or until golden brown, but still slightly pink in the center. Transfer the veal to the warm serving platter (with the mushrooms) and cover.

5. Pour the Marsala into the skillet (*be careful — liquid may splatter*) and stir in the seasoning mix and remaining 1 tablespoon butter. Bring to a boil and boil for 1 minute, scraping the bottom and along the sides of the skillet to release the browned bits. Pour the Marsala mixture through a fine-meshed strainer over the veal. Garnish the veal with the lemon wedges and serve at once as a main course.

CHAPTER 7

Mexican Magic

Mexican Seasoning Mix

Sopa de Tortilla

Guacamole

Red Snapper Veracruz

Chicken Enchiladas with Mole Sauce

Picadillo

Fresh Corn Soup with Pimientos

Mancha Manteles

Arroz Verde

Quesadillas with Guacamole

Burritos with Chilorio

Refried Beans

Salsa Fresca

Mole

MEXICAN COOKING is diverse and adventurous. Much of its appeal rests in the combination of its unusual and surprising flavor medleys, originating from a host of exciting ingredients.

My seasoning blend of chile powder, oregano, cumin, cinnamon, cayenne, cloves and allspice, frequently accompanied by chile peppers, onions and garlic, are the flavors we recognize as characteristic of Mexican cooking. Mexicans cook with a wide variety of foods—corn, fresh and dried beans, pumpkins, potatoes, tomatoes, citrus fruits and chocolate, among others—reflecting the influence of their ancient Aztec and Mayan ancestors.

That most ancient of foods, the *tortilla,* or little cake, is referred to as the "bread of Mexico." Thin, flat rounds made of either wheat or corn, *tortillas* are used today, just as they were in the days of the Aztecs, in a number of ways. They are stuffed, folded, sauced, buttered, cut into strips and fried, rolled and eaten plain, used in place of a spoon and dipped into foods, or torn and used to scoop up sauces. Sometimes *tortillas* are even used as plates!

In two recipes, you will find *tortillas* used in very different ways. In Chicken Enchiladas with Mole Sauce (page 101), flour *tortillas* are used to wrap another one of Mexico's equally famous preparations, *mole* (page 110), which comes from the Aztec word *molli,* meaning sauce flavored with chile. While the classic recipes for *mole* are time-consuming, my seasoning blend has helped to simplify the recipe yet still gives splendid results. In another recipe, corn *tortillas* are cut into strips and stirred into Sopa de Tortillas (tortilla soup), on page 99. Here the seasoning blend adds a spicy, sharp contrast to the mild chicken-tomato flavored broth.

Mexican cuisine is not always heavily spiced or hot. Guacamole

QUICKIES: EVERYDAY FOODS MADE INTERNATIONAL

South-of-the-Border Corn Bread
Stir 1 teaspoon *Mexican Seasoning Mix* into a single-loaf recipe or corn bread mix before baking.

Burger Anyone?
For burgers with an accent: Lightly sprinkle *Mexican Seasoning Mix*

over each side of a hamburger before grilling.

Always-Nice Nachos
Arrange some corn tortilla chips in a single layer on a baking sheet. Drizzle with some Mexican hot sauce, sprinkle with some shredded Monterey Jack cheese and *Mexican Seasoning Mix*. Bake in a preheated 375° F. oven about 10 minutes or until lightly toasted and the cheese is melted.

Tex-Mex Chili
Season homemade or canned chili with *Mexican Seasoning Mix* for an instant crowd-pleaser.

*This is pure "chile" (with an "e") powder, found in Mexican or Spanish specialty stores (see Source List). Or, you can substitute "chili" (with an "i") powder — a mixture of several herbs and spices—available at the supermarket.

(page 99), for example, a medley of avocados, cilantro and lime, has an unexpected, refreshing milder taste, accented by a hint of the seasoning blend. This is a departure from the traditional recipe that is usually unseasoned. A less well-known dish, Mancha Manteles or Tablecloth Stainer (page 104), a pork stew with apples and bananas, is daring in its mixture of ingredients. Somewhat monochromatic in color, but not in taste, this delicately flavored stew introduces one of my all-time favorite ingredients, the *tomatillo*, a Mexican green tomato, which has a slightly tart flavor, a cross between an apple and a lemon, and is quite delicious!

In short, I'm convinced that no matter which of the recipes you try, your family will be rushing south of the border for more!

Mexican Seasoning Mix

Makes about ¹/₂ cup

¼ cup chile powder*
2 tablespoons dried oregano leaves, preferably Mexican
    (Source list page 186)
1 tablespoon ground cumin
1¼ teaspoons ground cinnamon
1 teaspoon ground red (cayenne) pepper
½ teaspoon ground cloves
¼ teaspoon ground allspice

In a small bag or bowl (How-To page 11), combine the chile powder, oregano leaves, cumin, cinnamon, cayenne, cloves and allspice. Shake or stir until well blended. Transfer to a clean, dry, airtight glass container. Store up to 3 months away from heat, light or moisture. Shake well before using.

Sopa de Tortilla

(Mexican Tortilla Soup)
Servings: 4 (1½ cups each)
Preparation Time: About 5 minutes
Cooking Time: About 15 minutes

4 6-inch corn *tortillas,* cut in half, then into ½-inch-wide
   strips(available at supermarket)
6 cups canned low-sodium chicken broth
½ cup canned tomato purée
½ teaspoon *Mexican Seasoning Mix* (page 98)
Salt and freshly ground pepper to taste
5 scallions, green part only, thinly sliced, to garnish

1. Preheat the oven to 400° F.

2. Scatter the *tortilla* strips on a baking sheet in a single layer. Bake in the top third of the oven about 10 minutes or until crisp; reserve until ready to use.

3. Meanwhile, combine the chicken broth, tomato purée and seasoning mix in a nonreactive 4-quart pot over high heat. Stir until well blended and bring to a boil. Season with salt and pepper.

4. Place the *tortilla* strips on the bottom of a soup tureen and pour the hot soup over them. Sprinkle with the scallions and serve at once as a main course for 4 or as an appetizer for 6.

Roughing it in Mexico with Style
(Fast Vegetarian Menu for 4)
Sopa de Tortilla
Corn bread (supermarket — premade or mix)
Fresh Mango Salad
Limeade or Lemonade

Guacamole

(Mexican Avocado Sauce, Salad or Dip)
Servings: Makes about 3¼ cups, serving 4
Preparation Time: About 10 minutes
Cooking Time: None
(can be made up to 2 hours ahead)

3 medium-sized ripe avocados (about 1¼ pounds)
¼ cup fresh lime juice (2 to 3 small limes)
½ teaspoon *Mexican Seasoning Mix* (page 98)
1 small white onion, finely chopped

1 large ripe tomato, seeded and coarsely chopped
¼ cup finely chopped fresh cilantro (coriander) leaves
Salt and freshly ground pepper to taste

1. Halve the avocados lengthwise, remove the pits and reserve them. Scoop out the flesh into a nonreactive medium serving bowl and mash roughly with a fork. Gently stir in the lime juice, seasoning mix, onion, tomato and cilantro until well blended but still "chunky." Season with salt and pepper.

2. Place the reserved avocado pits in the guacamole to help prevent it from discoloring. Serve at once as a sauce, side dish or dip with tortilla chips. (NOTE: If unable to serve immediately, cover the bowl with plastic wrap and refrigerate up to 2 hours.)

Midsummer Celebration
*(Fast Vegetarian
Menu for 4)*
Cocktail: Tequila Sunrise
Red Snapper Veracruz
Arroz Verde (page 105)
Fresh Pineapple Wedges

Red Snapper Veracruz

Servings: 4
Preparation Time: About 5 minutes
Cooking Time: 15 to 20 minutes

4 (7-ounce) red snapper fillets or other mild, firm, white-fleshed fish
2 medium-sized ripe tomatoes, coarsely chopped
1 small white onion, minced
1 cup drained pimiento-stuffed Spanish green olives, coarsely chopped
2 tablespoons drained vinegar-packed capers, preferably large Spanish
½ teaspoon *Mexican Seasoning Mix* (page 98)
2 tablespoons fresh lime juice
Salt to taste

1. Preheat the oven to 400° F.

2. Arrange the fish fillets in a single layer, skinside-down, in the bottom of a 3-quart baking dish. In a nonreactive medium bowl combine the tomatoes, onion, ½ of the olives, 1 tablespoon of the capers, seasoning mix and lime juice and stir until well blended. Season with salt to taste. Ladle over the fillets until covered evenly with the sauce.

3. Cover the baking dish with aluminum foil and bake for 15 to 20 minutes or until the fish fillets are opaque throughout. Serve the

fillets on warm dinner plates with sauce ladled over each and sprinkle each fillet with some of the remaining chopped olives and 1 tablespoon capers. Serve at once as a main course.

Chicken Enchiladas with Mole

Servings: 4 (2 enchiladas each)
Preparation Time: About 15 minutes
Cooking Time: 20 to 25 minutes
(Mole can be made up to 3 days ahead)

2¾ cups shredded leftover cooked chicken
    (or fresh, made from 1½ pounds raw skinless,
    boneless chicken breasts)
⅓ cup sour cream or plain lowfat yogurt
1 cup firmly packed shredded Monterey Jack cheese
    (3-ounce piece)
1¼ teaspoons *Mexican Seasoning Mix* (page 98)
½ teaspoon salt
½ teaspoon freshly ground pepper
2 scallions, green part only, thinly sliced
8 7-inch white flour tortillas (available at supermarket)
1 recipe *Mole* (page 110)

1. Preheat the oven to 350° F.

2. Combine the shredded cooked chicken, sour cream, Monterey Jack cheese, seasoning mix, salt, pepper and scallions in a nonreactive medium bowl and stir until well blended. Lay the tortillas out on a work surface and spread ⅓ cup firmly packed chicken filling in a line down the center of each. Roll up each *tortilla* around the filling and transfer them in a single layer, seam-side-down, close together in a baking dish large enough to accommodate them; a 13-by-9-by-2-inch baking dish works well.

3. Ladle the *mole* over the *enchiladas,* making sure to cover the ends. Bake for 20 to 25 minutes until the *enchiladas* are heated through. Serve hot as a main course.

Festive Mexican Fare
(Entertaining Menu for 4)
Mexican cerveza (beer),
    such as Tecate served
    with a lime wedge
    and salt around rim
    of each glass
Tortilla chips
    (supermarket) and
Salsa Fresca (page 109)
Chicken Enchiladas with
Mole
Coconut Custard
Mexican Hot Chocolate

HINT: If you don't have any leftover cooked chicken, then poach some up to 2 days ahead. For a head start, the *mole* can be made up to 3 days ahead and stores very well.

Picadillo

(Mexican Minced Meat Dish)
Servings: 4 (1 cup each)
Preparation Time: About 15 minutes
Cooking Time: 20 to 25 minutes
(can be made up to 2 days ahead)

8 ounces extra-lean ground beef
8 ounces lean ground pork
2 cloves garlic, crushed
1 medium yellow onion, finely chopped
1 16-ounce can peeled whole tomatoes, drained and coarsely chopped
2 tablespoons apple-cider or red-wine vinegar
1½ teaspoons *Mexican Seasoning Mix* (page 98)
½ cup seedless raisins, "plumped" in ¼ cup brandy mixed with ¼ cup warm water for 10 minutes, then drained
½ cup slivered, blanched almonds, toasted (see left)
Salt and freshly ground pepper to taste

Cooked warm white rice, to serve

1. Combine the beef, pork, garlic and onion in a deep nonreactive 12-inch skillet over medium-high heat. Cook for 5 minutes, stirring often to break up the clumps of meat, or just until the beef and pork begin to brown. Carefully pour off the fat.

2. Stir in the drained chopped tomatoes, apple cider vinegar, seasoning mix and drained plumped raisins and bring to a boil. Reduce the heat to low and simmer, stirring occasionally, for 15 to 20 minutes or until slightly thickened.

3. Stir in the toasted almonds and season with salt and pepper. Using a slotted spoon, serve hot over rice as a main course or as a filling for *burritos* or *tacos*.

Fresh Corn Soup with Pimientos

Servings: 4 (1½ cups each)
Preparation Time: About 10 minutes
Cooking Time: About 20 minutes

1 small yellow onion, cut into eighths
1 whole clove garlic
5 cups fresh corn kernels (about 10 ears)
   or 2 10-ounce packages
   thawed frozen corn kernels (5 cups)
1 quart canned low-sodium chicken broth
½ teaspoon *Mexican Seasoning Mix* (page 98)
½ cup half-and-half, at room temperature
Salt and freshly ground white pepper to taste
1 4-ounce jar pimientos, drained, to garnish

1. Combine the onion and garlic in the bowl of a food processor
fitted with a metal blade or the container of a blender. Pulse about 5
times or until the onion and garlic are minced. Add the corn kernels
with 1 cup of the chicken broth and process about 3 minutes or until
puréed but not completely smooth, scraping down the sides of the
bowl as necessary.

2. Transfer the puréed corn mixture to a 4- to 6-quart pot over medium-high heat. Stir in the remaining 3 cups chicken stock and the seasoning mix until well blended and bring to a boil. Reduce the heat to
low and simmer, stirring occasionally, about 10 minutes or until the
corn is tender.

3. Stir ¼ cup of the hot soup into a small bowl with the half-and-half
until well blended, then stir back into the pot. Gently heat the soup
about 3 minutes more, stirring constantly, until the soup is heated
through and slightly thickened; do not let come to a boil. Season
with salt and pepper and serve at once garnished with the pimientos
as a main course for 4 or as an appetizer for 6.

Mancha Manteles

(Tablecloth Stainer)
Servings: 4 (2½ cups each)
Preparation Time: About 10 minutes
Cooking Time: 35 minutes
(can be made through step # 1 up to 2 days ahead)

1 quart canned low-sodium chicken broth
2 pounds lean boneless pork loin, trimmed and cut
   into ½-inch cubes
1½ teaspoons *Mexican Seasoning Mix* (page 98)
1 large white onion, finely chopped
12 fresh *tomatillos* (Mexican green tomatoes),
   papery husk removed and coarsely chopped
   or 2 11-ounce cans *tomatillos,* coarsely chopped
   (available at supermarket or Mexican grocery store)
2 medium-sized firm but ripe Granny Smith apples,
   peeled and each cut into 10 wedges
1½ cups fresh green peas (1½ pounds in pods)
   or 1 10-ounce package frozen green peas, thawed
3 large ripe but firm bananas

1. Combine the chicken broth, pork cubes and seasoning mix in a nonreactive 6- to 8-quart pot over high heat and bring to a boil. Reduce the heat to medium-low. Stir in the onion and *tomatillos* and cover. Simmer, stirring occasionally, for 30 minutes or until the pork is tender and no more pink remains.

2. Stir in the apples and peas and cook, uncovered, for 5 minutes or until the apples are tender but not falling apart. Slice the bananas into ¼-inch-thick slices and stir into the stew. Serve at once as a main course.

Arroz Verde

(Mexican Green Rice)
Servings: 4
Preparation Time: About 5 minutes
Cooking Time: About 30 minutes

3 whole cloves garlic
1 large green bell pepper, cut into 1-inch dice
3 scallions, green part only, cut into 1-inch-long pieces
½ cup firmly packed fresh cilantro (coriander) leaves
1 tablespoon olive oil or safflower oil
1 cup long-grain white rice
1¾ cups canned low-sodium chicken broth
2 teaspoons *Mexican Seasoning Mix* (page 98)
Salt and freshly ground pepper to taste

1. Add the garlic to the bowl of a food processor fitted with a metal blade or the container of a blender. Pulse the garlic about 3 times or until minced. Add the bell pepper, scallions and cilantro and pulse about 10 times more, scraping down the sides of the bowl in between, or until very finely chopped, and reserve.

2. Heat the olive oil in a heavy 3- to 4-quart saucepan over high heat. Stir in the rice until well coated with the oil. Stir in the chicken broth and seasoning mix and bring to a boil.

3. Reduce the heat to very low, and stir in the reserved garlic mixture until well blended. Cover the saucepan and cook for about 20 minutes, stirring once, or until almost all the liquid is absorbed. Remove the saucepan from the heat and let stand, covered, for 5 minutes more, until the rice is tender but not dry. Season with salt and pepper and serve at once as a side dish.

Quesadillas with Guacamole

Servings: 4 (2 each)
Preparation Time: About 20 minutes
Cooking Time: 15 minutes

HINT: This is already a super-simple recipe, but to get dinner on the table even faster, replace the homemade guacamole or *salsa fresca* with store-bought guacamole and prepared salsa picante, both products available from your local supermarket or gourmet store. Other useful time-saving ingredients are preshredded Monterey Jack cheese and canned jalapeño peppers, which can also be found in the supermarket.

Vegetable oil, to grease pan
8 7-inch white flour *tortillas*, 10-ounce package
    (available at supermarket)
2½ cups loosely packed shredded Monterey Jack cheese
    (6-ounce piece)
1 fresh jalapeño pepper, seeded, ribs removed and minced
    (How-To page 109) or 1 tablespoon minced drained canned
    jalapeño peppers (available at supermarket)
1 teaspoon *Mexican Seasoning Mix* (page 98)
3 scallions, green part only, thinly sliced
1 recipe *Guacamole* (page 99) or prepared guacamole (available
    at supermarket or gourmet store) or *Salsa Fresca* (page 109),
    or prepared salsa picante (available at supermarket), to serve

1. Preheat the oven to 400° F. Lightly grease a baking sheet.

2. Combine the Monterey Jack cheese, minced jalapeño pepper, sea-soning mix and scallions in a medium bowl. Gently toss together until well blended. Lay the *tortillas* out on a work surface. Sprinkle ⅓ cup loosely packed cheese filling evenly over half of each *tortilla*. Fold the uncovered half of each *tortilla* over the filled half, firmly pressing down to flatten, and seal the *tortilla* closed, forming a half-moon.

3. Arrange the *tortillas* on the prepared baking sheet and bake in the upper third of the oven about 15 minutes or until the cheese is melted and the *tortillas* are toasted and edges golden brown. Serve at once as a main course and pass the *Guacamole* or *Salsa Fresca* separately.

Carefree Mexican Meal
(Fast Menu for 4)
Cocktail: Margaritas
Quesadillas
   with Guacamole
Watercress and Orange
   Salad
Vanilla Ice Cream
   with Kahlúa

Burritos with Chilorio

(Burritos with Mexican Shredded Pork Filling)
Servings: 4 (2 each)
Preparation Time: About 15 minutes
Cooking Time: About 30 minutes
(Pork filling can be made up to 2 days ahead)

1½ pounds boneless pork, preferably from the shoulder
   or butt, trimmed and cut into ½-inch cubes
3 cloves garlic, crushed
2 tablespoons *Mexican Seasoning Mix* (page 98),
   mixed together with 3 tablespoons hot water
   and 1 tablespoon white vinegar
2 tablespoons safflower oil or vegetable oil
Salt and freshly ground pepper to taste
8 10-inch white flour *tortillas* (available at supermarket),
   wrapped in aluminum foil and kept warm in a very low oven
   until ready to use
1 cup *Refried Beans* (page 109) or canned refried beans, heated
1⅓ cups shredded Monterey Jack cheese (4-ounce piece)
Half small head lettuce, shredded

1 cup *Guacamole* (page 99) or prepared guacamole
   (available at supermarket or gourmet store) or sour cream
   or plain lowfat yogurt

1. Add the pork cubes to a 4- to 6-quart pot over high heat with
enough water to cover them by ½ inch and bring to a boil. Continue
to boil vigorously for about 20 minutes, stirring occasionally, or
until almost all the liquid has evaporated and the pork is cooked
through with no trace of pink, but not falling apart. Reduce the heat
to medium-low and cook the pork, stirring constantly, for 3 to 5
minutes more until just browned. Carefully pour off any grease and
transfer the pork cubes to the bowl of a food processor fitted with a
metal blade or the container of a blender and pulse about 8 times or
until coarsely chopped.

2. Return the pork to the pot along with the garlic and seasoning mix
combined with the water and vinegar, and place over medium-low

HINT: Don't forget about helpful appliances such as the food processor and blender. I often use the food processor to shred the pork filling in place of the traditional method of using two forks, which takes forever! Also, if you can't find the time to make refried beans, then purchase canned refried beans from the international section of the supermarket. I find homemade guacamole irresistible, but in a pinch, ready-made guacamole from your local gourmet store is a good substitute.

Chile or Chili?

Chile is the Spanish word for the fruit of the pepper plant from the *Capsicum* family. "Chili" is the American spelling, whereas the British spell it "chilley."

In common American usage, "chile" refers to the peppers ("chiles" being the plural) and "chili" is the Mexican-American stew-like dish *Chile con Carne*, which is a beef-based dish that is seasoned with chile peppers.

heat. Stir in the safflower oil until well blended. Cook, stirring constantly, scraping the bottom and around the sides of the pot to release any browned bits, about 5 minutes or until the pork is heated through and the flavors have blended. (NOTE: The mixture will be rather dry; stir well so that it does not stick to the bottom of the pot.) Season with salt and pepper.

3. Working quickly, place ¼ cup of the pork filling along the bottom half of a warm *tortilla*, followed by 2 tablespoons of heated refried beans. Then top the beans with a heaping tablespoon Monterey Jack cheese and some lettuce. Fold the sides of the *tortilla* over the filling but not all the way to the center, then roll the bottom half of the *tortilla* up and over the filling, while folding the top half of the *tortilla* over the bottom half. Repeat the process with the remaining *tortillas* and fillings. Serve the *burritos* at once as a main course with *guacamole* or sour cream.

Refried Beans

Servings: About 2½ cups
Preparation Time: About 5 minutes
Cooking Time: None
(can be made up to 3 days ahead)

Here is my quick "lard-free" (not fried) version of refried beans, yet they are still just as creamy and unctuous. Not only is this recipe better for you, but it is much prettier — reddish-mauve in color!

2 15½-ounce cans red kidney beans, drained,
   reserving ½ cup of the liquid
2 cloves garlic, crushed
Salt to taste

Transfer the beans with the ½ cup reserved liquid to the bowl of a food processor fitted with a metal blade. Process the beans about 2 minutes, scraping down the sides of the bowl as necessary, or just until the mixture has a paste-like consistency and is still slightly rough in texture, not completely smooth. Pulse in the crushed garlic until well blended and season with salt to taste. Serve warm or at room temperature as a condiment.

Salsa Fresca

(Mexican Fresh Tomato Sauce)
Servings: About 3 cups
Preparation Time: About 15 minutes
Cooking Time: None

1 pound ripe tomatoes (about 4 medium), finely chopped
1 cup finely chopped white onion
2 fresh jalapeño peppers, seeded, ribs removed and minced
   (How-To, this page) or 2 tablespoons minced drained
   canned jalapeño peppers (available at supermarket)
¼ cup fresh lime juice (2 to 3 small limes)
¼ cup finely chopped fresh cilantro (coriander) leaves
Salt and freshly ground pepper to taste

In a medium nonreactive bowl combine the tomatoes, onion,

HANDLE WITH CARE

Handling Fresh, Dried or Canned Chiles
It is advisable to wear rubber gloves when handling chiles and never touch your face — eyes or nose — because the oil from the chiles can act as an irritant to your skin and mucous membranes. After handling the chiles, wash your hands, cutting board and knife with warm soapy water. If you do get chile oil on your skin and feel a burning sensation apply a paste of baking soda and cold water (a ratio of 2:1) to the affected area and allow to dry, then wipe off.

To Prepare a Fresh Chile
Before cutting the chile pepper, rinse it and pull the stem out under cold running water. The heat of the chile (an alkaloid called "capsaicin") is more concentrated in its seeds and ribs than in its meat, so to prepare the chiles for cooking, cut the pod in half lengthwise and brush out and discard the seeds. Using a sharp paring knife, cut out the fleshy ribs and discard. The chile can now be used or it can be soaked briefly in lightly salted cold water to help reduce some of the heat.

To Prepare a Dried Chile

Dried chiles should be stemmed, de-ribbed and seeded before being used; they do not require washing.

Grinding Dried Chiles

In general, a large chile pod, such as an *ancho*, will yield when ground one tablespoon of chile powder.

You can use an electric spice grinder or blender to grind chiles. If you have leftover chile powder, store the powder in a clean, dry, airtight glass container up to 3 months away from heat, light or moisture.

To Grind Large Dried Chiles

Remove the stem, seeds and ribs from the dried pepper pod and grind.

To Grind Small Dried Chiles

Remove the stem and grind the entire pepper pod.

To Prepare Canned Chiles

Always drain canned chiles and rinse them in cold water to remove as much of the brine they are packed in as possible.

jalapeño peppers, lime juice and cilantro and stir until well blended. Season with salt and pepper. (NOTE: If the tomatoes aren't ripe and fairly sweet, add 1 teaspoon sugar, or to taste.) Serve at once as an accompaniment to Mexican food.

Mole

(Mexican Chile Sauce)
Servings: About 2½ cups
Preparation Time: About 15 minutes
Cooking Time: 2 minutes
(can be made up to 3 days ahead)

2 ounces (¾ cup) sliced almonds, toasted (How-To page 102)
5 ounces (1 cup) unsalted peanuts
½ cup seedless raisins
1 cup finely chopped white onion
3 cloves garlic, crushed
1 8-ounce can tomato sauce
¾ cup canned low-sodium chicken broth
1 teaspoon *Mexican Seasoning Mix* (page 98)
1½ ounces unsweetened chocolate, coarsely chopped
Salt and freshly ground pepper to taste

1. Combine the toasted almonds, peanuts and raisins in the container of a blender or the bowl of a food processor fitted with a metal blade. Process about 3 minutes or until the mixture is very finely ground, almost pulverized. Add the onion, garlic and tomato sauce and process for 3 minutes more, scraping down the sides of the bowl as necessary or until the mixture is well blended and smooth. (NOTE: If necessary, force the mixture through the finest blade of a food mill or coarse sieve into a medium bowl, until the mixture is as smooth as possible.)

2. Transfer the almond mixture to a 2- to 3-quart saucepan over medium heat. Stir in the chicken broth, seasoning mix and chocolate pieces until well blended. Heat about 2 minutes, stirring constantly, just until the chocolate has melted and the sauce has the consistency of heavy cream. Season to taste with salt and pepper and serve warm.

Spanish Seasoning Mix

Sopa de Ajo con Huevos

Arroz con Pollo

Tortilla Española

Chick-Pea and Sausage Stew

Huevos a la Flamenca

Empanada de Lomo

Spanish-Style Green Beans

Seafood Paella

Lima Beans with Ham

Chicken with Romesco-Style Sauce

CHAPTER 8

THE SPIRIT OF SPAIN

SPAIN IS A COUNTRY with a hot climate, vivid landscape and compelling culture whose cuisine is equally spirited. Spanish food, like that of all countries, varies from region to region. Overall uncomplicated, but unusual combinations of fresh ingredients, rich and subtly seasoned — not necessarily "hot" or even highly spiced — mark the cooking. My seasoning blend of cumin, paprika, saffron, mint and cayenne captures the essence of this style of cooking and makes these dishes come alive with flavor.

Tomatoes, onions and garlic are the foundation of many dishes, and, as in most Mediterranean countries, olive oil generally replaces butter with only a few exceptions. Spain's olive oil is a primary ingredient in the nation's cuisine, lending the food much of its unique flavor.

In recreating Spanish dishes in your home, you can choose one of the most cherished of seafood dishes, Seafood Paella (page 121). The "spirit" of this dish resides in the fresh flavors of the sea offset by grains of fluffy rice, stained with the sunny color of saffron and adorned with pimientos. In this dish, the seasoning blend is used not only for its flavor but its color as well.

In Spanish-Style Green Beans (page 120), the seasoning mix adds a slightly hot accent to this honest vegetable dish. In Chick-Pea and Sausage Stew (page 116) the herbs and spices lend more depth to the stronger flavors of some of Spain's favored ingredients, namely, chick-peas, *chorizo* (spicy pork sausage) and green bell peppers.

In Sopa de Ajo (garlic soup with poached eggs), page 112, the mixture of ingredients may strike you as an odd medley but don't be fooled, it's delicious. In this recipe, the bread (I used croutons) does double-duty, for its wonderful flavor and texture.

QUICKIES: EVERYDAY FOODS MADE INTERNATIONAL

Spanish Rice

Toss together buttered warm rice with some thinly sliced scallions, drained capers, *Spanish Seasoning Mix*, salt and pepper.

Say "Cheese"

To perk up a grilled cheese sandwich, sprinkle

the cheese with *Spanish Seasoning Mix* before grilling.

Best Bean Salad
Follow the Double-Duty Dressing quickie recipe (page 54), but season with *Spanish Seasoning Mix* instead of the *Greek Seasoning Mix*. Combine with drained canned garbanzo or red kidney beans until well blended and season with crushed garlic and finely chopped fresh parsley.

Wake-Up Breakfast
Cook scrambled eggs with a pinch of *Spanish Seasoning Mix*.

HINT: Packaged garlic-flavored croutons available from the supermarket bread aisle save time because you do not have to prepare them yourself. The croutons dissolve and thicken this rich Spanish soup.

Huevos a la Flamenca (colorful baked eggs) on page 117 also epitomizes Spanish cuisine in as much as it begins with a few simple fixings — eggs, peas, and a few other basic ingredients — but becomes ablaze with color when assembled. When you serve it, don't be surprised if your guests end their meal on a typically Spanish note — olé!

Spanish Seasoning Mix
Makes about 1/2 cup

¼ cup ground cumin
2 tablespoons paprika
1 1-gram package saffron threads or 2 firmly packed teaspoons (available at supermarket or gourmet store or see Source List page 186)
1 tablespoon dried mint leaves
1 teaspoon ground red (cayenne) pepper

In a small bag or bowl (How-To page 11), combine the cumin, paprika, saffron threads, mint and cayenne. Shake or stir until well blended. (NOTE: Be especially careful to distribute the saffron threads evenly.) Transfer to a clean, dry, airtight glass container. Store up to 3 months away from heat, light or moisture. Shake well before using.

Sopa de Ajo con Huevos
(Garlic Soup with Poached Eggs)
Servings: 4 (1⅔ cups each)
Preparation Time: About 5 minutes
Cooking Time: About 25 minutes

Legend has it that this simply flavored Spanish soup came about because peasants had little else but garlic and day-old bread in their pantries. With the addition of eggs from their chickens and water from their well, they developed a broth-like soup that could curb any appetite. Today this well-

known Spanish soup is made with chicken stock instead of water and I've added some spices to please the palate.

1 medium head garlic (about 12 cloves), each clove
   peeled and cut in half lengthwise
1 6-ounce (4 cups) package garlic- or onion- and
   garlic-flavored croutons (available at supermarket)
1½ quarts canned low-sodium chicken broth
1 teaspoon *Spanish Seasoning Mix* (page 112)
Salt and freshly ground pepper to taste
4 large eggs
3 tablespoons finely chopped fresh parsley, to garnish

A tomato and onion salad, to serve

1. Preheat the oven to 375° F.

2. Combine the garlic and croutons in the bowl of a food processor fitted with a metal blade and process about 1 minute or until finely ground.

3. Transfer the garlic mixture to a heavy 6-quart pot along with the chicken broth and seasoning mix and place the pot over high heat. Bring to a boil and boil for 3 minutes, stirring occasionally. Season with salt and pepper.

4. Place 4 ovenproof 2-cup soup bowls on a baking sheet. Divide the soup evenly among the 4 bowls, filling each ¾ full. (NOTE: Spanish earthenware is the traditional choice.) One-at-a-time, break each egg into a saucer, then slide the egg from the saucer into each bowl, so that the yolk does not break.

5. Bake on the lower rack of the oven for 15 to 18 minutes or until the whites just turn opaque and the yolks are poached. Be *very* careful not to overcook, as the eggs will continue to cook even after being removed from the oven. Sprinkle the soup with the parsley and serve immediately as a main course with a simple salad such as a tomato and onion salad. Instruct diners to use their soup spoons to break the egg yolks and mix them into the soup.

Arroz con Pollo

(Chicken with Rice)
Servings: 4 to 6
Preparation Time: About 15 minutes
Cooking Time: About 45 minutes

3½ pounds drumsticks and split chicken breasts (with ribs)
2 tablespoons olive oil, preferably Spanish (available at supermarket)
2 medium white onions, finely chopped
3 cloves garlic, crushed
1 28-ounce can whole plum tomatoes, crushed
1½ tablespoons *Spanish Seasoning Mix* (page 112)
2 cups long-grain white rice
1 quart canned low-sodium chicken broth
1 teaspoon salt
1 cup fresh (1 pound in pods) or thawed frozen green peas

1. Preheat the broiler.

2. Rinse the chicken pieces well and pat dry with paper towels. Arrange the chicken on a broiler pan. Line the bottom pan with aluminum foil. Broil 4 inches from the heat source for 6 minutes or until the skin is crisp and golden brown. (NOTE: The chicken will not be completely cooked as it will be cooked more later.) When the chicken is cool enough to handle, remove and discard the skin.

3. Meanwhile, heat the olive oil in a heavy 6-quart nonreactive pot over medium-high heat. Add the onions and garlic and cook, stirring, for 4 minutes or until the onions are soft. Stir in the tomatoes and cook for 5 minutes, stirring often. Stir in the seasoning mix, rice, chicken broth and salt until well blended. Stir in the partially cooked, skinned chicken pieces, making sure they are completely immersed and bring to a boil.

4. Reduce the heat to low, partially cover and cook for 25 minutes, stirring once after 15 minutes, or until the chicken is completely cooked and the rice tender but not dry. (The rice should absorb almost all the liquid.)

5. Stir in the peas and cook, covered, about 4 minutes or until the

HINT: Not only does broiling the chicken save time, it is also healthier for you than the traditional method of frying. The skin must be left on to keep the chicken moist while broiling, but afterwards remove it to reduce the fat content of the meal. Another tip: To save more time, use a food processor to chop the onions.

Cozy Evening in Spain
(One-Dish Menu for 4 to 6)
Arroz con Pollo
Tomato and Onion Salad
Orange Sherbet
    (supermarket)
Wine: Chilled white
    Spanish Rioja

peas are tender. Let stand, uncovered, for 5 minutes before serving hot as a main course.

Tortilla Española
(Spanish Omelette)
Servings: 2
Preparation Time: About 10 minutes
Cooking Time: 20 to 25 minutes

In Spain, a tortilla is an omelette, but it is different from a French omelette in that the Spanish version is cake-like, about 1½ inches thick.

4 large eggs
2 large egg whites
1 teaspoon *Spanish Seasoning Mix* (page 112)
½ teaspoon salt
½ teaspoon freshly ground pepper
1 pound (2 medium) boiling potatoes
4 tablespoons olive oil, preferably Spanish (available at supermarket)
1 medium yellow onion, thinly sliced
2 scallions, green part only, thinly sliced, to garnish

A garden salad, to serve

1. Combine the eggs, egg whites, seasoning mix, salt and pepper in a large bowl, whisk until blended and reserve.

2. Preheat the oven to 350° F.

3. Peel and cut the potatoes into ⅛-inch-thick slices or use the thin slicing disk of the food processor to expedite the slicing. Stack the potato slices in small piles and cut each pile crosswise into quarters. Add 3 tablespoons of the olive oil to a heavy 10-inch ovenproof skillet. Rotate the skillet so the oil coats the side and bottom evenly. Heat the oil over medium heat.

4. Add the onion and potatoes to the skillet and cook, stirring often, for 3 minutes or until the onion is soft and the potatoes are crisp-tender. Using a slotted spoon, transfer the mixture to the medium bowl with the egg mixture.

HINT: I highly recommend owning a full nonstick cookware system.

However, if you are only going to purchase one pan for now, make it a 10-inch ovenproof skillet — a good all-around pan — and especially perfect for omelettes, where nonstick performance is so crucial; using lots of oil to prevent sticking is not the solution.

It is always good practice to have all of your ingredients prepared and measured-ready-to-be-cooked. It saves time because you don't stop what you are doing and interrupt the cooking process; it is especially important when working with potatoes, since they will begin to discolor once cut.

Soulful Spain
(Vegetarian Menu for 2)
Cocktail: Sangría (Spanish wine and fruit punch)
Tortilla Española
Spanish-Style Green Beans (page 120)
Flan (Spanish caramel custard)

GARBANZO CHIC

Known as the "chick-pea" or by the Spanish *garbanzo* or the Italian *ceci*, garbanzos are typically beige to yellow in color. Though they share similar traits to a bean, these plump wonders are, in fact, a member of the pea family, the seed of the chick-pea plant. They are extremely nutritious, an admirable source of low-fat protein and rich in calcium, iron and B vitamins.

Back in Time

Garbanzos were first cultivated in North Africa and the Middle East (Cont'd on page 117)

HINT: I call for canned chick-peas (already cooked) instead of the dried. This saves a tremendous amount of time since both presoaking and cooking times are avoided. Also, this one-dish meal can be made ahead up to 2 days. It reheats very well.

TIP: Mixed vegetable juice works well in this recipe. I like to use "V-8™ 100% vegetable juice."

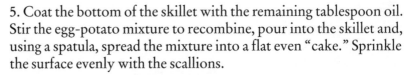

5. Coat the bottom of the skillet with the remaining tablespoon oil. Stir the egg-potato mixture to recombine, pour into the skillet and, using a spatula, spread the mixture into a flat even "cake." Sprinkle the surface evenly with the scallions.

6. Transfer the skillet to the preheated oven and bake on the lower rack of the oven for 15 to 20 minutes or until the potatoes are tender and the egg mixture is thoroughly set but not dry. Let stand for 5 minutes before cutting. To serve, cut the omelette around the outer edge, then into 4 wedges; serve hot or at room temperature as a main course for 2 with a garden salad.

Chick-Pea and Sausage Stew

Servings: 4 (2 cups each) to 6 (1⅓ cups each)
Preparation Time: About 10 minutes
Cooking Time: 25 minutes
(can be made up to 2 days ahead)

1½ tablespoons olive oil, preferably Spanish (available at supermarket)
1 pound fresh *chorizo* (spicy fresh pork sausage) or other spicy fresh pork sausage, cut on the diagonal into ¼-inch-thick slices (available from gourmet store or see Source List page 186)
1 large white onion, finely chopped
1 medium green bell pepper, finely chopped
3 cloves garlic, crushed
1 28-ounce can crushed tomatoes
1 11.5-ounce can (1¼ cups) mixed vegetable juice (available from supermarket)
2 teaspoons *Spanish Seasoning Mix* (page 112)
3 15-ounce cans chick-peas *(garbanzos)*, drained and rinsed
Salt and freshly ground pepper to taste

Crusty bread, such as olive bread, to serve (optional)

1. Heat the olive oil in a heavy nonreactive 6-quart pot over medium-high heat. Add the sausage and fry about 5 minutes or until browned. Stir in the onion, bell pepper and garlic and cook, stirring often, for 4 minutes, or until the onion is soft and bell pepper crisp-tender.

2. Stir in the tomatoes, vegetable juice, seasoning mix and chickpeas and bring to a boil. Reduce the heat to low, and cook for 15 minutes, stirring occasionally. Season with salt and pepper and serve hot as a main course accompanied with olive bread if desired.

Huevos a la Flamenca
(Spanish-Style Colorful Baked Eggs)
Servings: 2
Preparation Time: About 10 minutes
Cooking Time: 20 minutes

For its distinctive flavor, this Spanish main dish uses a seasoned base sauce known as sofrito ("lightly fried") — a favorite component, usually composed of onion, garlic and tomatoes, but with several variations depending on the region. Classically, this dish also uses serrano ham; however, it can be difficult to find in the United States and prosciutto is an acceptable substitute.

2 tablespoons olive oil, preferably Spanish (available at supermarket)
1 medium yellow onion, finely chopped
2 cloves garlic, crushed
1 16-ounce can peeled whole tomatoes, drained and crushed
1 teaspoon *Spanish Seasoning Mix* (page 112)
1 4-ounce slice *prosciutto* (Italian cured ham), finely chopped
¼ teaspoon salt
¼ teaspoon freshly ground pepper
4 large eggs
½ cup fresh (8 ounces in pods) or frozen green peas, thawed
4 cooked asparagus spears, cut into 2-inch-long pieces
1 4-ounce jar sliced pimientos (available at supermarket), drained
2 tablespoons pale dry Sherry (optional)

1. Preheat the oven to 400° F.

2. Heat the olive oil in a heavy 10-inch skillet over medium heat. Add the onion and garlic and cook, stirring often, about 5 minutes or until soft but not brown. Stir in the tomatoes, seasoning mix, *prosciutto*, salt and pepper and cook for 2 minutes, stirring often, or until the mixture is just heated through. Reserve at room temperature until ready to use.

around 5000 B.C. They were a staple in the diet of ancient Romans, who christened them *arietinum* (ram-like) since the peas resemble rams heads with horns curling over the sides. The West embraced chick-peas by the Spanish name *garbanzos*, since they were introduced to Europe by the Moors via Spain, where garbanzos have become an essential component of Spanish cuisine.

The Traveling Pea
The well-liked *garbanzo* has found its way to many international dinner tables. The assets of this pea are far-reaching and they are used throughout the world, especially in the cuisines of Spain, the Mediterranean, South America, North Africa, the Middle East and India. They are employed in appetizers, soups, main courses, side dishes, even desserts. They are also ground into flour, and toasted and eaten like nuts.

HINT: To save time, presteam or microwave the asparagus. Sometimes cooked asparagus can even be found at your local supermarket "salad bar."

3. Spread the onion mixture evenly in the bottom of a 8-inch-square baking dish. One at a time, break an egg into a saucer, then slide the egg from the saucer into each of the four corners of the dish. Make little piles of the peas in between the eggs and arrange the asparagus in parallel rows on either side of the eggs, scattering the pimiento strips decoratively over all. Sprinkle the eggs with the Sherry if desired.

4. Bake on the middle rack of the oven about 12 minutes or until the egg whites are opaque and firm and the yolks poached, being careful not to overcook. Serve at once directly from the baking dish for 2 as a light main course or as part of brunch for 4.

Empanada de Lomo
(Spanish Pork-Filled Pie)
Servings: 4
Preparation Time: About 20 minutes
Cooking Time: 50 to 55 minutes
(can be made up to 2 days ahead)

Although empanadas originated in Mexico, they are widely enjoyed throughout Latin America, and have become a Spanish specialty. To save time, instead of the traditional two-crusted pie, I have modified the recipe as a single-crust pie.

PASTRY: or substitute half (1 crust) a 15-ounce package
　　refrigerated premade pie crusts for a 9-inch pie
　　(package contains 2 crusts), available at supermarket
2½　cups unbleached white flour, plus more to dust
½　teaspoon baking powder
½　teaspoon salt
4　tablespoons (½ stick) unsalted butter
　　or unsalted margarine, cut into 8 pieces
1　large egg, lightly beaten
½　cup ice water

FILLING:
2　tablespoons olive oil, preferably Spanish (available at supermarket)
1　large white onion, finely chopped
3　cloves garlic, crushed

1 pound boneless trimmed pork loin, cut into ½-inch dice
4 ounces fresh *chorizo* sausage (spicy fresh pork sausage)
 or other spicy fresh pork sausage, cut into ¼-inch-thick slices
 (available from gourmet store or see Source List page 186)
1 medium green bell pepper, cut into ⅛-inch-thick strips
1 medium red bell pepper, cut into ⅛-inch-thick strips
1½ teaspoons *Spanish Seasoning Mix* (page 112)
¼ cup pale dry Sherry
½ teaspoon salt
1 teaspoon freshly ground pepper
2 tablespoons milk, to glaze (optional)

1. To prepare the pastry: In the bowl of a food processor fitted with a metal blade combine the flour, baking powder and salt and pulse twice to mix. Add the butter and pulse about 8 times or until the mixture is the consistency of coarse cornmeal. Pulse in the egg until well blended. Then, while pulsing the machine, add the ice water through the feed tube, ⅛ cup at a time, scraping down the sides of the bowl as necessary. Process until the dough is moist and just hangs together. (NOTE: Do not let the dough form into a ball in the processor.) Remove the dough from the bowl, form into a flat disk, wrap in waxed paper and refrigerate until ready to use.

2. To make the filling: Heat the olive oil in a heavy 4- to 6-quart pot over medium-high heat. Add the onion and garlic and cook, stirring often, about 4 minutes or until soft but not browned. Add the pork and *chorizo* and cook, stirring often, about 8 minutes or until browned. Stir in the green and red bell pepper strips and cook, stirring often, for 6 minutes more or until the peppers are just tender. Stir in the seasoning mix, Sherry, salt and pepper and bring to a boil. Remove the pot from the heat and reserve until ready to use.

3. Preheat the oven to 375° F.

4. On a lightly floured work surface, roll out the dough ¼ inch thick. (If using a prepared refrigerated single pie crust, unfold it but do not roll out and proceed with recipe.) Using a deep 1-quart oven-proof round casserole (with a 9-inch diameter), trim the dough to fit the top of the casserole with a ½-inch overhang. Either cut a steam vent with a small cookie cutter or make 2 diagonal slashes in the center of the crust to expose the filling.

HINT: If you are watching the clock, substitute a premade pie crust available from the supermarket. I like to use Pillsbury's "All-Ready Pie Crusts."® All you have to do is unfold and bake — you don't have to even touch your rolling pin. This will reduce the preparation time by about 10 minutes because you don't need to assemble dough ingredients as in step #1.

Or, the homemade pie dough can be made up to 1 day ahead, wrapped in waxed paper and refrigerated. Then roll out the day of serving. The filling can be made up to 2 days ahead. Or, prepare the entire pie, glaze if desired, and bake up to 2 days ahead. Let cool, wrap and refrigerate. Reheat in oven just before serving.

5. Transfer the filling to the casserole and lightly moisten the edges of the rim of the casserole with water. Place the crust gently on top and crimp the edges to seal. Brush the crust lightly with the milk to glaze if desired.

6. Bake for 30 to 35 minutes or until the crust is crisp and delicately browned. Serve hot as a main course.

Spanish-Style Green Beans

Servings: 4
Preparation Time: About 10 minutes
Cooking Time: 15 minutes

In Spain this vegetable dish is served as a separate course, but it works nicely as a side dish to an entrée as well.

1 pound green beans, trimmed
3 tablespoons unsalted butter or unsalted margarine
3 cloves garlic, crushed
1 teaspoon *Spanish Seasoning Mix* (page 112)
¼ teaspoon salt

1. Add the green beans to a 3-quart saucepan of lightly salted boiling water over high heat. Return to a boil and cook about 5 minutes or until the beans are crisp-tender and drain in a colander.

2. Melt the butter in a heavy 12-inch skillet over medium-high heat. Add the beans and cook, stirring often, about 9 minutes or until dappled golden brown and completely tender. Remove the skillet from the heat and stir in the garlic, seasoning mix and salt until well blended. Serve at once as a side dish.

Seafood Paella

Servings: 4
Preparation Time: About 20 minutes
Cooking Time: About 35 minutes

The name paella originates from the pan in which this dish is traditionally cooked and served, the paellera—a pan large and shallow, with two loop handles, made of heavy, iron, aluminum or Spanish earthenware. A heavy deep ovenproof 12- to 14-inch skillet is a fine substitute. Paella can be made with a variety of possible ingredients: lobster, clams, squid, chicken, rabbit and string beans. Olive oil, rice and saffron are always used.

1   tablespoon olive oil, preferably Spanish (available at supermarket)
1   medium yellow onion, finely chopped
1   cup long-grain white rice
1   tablespoon *Spanish Seasoning Mix* (page 112),
       soaked in 2 cups boiling water
½   teaspoon salt
3   cloves garlic, crushed
1   4-ounce jar sliced pimientos, drained (available at supermarket)
1½ cups fresh (1½ pounds in pods) or frozen green peas, thawed
1   pound monkfish steaks, or other firm mild white fish steaks,
       central bone removed and cut into 2-inch-wide pieces
12 small mussels, soaked, scrubbed and debearded (see Tip this page)
12 ounces jumbo shrimp (21 to 25 to the pound),
       shelled and deveined (How-To page 15)
½   cup finely chopped fresh parsley, to garnish
Lemon wedges, to serve

1. Heat the olive oil in a deep heavy 12-inch ovenproof skillet over medium-high heat. Add the onion and rice and cook, stirring frequently, for 4 to 5 minutes or until the onion is soft but not browned. Add the seasoning mix with the soaking water and salt and bring to a boil, stirring occasionally.

2. Preheat the oven to 350° F.

3. Reduce the heat to low, cover and simmer, undisturbed, for 6 to 8 minutes or until the rice is tender (be sure to test the rice in the bottom of the skillet also) and no longer soupy but some liquid remains.

HINT: To save time, I recommend using long-grain rice, which cooks faster than the typical Spanish choice of short stubby rice.

TIP: Soak the mussels in cold salted water sprinkled with 1 tablespoon cornmeal and refrigerate for at least 2 hours or up to 6. This helps rid them of sand. Drain and rinse the mussels, discarding any that float to the surface or have shells that are open and don't close when tapped several times.

Turn off the heat, stir in the garlic, pimientos and peas until well blended. Gently place the monkfish pieces in the rice mixture, placing a few pieces on the surface also. Transfer the skillet to the oven and bake, uncovered, for 8 minutes.

4. Gently stir the mixture once, then arrange the mussels (in their shells) on their sides on top of the rice mixture. Repeat with the shrimp. Bake for 12 minutes more, depending on size of mussels, or until the mussels have opened, the shrimp are pink and the monkfish opaque throughout.

5. To serve, sprinkle with the parsley and serve the *Paella* at once as a main course. Pass with lemon wedges for the diners to squeeze over the *Paella* before eating.

Lima Beans with Ham

Servings: 4
Preparation Time: About 5 minutes
Cooking Time: 10 minutes

Tapas are small dishes that are served as appetizers with cocktails, in other words, bar snacks or Latin hors d'oeuvres. They can be as simple as a few olives in a dish, or as substantial as stuffed peppers. This dish is a traditional tapa but makes for a fabulous accompaniment to a main course.

2 tablespoons olive oil, preferably Spanish (available at supermarket)
2 10-ounce packages frozen lima beans, thawed
2 tablespoons dry white wine
3 cloves garlic, crushed
1 4-ounce slice *prosciutto* (Italian cured ham), finely diced
1¼ teaspoons *Spanish Seasoning Mix* (page 112)
2 tablespoons unsalted butter or unsalted margarine, cut into quarters
Salt and freshly ground pepper to taste

Heat the olive oil in a nonreactive heavy 10-inch skillet over medium heat. Add the lima beans, wine, garlic, *prosciutto* and seasoning mix and stir until well blended. Cover with a lid or aluminum foil and cook about 8 minutes, stirring occasionally, or until the lima beans are tender but not mushy. Stir in the butter pieces until melted. Season with salt and pepper and serve at once as a side dish.

Chicken with Romesco-Style Sauce

Servings: 4
Preparation Time: About 15 minutes
Cooking Time: About 20 minutes
(Sauce can be made up to 3 days ahead)

Romesco is a glossy, cold, brightly colored Spanish sauce with a bite. The red romesco pepper, also called a ñora pepper, lends its name to this sauce. The pepper is indigenous to Catalonia, but my seasoning mix contains paprika and cayenne, which approximate the flavor of this pepper. There are as many variations of Romesco sauce as there are mustards, but they all have in common a smooth texture and marvelous flavor. The sauce should be hot to taste but not overwhelming or fiery. Romesco sauce is primarily served with fish and shellfish but it is also fabulous with chicken, as you will soon find out.

I like to keep this sauce on hand for last-minute entertaining. It happens to work double-duty, not just as a sauce, but as a dip that is excellent when served with crudités.

SAUCE: (Makes 1⅔ cups)
1 ½-inch-thick slice of white bread, including crust, torn into small pieces
¼ cup red-wine vinegar
2 cloves garlic, cut in half lengthwise

HINT: Quick-Thaw Method: It is easy to thaw food unattended in the refrigerator by simply leaving it in its original wrapper overnight. Or, if it is in an airtight and waterproof freezer container, set it in a bath of cold (not warm) water until the food is sufficiently thawed for easy removal from its container. I do not recommend using a microwave oven for thawing as the outer areas tend to get cooked by the time the center has defrosted.

Even though thawing at room temperature takes about half the time as the refrigerator method, do it only as a last resort. Also, once thawed at room temperature, the food must be used at once, as bacteria can set in and nutritional values start to decrease.

2¼ ounces (½ cup) slivered blanched almonds, toasted
    (How-To page 102)
1 medium-sized ripe tomato, seeded and coarsely chopped
1 teaspoon *Spanish Seasoning Mix* (page 112)
½ teaspoon salt
1 teaspoon freshly ground pepper
½ cup olive oil, preferably Spanish (available at supermarket)

CHICKEN:
1½ cups dry white wine
1½ pounds (4 breast halves) skinless, boneless chicken breasts
½ cup drained Spanish pimiento-stuffed green olives,
    coarsely chopped, to garnish (available at supermarket)

1. To make the sauce: Soak the bread in the vinegar until soft. Meanwhile, in the bowl of a food processor fitted with a metal blade or the container of a blender, pulse the garlic and almonds about 30 seconds or until very finely chopped. Add the bread with vinegar, the tomato, seasoning mix, salt and pepper. Process for 1 minute or until well blended. With the machine running, add the oil in a thin, steady stream, scraping down the sides of the bowl as necessary, until all the oil is incorporated and the sauce is smooth and sauce-like. Cover the sauce and refrigerate until ready to serve. Bring back to room temperature and whisk to recombine before serving. (NOTE: The sauce is best when refrigerated about 4 hours before serving so flavors can mingle.)

2. To prepare the chicken: Combine 1½ cups water and the wine in a deep 10-inch nonreactive skillet over medium-low heat. Bring almost to a boil, then reduce the heat to low. Add the chicken breasts, cover the skillet with a lid or aluminum foil and gently simmer (poach) the chicken breasts for 15 minutes or until cooked through. (NOTE: Be careful not to overcook; the poaching liquid should barely tremble during cooking time; if the liquid comes to a full simmer or boil, reduce the heat to very low.)

3. To serve, using a slotted spoon, transfer the chicken breasts to individual dinner plates and spoon Romesco sauce over each. Garnish with chopped olives. Serve as a main course. (Reserve the poaching liquid for another use, such as a base for chicken stock.)

CHAPTER 9

SCANDINAVIAN SMÖRGÅSBORD

Scandinavian Seasoning Mix

Swedish Meatballs

Cucumber Salad

Yellow Pea Soup with Bacon

Swedish-Style Chicken

Poached Salmon Steaks with Mustard Sauce

Gravlax

Swedish Creamed Potatoes

Cauliflower with Dilled Egg

Lamb with Dill Sauce

Lihamurekepiiras

WHAT IS TYPICAL of Scandinavian cuisine? Fish plays an important role, game is plentiful and among the seasonings dill is preeminent. You will also find dishes with pork and poultry and a characteristic preference for beets, cucumbers, potatoes, horseradish, apples, cream and butter.

Scandinavian cuisine is noteworthy because the ingredients used remain genuine and "fresh" in flavor: Fish tastes of the sea, mushrooms of the earth and herbs of the fields. One such example is the world-famous Scandinavian delicacy Gravlax (page 132), salmon that is cured simply with salt, sugar, peppercorns and fresh dill. In this recipe the versatile Scandinavian seasoning blend containing dillweed, marjoram, caraway and nutmeg, is also used in the "dry rub" to cure the salmon, adding even more flavor without extra effort.

Simple recipes are enhanced by the seasoning mix. Cauliflower with Dilled Egg (page 134), is a good example. Swedish Creamed Potatoes (page 133), made with skim milk in place of cream, is another.

You will find a number of recipes in this chapter that are part of that glorious table called *smörgåsbord*. A Scandinavian way of starting a meal, *smörgåsbord* is a buffet consisting of dozens of varieties of hors d'oeuvres and a number of light entrées. It can be quite modest or very elaborate, the common factor being attention to decorative and appetizing detail.

This chapter is like a *smörgåsbord*; it includes a delicious sampling of typical preparations along with actual traditional *smörgåsbord* recipes, such as tangy Cucumber Salad (page 128) and Swedish Meatballs (page 126).

You can even hold your own *smörgåsbord!* Offer it not as an

QUICKIES: EVERYDAY FOODS MADE INTERNATIONAL

Passionate Potatoes
Season homemade or deli potato salad with *Scandinavian Seasoning Mix.*

The Only Omelette
Sprinkle a prepared omelette with some *Scandinavian Seasoning Mix* for a touch of elegance.

Scandinavian Scallops
Sauté scallops in a little
vegetable oil just until
opaque but still springy to
the touch. Season with
*Scandinavian Seasoning
Mix,* finish with some
butter and serve at once.

Egg Salad Special
Season your homemade
or deli egg salad with
*Scandinavian Seasoning
Mix* for "egg-ceptional"
sandwiches!

overture to the main course but as the meal itself. All you'll have left
to do is raise your glass of *aquavit* and toast the tantalizing tastes of
Scandinavia — *"skoal!"*

Scandinavian Seasoning Mix

Makes about 1/2 cup

¼ cup dried dillweed
3 tablespoons dried marjoram leaves
2 teaspoons caraway seeds
1 teaspoon ground nutmeg

In a small bag or bowl (How-To page 11), combine the dillweed,
marjoram, caraway seeds and nutmeg. Shake or stir until well blended. Transfer to a clean, dry, airtight glass container. Store up to 3
months away from heat, light or moisture. Shake well before using.

Swedish Meatballs

Servings: 4 to 6
Preparation Time: About 20 minutes
Cooking Time: About 30 minutes

*In the Swedish manner, meatballs are served as a main course with cream
gravy, and for a complete meal, I suggest serving them over a bed of noodles.
However, if they are to be an hors d'oeuvre or part of a smörgåsbord, they
should be formed into smaller balls and served without gravy.*

MEATBALLS:
8 ounces extra-lean ground beef
4 ounces extra-lean ground veal
4 ounces ground lamb
½ cup minced white onion
½ cup unseasoned dry bread crumbs
1½ teaspoons *Scandinavian Seasoning Mix* (above)
3 tablespoons club soda or seltzer water
1 large egg

1 pound wide egg noodles, to serve

GRAVY: (Makes 2 cups)

4 tablespoons (½ stick) unsalted butter or unsalted margarine
¼ cup unbleached white flour
2 cups canned low-sodium beef broth
Salt and freshly ground pepper to taste
2 scallions, green part only, thinly sliced

1. To prepare the meatballs: Combine the beef, veal, lamb, onion, bread crumbs, seasoning mix, club soda and egg in a medium bowl and mix until well blended.

2. Spoon a heaping teaspoon of the mixture and with your hands shape into tightly packed balls about 1-inch in diameter. Repeat process until you have about 4 dozen meatballs and reserve.

3. Meanwhile, prepare the noodles: Add the noodles to a 6- to 8-quart pot of boiling water over high heat. Return to a boil and cook for 7 to 9 minutes, stirring occasionally, or until *al dente* (slightly firm to the bite). Drain and transfer the noodles to a warm serving platter. Cover and keep warm until ready to serve.

4. While noodles are cooking, make the gravy: In a heavy 2½- to 3-quart saucepan melt the butter over low heat. Add the flour and cook for 2 minutes, whisking constantly; do not let the *roux* brown. Gradually pour in the beef broth, while whisking constantly across the bottom and along the sides of the saucepan, until well blended and smooth.

5. Raise the heat to medium and bring the gravy to a simmer, whisking often. Drop in the reserved meatballs a handful at a time, and cover. Do not stir. Cook about 15 minutes, or until the meatballs are cooked through and no pink remains. Using a slotted spoon, scatter the meatballs over the bed of noodles, cover and reserve.

6. Season the gravy with salt and pepper and stir in the scallions until well blended. Ladle the gravy over the meatballs and noodles and serve hot as a main course.

HINT: The meatballs should be light in texture and tender. To achieve this, don't handle the meat mixture too much. My secret to extra lightness is club soda. Traditionally, Swedish meatballs are fried, but these directions are for boiling, a much healthier method of cooking. Also, see page 63 for extra work-saving tips for shaping meatballs.

Cucumber Salad

Servings: 4 to 6
Preparation Time: About 10 minutes
Cooking Time: None
Chilling Time: 2 hours to overnight
(can be made up to 1 day ahead)

TIP: When preparing the ingredients, use a food processor to mince the red onion. Remove the onion and metal chopping blade, then fit the processor with a fine slicing disk and slice the cucumbers.

A smörgåsbord *is a widely varied buffet of open sandwiches, pickled fish, meats, vegetables, eggs and salads served in Scandinavian countries as hors d'oeuvres or as the meal itself. This salad is customarily part of a smörgåsbord. I love its refreshing attributes as a "palate-cleanser." Usually the salad accompanies meat and fish dishes and typically is made with sour cream, but I have substituted a healthier lowfat yogurt.*

1 medium red onion, minced
¼ cup white vinegar
⅔ cup plain lowfat yogurt
2 tablespoons sugar
1 teaspoon *Scandinavian Seasoning Mix* (page 126)
3 tablespoons finely chopped fresh dillweed
¼ teaspoon salt
½ teaspoon freshly ground pepper to taste, preferably white pepper
2 large cucumbers, peeled and very thinly sliced

Combine the onion, vinegar, yogurt, sugar, seasoning mix, dillweed, salt and pepper in a medium glass salad bowl and mix until well blended. Add the cucumbers and gently toss with the dressing until coated evenly. Cover the bowl and refrigerate for at least 2 hours, preferably overnight, or until the salad is chilled and the flavors are well blended. Serve cold as a side dish.

Yellow Pea Soup with Bacon

Servings: 4 (2½ cups each)
Preparation Time: About 15 minutes
Cooking Time: 70 minutes
(can be made up to 2 days ahead)

This soup, made with Swedish yellow peas, is a favorite throughout Scandi-

navia. Each country has its own version, cooked with salted pork, ham or bacon to add flavor; these are either eaten separately or as part of the soup.

Outside Scandinavia, yellow Swedish peas can be difficult to find. Domestic dried yellow split peas can be used, and though they are slightly different in flavor, they still make for a splendid soup!

3 quarts canned vegetable broth or 3 quarts made from vegetable
  bouillon cubes, following package directions (available at supermarket)
1 pound dried yellow split peas, rinsed and picked over
1 medium white onion, coarsely chopped
3 ribs celery, finely chopped
8 ounces Canadian bacon, cut into ¼-inch dice (available at supermarket)
2 teaspoons *Scandinavian Seasoning Mix* (page 126)
Salt and freshly ground pepper to taste
3 tablespoons finely chopped fresh chives

Dark rye bread, to serve

1. Combine the vegetable broth, split peas, onion and celery in an 8-quart pot over high heat. Bring to a boil. Then reduce the heat to medium-low and partially cover. Cook, stirring occasionally, for 50 minutes, skimming the surface occasionally.

2. Stir in the Canadian bacon and seasoning mix and cook for 20 minutes more, stirring occasionally, or until the peas are tender and beginning to fall apart. The soup should have the consistency of heavy cream. Season with salt and pepper and stir in the chives until well blended. Serve hot as a main course accompanied with sliced dark rye bread.

Swedish-Style Chicken

Servings: 4
Preparation Time: About 5 minutes
Cooking Time: 25 minutes

This recipe is so easy that you will want to make it for the most informal get-togethers, yet it makes for an elegant presentation. The chicken is also delicious sliced in a supper salad.

4 skinless, boneless chicken breasts (about 1¼ pounds)

2 teaspoons dry gin
2 teaspoons *Scandinavian Seasoning Mix* (page 126)
4 tablespoons (½ stick) unsalted butter or unsalted margarine, diced
Salt and freshly ground pepper to taste

4 sprigs fresh dillweed, stemmed, to serve

1. Preheat the oven to 350° F.

2. Arrange the chicken breasts in a nonreactive 2-quart baking dish. Drizzle ½ teaspoon of the gin evenly over each chicken breast. Sprinkle each breast evenly with ½ teaspoon of the seasoning mix, then dot each with 1 tablespoon butter. Cover the dish with aluminum foil and bake for 25 minutes or until the chicken tests done when pierced in the thickest part and the juices run clear.

3. Using a slotted spoon, transfer the chicken breasts to individual heated plates and ladle some of the juices over them. Sprinkle with salt and pepper and to serve garnish each with a sprig of dill.

Speedy Scandinavia
(Fast Menu for 4)
Cocktail: Gin and Tonic
   with Lime Twist
Poached Salmon Steaks
   with Mustard Sauce
Swedish Creamed Potatoes
   (page 133)
Steamed Fresh
   (or Frozen) Spinach
   with Butter
Applesauce
   with Cinnamon
   (supermarket)

Poached Salmon Steaks with Mustard Sauce

Servings: 4
Preparation Time: About 10 minutes
Cooking Time: 10 to 15 minutes
(sauce can be made up to 3 days ahead)

To save time, I poach salmon steaks instead of a whole salmon, and use bottled clam juice and water as a substitute for fish stock. Typically the sauce is made with egg yolk, but this egg-free version is better for you and maintains a silky texture, while offsetting the richness of the salmon. The Swedish mustard called for, is delicious — sweet but tangy. It is available mild or spicy; use mild for this recipe. Smooth Dijon mustard made with white wine can be substituted with equally delectable results.

SALMON:

2 8-ounce bottles clam juice (available at supermarket)

¼ cup hot water

2 teaspoons *Scandinavian Seasoning Mix* (page 126)

4 8-ounce salmon steaks, about 1 inch thick

4 fresh dill sprigs, to garnish

MUSTARD SAUCE: (Makes about 1 cup)

2 tablespoons white-wine vinegar

¼ cup mild Swedish mustard (available at gourmet shop
    or see Source List page 186) or other mild, pale brown
    sweet mustard, such as Dijon-style made with white wine
    (available at supermarket)

1 tablespoon honey

⅔ cup vegetable oil

1. To prepare the salmon: Combine the clam juice, water and seasoning mix in a deep nonreactive 10-inch skillet over medium-low heat. Bring almost to the boil, then reduce the heat to low and add the salmon steaks. (NOTE: There should be enough poaching liquid to just cover the salmon steaks; if not, add a little more hot water.) Cover the skillet with a lid or aluminum foil and gently simmer (poach) the salmon steaks for 10 minutes or until just opaque, springy with a slight resistance to the touch, yet slightly pink in the center. (NOTE: Be careful not to overcook. The poaching liquid should barely tremble during cooking time; if the liquid comes to a full simmer or boil, reduce the temperature to very low.)

2. Meanwhile, to prepare the sauce: Combine the vinegar, mustard, honey and vegetable oil in a small nonreactive bowl. Whisk together until well blended and smooth. Whisk to recombine just before serving.

3. To serve, carefully transfer the fragile salmon steaks to individual dinner plates, leaving the poaching liquid behind. Using your fingers, gently lift out and discard the central bone from each, being careful not to tear the flesh. Serve hot and spoon some of the mustard sauce over each salmon steak. Garnish each serving with a dill sprig. Or, refrigerate and serve chilled with the mustard sauce and garnish with dill as a main course.

Gravlax

(Marinated Salmon)
Servings: 6 as a main course, 8 to 10 as an appetizer
Preparation Time: About 10 minutes
Cooking Time: None
Marinating Time: 36 to 48 hours

TIP: Make sure to purchase very fresh salmon (not having been previously frozen), and preferably Norwegian, from a reliable fishmonger.

Gravlax is served like smoked salmon, yet it is more delicate in flavor since it is cured but not smoked. Most Scandinavians use rather more salt than sugar to cure the raw salmon, but I prefer a slightly sweeter result. Don't be put off by the lengthy marination time, as it is necessary to achieve the correct balance of flavors. Not only is gravlax easy to prepare, but it is more economical when you make it yourself. Remember that it can be served as an appetizer or main course—and a little goes a long way—it is rich!

1 2¼- to 2½-pound center-cut fresh salmon fillet; ask fishmonger
   to bone, skin and fillet, then wipe clean with damp paper towels
¼ cup kosher (coarse) salt (available at supermarket)
¼ cup sugar
4 teaspoons whole black peppercorns, crushed
1 tablespoon *Scandinavian Seasoning Mix* (page 126)
1 1½-ounce bunch fresh dill, finely chopped
   (about 1 cup), reserving 1 teaspoon for garnish

1 recipe *Dill Sauce* (page 135), to serve
Thinly sliced dark pumpernickel bread, to serve

1. Lightly run one of your fingers along the fleshy surface of the salmon to determine if all the bones have been removed.

(NOTE: There is a central line of small bones that extends down into salmon fillets.) If there are any remaining, pull them out with a small tweezers, strawberry huller or pair of small needle-nosed pliers. Cut the salmon in half lengthwise, along the central line where the bones were, to form two long salmon fillets.

2. Combine the salt, sugar, crushed peppercorns, seasoning mix and dill in a small nonreactive bowl and stir until well blended. Rub this mixture in an even layer over the rounded surface of each salmon fillet.

3. Place the fillets seasoning-to-seasoning-side against one another, "sandwiching" them together. Carefully slide the "sandwiched" fillets into a large clear self-sealing plastic bag, push all the air out and seal the top. Place the bag in another self-sealing bag, pushing all the air out and sealing the top. Then place on a baking sheet and put in the refrigerator. Place a cutting board or some heavy cans on top of the salmon to weight down, distributing the weight evenly.

4. Refrigerate for 36 to 48 hours. Every 12 hours, baste the fish with juices that have accumulated, and flip over the salmon fillets (placing the top piece on bottom and bottom piece on top), resealing the bags and replacing the cutting board or cans.

5. Drain the fish, discarding any liquid. Using the dull edge of a dinner knife, scrape off the dill and seasonings and discard. Pat dry the fillets with paper towel and place the fish on a cutting board, flat-side-down.

6. To serve, using a very sharp knife, preferably a salmon knife, slice thinly crosswise almost parallel to the board, at an angle, into about ¹⁄₁₆-inch-thick slices. Sprinkle the slices with the reserved teaspoon chopped dill and serve with the Dill Sauce and thinly sliced dark pumpernickel bread. (NOTE: *Gravlax* will keep wrapped tightly in plastic wrap in the refrigerator up to 1 week.)

Swedish Creamed Potatoes

Servings: 4
Preparation Time: About 15 minutes
Cooking Time: About 50 minutes

Because boiling potatoes hold their shape during cooking and stew instead of disintegrating, they work better than baking potatoes in this soothing and simple dish.

3½ tablespoons vegetable or corn oil
1   medium white onion, thinly sliced
1¾ pounds boiling potatoes (about 5 medium),
     peeled and cut into ½-inch dice
1¼ cups skim milk, at room temperature

TIP: Prepare all the ingredients before peeling and dicing the potatoes. Cut potatoes will discolor.

½ teaspoon *Scandinavian Seasoning Mix* (page 126)
½ teaspoon salt
2 tablespoons finely chopped fresh parsley, to garnish

1. Heat the oil in a heavy 5-quart pot over medium heat. Add the onion and potatoes and cook about 12 minutes, stirring often, or until the onion is soft and the potatoes crisp-tender (just half-cooked).

2. Reduce the heat to low and add the milk, seasoning mix and salt. Simmer for 30 to 35 minutes, gently stirring the mixture often, or until the potatoes are fully cooked and the sauce has thickened and become "creamy." Transfer the potato mixture to a shallow serving bowl and sprinkle with the parsley. Serve at once as a side dish.

Cauliflower with Dilled Egg

Servings: 4
Preparation Time: About 5 minutes
Cooking Time: About 10 minutes

4 tablespoons (½ stick) unsalted butter or unsalted margarine
3 scallions, green part only, thinly sliced
2 large hard-cooked eggs, finely chopped
1 teaspoon *Scandinavian Seasoning Mix* (page 126)
½ teaspoon salt
½ teaspoon freshly ground pepper
1 medium head cauliflower (about 1½ to 2 pounds), cut into florets

1. To prepare the sauce: In a heavy nonreactive 1-quart saucepan melt the butter over low heat. Stir in the scallions and cook for 1 minute, stirring. Remove from heat; stir in the hard-cooked eggs, seasoning mix, salt and pepper until well blended and reserve until ready to use.

2. Add the cauliflower to a 3-quart saucepan of boiling water over high heat. Boil the cauliflower for 8 minutes or until tender. Drain in a colander and transfer to a serving bowl. Toss the cauliflower together with the egg mixture until well coated and serve at once as a side dish.

Lamb with Dill Sauce

Servings: 4
Preparation Time: About 10 minutes
Cooking Time: 7 to 10 minutes
(Sauce can be made up to 2 days ahead)

Traditionally this dish is prepared by boiling a lamb roast, which can take several hours to reach the proper tenderness. Not only is it time-consuming, but many Americans, though they like boiled corned beef, do not enjoy the flavor or texture of boiled lamb. To give this dish appeal, I have broiled lamb chops as a variation on the classic preparation.

DILL SAUCE: (Makes about 1 cup)

¼ cup mild Swedish mustard (available at gourmet shop
    or Source List [page 186] or other mild, pale brown sweet mustard,
    such as Dijon-style made with white wine,
    available at supermarket)
1 tablespoon honey
1 teaspoon *Scandinavian Seasoning Mix* (page 126)
3 tablespoons finely chopped fresh dillweed
2 tablespoons fresh lemon juice
⅔ cup vegetable oil

LAMB:

8 rib lamb chops, about 1 to 1½ inches thick,
(4 to 6 ounces each), at room temperature

1. Preheat the broiler.

2. To make the Dill Sauce: Combine the mustard, honey, seasoning mix, dillweed, lemon juice and vegetable oil in a small nonreactive bowl. Whisk together until well blended and smooth. Whisk to recombine just before serving.

3. To prepare the lamb chops: Arrange the lamb chops on the top half of a broiler pan. (NOTE: Line the bottom pan with aluminum foil.) Broil 4 inches from the heat source for 4 to 6 minutes on one side. Using long-handled tongs, flip the chops over and broil for 3 to 4 minutes more for medium-rare, depending on thickness. Be careful not to overcook; remember that the lamb chops will continue to cook slightly even after removed from the broiler.

4. To serve, divide the chops evenly among 4 individual dinner plates, ladle some of the sauce over each and serve at once as a main course.

Scandinavian Dinner Party

(Entertaining Menu for 4 to 6)
Akvavit ("aquavit" — water of life — Scandinavian liquor with caraway flavor)
Gravlax (page 132)
Pumpernickel Bread
Scandinavian Dill Sauce (page 135)
Lihamurekepiiras
Scandinavian Cucumber Salad (page 128)
Boiled New Potatoes with Butter
Tapioca (supermarket — mix)

Lihamurekepiiras
(Meat Loaf Wrapped in Sour-Cream Pastry)
Servings: 4 to 6
Preparation Time: About 1¼ hours
Cooking Time: 45 to 50 minutes
(Dough can be prepared up to 1 day ahead.)

PASTRY:

3 cups unbleached white flour, plus more to dust
1 teaspoon salt
12 tablespoons (1½ sticks) unsalted butter or unsalted margarine, cut into 12 slices and chilled
½ cup sour cream
2 large eggs, lightly beaten

FILLING:

3 tablespoons unsalted butter or unsalted margarine
4 ounces mushrooms, thinly sliced

1 pound extra-lean ground beef
1 cup finely chopped onion
2 teaspoons *Scandinavian Seasoning Mix* (page 126)
3 scallions, green part only, thinly sliced
4 ounces Emmental cheese, shredded (1⅓ cups)
¼ cup skim milk
½ teaspoon salt
½ teaspoon freshly ground pepper

1 large egg, lightly beaten with 1 tablespoon
   skim milk, to glaze
Sour cream, to serve (optional)

Lingonberry preserves, to serve (optional)

1. To prepare the pastry: In the bowl of a food processor fitted with a metal blade combine the flour and salt and pulse twice to mix. Add the butter and pulse about 6 times or until the mixture is the consistency of coarse cornmeal. Pulse in the sour cream and eggs until well blended and the dough just hangs together, scraping down the sides of the bowl as necessary. (NOTE: Do not let the dough form into a ball in the processor.) Remove the dough from the bowl, divide in half evenly and form into 2 flat disks. Wrap each in waxed paper and refrigerate for 1 hour or until ready to use.

2. To make the filling: Melt the butter in a 10-inch skillet over medium-high heat, add the mushrooms and sauté about 4 minutes or until lightly browned. Drain, and let cool to room temperature. In a medium bowl mix together the beef, onion, seasoning mix, scallions, Emmental cheese, skim milk and salt and pepper until well blended. Gently fold in the mushrooms until well blended.

3. Preheat the oven to 375° F.

4. On a lightly floured work surface, roll out each dough half to a ⅛-inch thickness. Trim one of the sheets to a 10-inch-long-by-8-inch-wide rectangle, reserving any pastry scraps. Transfer the trimmed sheet to the bottom of a baking sheet.

5. Firmly pack the meat mixture into an 8-inch-long-by-4-inch-wide-by-2-inch-tall mound down the center of the pastry on the baking sheet, leaving a margin on the sides and at both ends. Press

Gjetost (Norway) — Semi-soft, creamy, goats' milk cheese or blend of cows' and goats' milk, caramel-like color and flavor. Traditionally sliced thinly and eaten for breakfast or on spiced fruit cake for Christmas.

Danish Blue (Denmark) — Firm, sharp blue-veined cows' milk cheese, not as crumbly or pungent as most blue cheese.

Havarti (Denmark) — Semi-soft, with a mild, buttery flavor, sliceable cows' milk cheese with innumerable irregular holes. Available with fresh dillweed or caraway seed as well.

Fontina/Fontal (Denmark) — Semi-soft, supple, mild, buttery cows' milk cheese.

Emmental (Switzerland/ Finland) — Semi-soft, smooth, buttery, slightly nutty cows' milk cheese. Melts beautifully; large random holes throughout. Though Emmental is definitely Swiss and not Finnish in origin, it is the most important cheese of the Finnish dairy industry and has been produced in Finland since 1856.

gently on the filling to mold it into a rectangular "loaf."

6. Trim the edges of the pastry to leave a 1-inch-wide border. Dip a pastry brush into the egg glaze and lightly brush on the surface of the border. Lay the remaining pastry sheet over the filling and press the edges of dough together to encase the filling. Trim the edge of the second pastry sheet to conform to the first. Press the back of a fork (using the tines) into the pastry border around the loaf, to seal the edges.

7. Use the reserved pastry scraps to make decorations on the pastry, cutting them into designs with a knife or cookie cutter. Brush the surface of the pastry with the egg glaze, sticking the pastry decorations on in a pleasing pattern. Lightly brush some more of the egg glaze on the surface of the pastry and prick the top of the pastry in several places with a fork, along the length of the pastry to allow steam to escape.

8. Bake the pastry for 35 to 40 minutes or until the crust is a delicate golden brown and crisp. Let stand for 5 minutes before serving. Slice thickly and serve hot as a main course accompanied with a dollop of sour cream and some lingonberry preserves if desired.

CHAPTER 10

INDIA AROMATICA

Indian Seasoning Mix

Cucumber Raita

Gingered Eggplant

Okra with Onion Sauce

Beef in Fragrant Spinach Sauce

Savory Chicken

Tandoori-Style Chicken

Chicken in Spice Gravy

Lamb Korma

Lentil Dal

Mulligatawny Soup

THE GENIUS OF INDIAN COOKING lies in the visionary use of spices. Some herbs and spices are used as aromatics, others provide coloring, while still others function as souring agents. There are spices that give a hot taste to food and others that thicken or tenderize a dish. The seasoning blend that I've made from cinnamon sticks, coriander seeds, cumin seeds, black peppercorns, cardamom seeds and whole cloves that are toasted then ground, makes this exotic cuisine very accessible to home cooks.

What we know as "curry powder," commercial blends of commonly used Indian spices does not exist in India, though other seasoning blends are used. My blend is a great starter for "curry," which in India refers not to a taste, but to a dish with a sauce, as with Chicken in Spice Gravy (page 147). In this recipe, the addition of turmeric and cayenne provides not only aroma and flavor, but a remarkable golden color as well.

Depending on how spices are used — whole, ground, roasted, fried —they can vary in intensity and texture, relative to the other spices in the blend. For example, in Lamb Korma (page 148), the seasoning mix is as important for the slightly coarse quality it gives the sauce as for its flavor.

Since many Indians are vegetarians, they have created a number of ways to cook vegetables. Gingered Eggplant (page 141) is an example of a "dry" or almost sauce-free dish, while Okra with Onion Sauce (page 142) is closer to a "wet" or thickly sauced preparation.

In India, meals are enhanced with a variety of condiments that tease the palate with contrasting flavors of sweet, sour, hot and salty, and balance the meal with added protein and vitamins. The condiments range from simply seasoned vegetables like chopped onions and tomatoes to chutneys and pickles. There are also yogurt relishes such as Cucumber Raita (page 141), a remarkably refreshing condiment that is scented with fresh mint, lightly fired with cayenne, and

QUICKIES: EVERYDAY FOODS MADE INTERNATIONAL

Delicious Dip

Stir *Indian Seasoning Mix* into sour cream to taste. Season with salt and pepper and refrigerate, covered, at least 3 hours, preferably overnight.

Very Veggie

To give a taste-lift to frozen lima beans, cook the beans as directed, and stir in some cream cheese, a pinch of *Indian Seasoning Mix*, salt and pepper.

Savory Spinach Salad

Follow the Double-Duty

Dressing quickie recipe (page 54), but season with *Indian Seasoning Mix* in place of the *Greek Seasoning Mix*. Toss dressing with some fresh spinach and garnish with thinly sliced hard-cooked eggs for a salad-on-the-go.

India-Inspired Pita Snacks
Blend together some softened butter (or margarine) and season with a touch of *Indian Seasoning Mix*, salt and pepper. Spread onto quartered small pita breads for a spicy snack or supper starch.

TIP: ½ tablespoon = 1½ teaspoons

*To break cinnamon sticks: Place the cinnamon sticks on the foil-lined baking sheet and place a rolling pin or heavy skillet on top of them, lean your weight onto the rolling pin or skillet and rock back and forth until the cinnamon is crushed into small pieces.

**Break open cardamom pods by squeezing them between your thumb and forefinger to break open the husks to reveal the brown seeds inside. Using your fingertips, push out the seeds, discarding the husks.

wonderfully cooling in the presence of a curry.

For a fragrant Indian dinner at home, just rely on the spice blend to recreate some of your restaurant favorites.

Indian Seasoning Mix
Makes about ½ cup

Indians use spices lavishly and cook with a great variety of them! However, the modern technique of using a seasoning blend as a base still saves a lot of time and is a much less arduous way to cook!

2   3½-inch-long cinnamon sticks, broken into small pieces*
3   tablespoons coriander seeds (available at supermarket
      or gourmet store or see Source List page 186)
1½   tablespoons cumin seeds
1½   tablespoons whole black peppercorns
1½   teaspoons cardamom seeds,
      from about 27 green cardamom pods**
      (available at gourmet store or see Source List page 186)
1½   teaspoons whole cloves

1. Preheat the oven to 200° F.

2. Spread out all the spices in a single layer on an aluminum-foil-lined baking sheet. Bake on the center rack of the oven for 15 minutes, stirring once or twice (the aroma of the spices will come forth). Transfer the mixture to a small heatproof bowl and let cool completely at room temperature.

3. Pulverize the mixture to a fine powder in an electric spice or coffee grinder or in a blender. (NOTE: The cinnamon may still be a little coarse but you can sift the spices and grind the coarse pieces again.)

4. Transfer the mixture to a small bag or bowl (How-To page 11) and shake or stir until well blended. Transfer to a clean, dry, airtight glass container. Store up to 3 months away from heat, light or moisture. Shake well before using.

(NOTE: Loose cardamom seeds can also be purchased at a gourmet store or Indian grocery store or see Source List page 186.)

Cucumber Raita

Servings: About 2¼ cups
Preparation Time: About 5 minutes
Cooking Time: None
Chilling time: 2 hours (can be made up to 1 day ahead)

A raita is a refreshing Indian condiment made with a yogurt base that is frequently served chilled with curries. This cucumber-mint raita acts to cool any highly seasoned Indian meal.

1 small (8-ounce) cucumber, peeled and coarsely grated
2 8-ounce containers plain lowfat yogurt
3 tablespoons firmly packed minced fresh mint
¼ teaspoon *Indian Seasoning Mix* (page 140)
⅛ teaspoon ground red (cayenne) pepper
½ teaspoon salt

Squeeze the grated cucumber flesh between your hands to remove and discard excess juice. Combine the yogurt, cucumber, mint, seasoning mix, cayenne and salt in a nonreactive medium bowl. Stir together until well blended. Cover tightly with plastic wrap and refrigerate until well chilled, about 2 hours.

Gingered Eggplant

Servings: 4
Preparation Time: About 15 minutes
Cooking Time: About 20 minutes
(can be made up to 1 day ahead)

Fresh ginger is sold in two forms: young and mature. Young ginger has a soft, thin pink-tinged tan skin, which can be scraped off. The semi-hard tan peel of mature ginger must be removed by peeling. Mature ginger is available in most supermarket produce areas and though it is tasty, young ginger is more aromatic. If you have a chance to go to an Oriental market during the springtime and purchase the young ginger, use it for this boldly flavored dish! Turn to page 169 "The Gift of Ginger" for more tidbits on fresh ginger.

1 3-inch-long by 1-inch-wide piece of fresh ginger, peeled and thinly sliced

HINT: Attach the large-holed grating disk to your food processor and use it to grate the cucumber in place of the standard metal box grater.

PEPPERCORNS: THE RICH AND FAMOUS

Take Two Peppercorns and Call Me in the Morning . . .
Pepper has a long and dramatic history. It was widely used in India and China before being introduced to the West by the Romans. The exact date is not known, but Hippocrates was prescribing pepper medicinally in the fifth century B.C.

The Treasure Chest
Europeans favored pepper over all other Eastern spices. From the tenth through the 18th centuries, the European powers of Venice, Portugal and Spain vied for control of the lucrative pepper trade. Indeed, the famous voyage of Christopher Columbus, as with most of the explorers, was undertaken to find the treasure of this spice.

HINT: This recipe works well doubled for a vegetarian main dish: Just increase the size of the skillet and cooking times accordingly, and season to taste. I find that thawed frozen okra is more suitable for use in this recipe because it cooks faster than fresh. As a consequence, the sauce and spices don't burn while the okra cooks.

TIP: To prepare okra: Trim-off the ends from both fresh or frozen. If using fresh okra, scrape off the surface fuzz.

¼ cup finely chopped fresh cilantro
¼ cup hot water
2 teaspoons *Indian Seasoning Mix* (page 140)
1 1-pound unpeeled eggplant, cut into ½-inch dice
½ cup hot water
2 tablespoons unsalted butter or unsalted margarine, cut into quarters
1 tablespoon fresh lemon juice
Salt and freshly ground pepper to taste

1. Combine the ginger, cilantro, the ¼ cup hot water and the seasoning mix in the bowl of a food processor fitted with a metal blade or the container of a blender. Process about 1 minute or until the mixture is finely chopped, scraping down the sides of the bowl as needed.

2. Add the eggplant to a heavy nonreactive 10-inch skillet over medium heat. Stir in the ½ cup hot water and ginger mixture. Cover the skillet with a lid or aluminum foil and cook, stirring occasionally, for 10 to 15 minutes or until the eggplant mixture is nearly dry and the eggplant is very tender. Stir in the butter pieces until melted, then the lemon juice until well blended. Season with salt and pepper and serve hot as a side dish.

Okra with Onion Sauce

Servings: 4
Preparation Time: About 15 minutes
Cooking Time: 15 minutes
(can be made up to 1 day ahead)

Nowadays, ghee (Indian-style clarified butter) is not much used in India because it is expensive to make. Since many American home cooks are short on time and want to be thrifty, I have replaced ghee with vegetable oil for cooking at high temperatures and finished the dish with butter for more flavor. This dish is scrumptious — even without the ghee.

2 medium yellow onions, quartered
3 whole cloves garlic
1 2-inch-long by 1-inch-wide piece of fresh ginger, peeled and thinly sliced
¼ cup hot water
3 tablespoons vegetable oil

1 tablespoon tomato paste

1¾ teaspoons *Indian Seasoning Mix* (page 140)

2 10-ounce packages frozen whole baby okra, thawed and cut into ½-inch-wide slices (available at supermarket)

¾ cup hot water

3 tablespoons unsalted butter or margarine, quartered

Salt and freshly ground pepper to taste

1. Combine the onions, garlic, ginger and the ¼ cup hot water in the bowl of a food processor fitted with a metal blade or the container of a blender. Process about 2 minutes or until the mixture is finely chopped, scraping down the sides of the bowl as needed.

2. Heat the vegetable oil in a heavy nonreactive 10-inch skillet over medium-high heat. Add the onion mixture and cook, stirring often, for 3 minutes.

3. Reduce the heat to low, stir in the tomato paste, seasoning mix, okra and the ¾ cup hot water. Cover the skillet with a lid or aluminum foil, and cook, stirring often, for 10 minutes or until the okra is tender. Stir in the butter pieces until melted and season with salt and pepper. Serve hot as a side dish.

Beef in Fragrant Spinach Sauce

Servings: 4 to 6
Preparation Time: About 20 minutes
Cooking Time: About 65 minutes
(can be made up to 2 days ahead)

2 medium white onions, cut into quarters

3 whole cloves garlic

1 3-inch-long and 1-inch-wide piece of fresh ginger, peeled and thinly sliced

1½ tablespoons *Indian Seasoning Mix* (Page 140)

2 cups hot water

2½ pounds trimmed, boneless beef chuck, preferably from shoulder or leg, cut into 1-inch cubes

3 medium-sized ripe tomatoes, coarsely chopped

3 pounds fresh spinach, stemmed, washed thoroughly,

Peppercorn Poll
Pepper is actually a berry —called a peppercorn— from the plant *(Piper nigrum);* a climbing vine that grows to 30 feet in height and is native to India's Malabar. Pepper still grows in India, but today's major producers are Brazil, Indonesia and Malaysia. Most connoisseurs agree that the *Telicherry* (grown in the north Malabar coast) is the finest black peppercorn, while the best white peppercorns come from Muntok near Sumatra, Indonesia.

TIP: Basmati rice, a tasty, nutty rice from India, is a fantastic partner with this dish. Although this rice is delicious, it can be difficult to find and is time-consuming to prepare, so I encourage you to use either Texmati rice from the United States another fragrant long-grain rice, or, any brand of rice that is referred to as "aromatic" on the label. These are available from the supermarket.

To plan your meal, start cooking the rice at the beginning of step # 3 so that it is cooked in time to serve.

Definitely invest in a
peppermill and grind your
own peppercorns! The
aroma and flavor of
pepper is at its peak when
the whole peppercorn
kernel is just broken open.
Pre-ground or precracked
peppercorns do not have
the same "punch."

◆ Green Peppercorns: The
Piper nigrum berry begins
its life green. The peppercorns are not only literally
green (in color), but also
"green" in the figurative
sense, underripe. The
berries are then dried or
pickled when still fresh
(not dried) in vinegar or
brine, which retains their
soft texture. Green pep-
percorns are more mellow
and fruity, but still have
the characteristic pepperiness of black pepper. If
they are pickled in vine-
gar, they will also have an
acidic "kick," to their
flavor.

drained and coarsely chopped
¾ cup sour cream, at room temperature
Salt and freshly ground pepper to taste

Cooked white rice, (follow package directions) to serve

1. Combine the onions, garlic, ginger and seasoning mix in the bowl
of a food processor fitted with a metal blade or the container of a
blender. Process about 1 minute or until the mixture is well blended
and finely chopped, scraping down the sides of the bowl as necessary.

2. Combine the 2 cups hot water, the onion mixture, beef, tomatoes
and spinach in an 8-quart pot over medium-low heat and stir until
well blended. (NOTE: The tomatoes and spinach will "give off" more
cooking liquid.) Partially cover and cook for 30 minutes, stirring
often.

3. Reduce the heat to low, then simmer, uncovered, for 30 minutes
more, stirring occasionally, or until the beef is cooked through and
tender. Stir ½ cup of the hot liquid from the pot into a small bowl
with the sour cream until mixed, then stir this mixture back into the
pot until well blended. Season with salt and pepper and serve at once
alongside rice as a main course.

Savory Chicken

Servings: 4
Preparation Time: About 15 minutes
Cooking Time: About 45 minutes
(can be made up to 2 days ahead)

*The nice, simple cooking technique here keeps the chicken from drying out
by sealing in the natural juices while flavoring and tenderizing the meat.
Though it is not imperative for good flavor, this dish is at its finest when the
baste is applied to the chicken ahead of time. Just spread the marinade evenly all over the chicken, place in a 9-inch-square nonreactive baking dish and
cover. This takes about 15 minutes to prepare, so I do it before I leave for
work. The chicken marinates while I'm away and when I get home it is
ready to bake. Marinate at least 3 hours, preferably overnight in the refrigerator. Bring the chicken to room temperature before roasting.*

4 whole chicken leg pieces (with thighs attached), about 2½ pounds, skinned and pricked all over with the tines of a fork
1 tablespoon vegetable oil
3 whole cloves garlic
1 3-inch-long by 1-inch-wide piece of fresh ginger, peeled and thinly sliced
1 tablespoon *Indian Seasoning Mix* (page 140)
1 tablespoon paprika
1 teaspoon salt
1 teaspoon freshly ground pepper
½ cup plain lowfat yogurt

1. Preheat the oven to 450° F.

2. Combine the vegetable oil, garlic, ginger, seasoning mix, paprika, salt, pepper and yogurt in the bowl of a food processor fitted with a metal blade or the container of a blender. Process about 1 minute or until it is a well blended, fairly smooth mixture, scraping down the sides of the bowl as necessary.

3. Arrange the pricked chicken pieces on a flat wire rack across an aluminum foil-lined roasting pan. Spread the yogurt mixture evenly over the chicken pieces. Bake on the middle rack of the oven for 35 to 40 minutes until the top is crispy, the chicken tests done when pierced in the thickest part and the juices run clear. Serve hot as a main course.

Tandoori-Style Chicken

Servings: 4
Preparation Time: About 15 minutes
Cooking Time: 15 minutes
Marinating Time: 8 hours to overnight

Indian cooks use a high-temperature clay oven called a tandoor. *I have adapted this recipe so you can use a conventional oven with equally tempting results.* Tandoori *chicken is a golden-red color, almost orange, like the color of lobster shell. Interestingly enough, the color comes not from the seasonings but food coloring!* Tandoori *chicken is usually made with halved whole chickens, which take a while to cook and can be a nuisance to serve since they require carving. I use chicken breasts here; they*

◆ Black Peppercorns: These peppercorns are harvested when underripe, but are allowed to mature longer than green peppercorns. They are usually dried under the sun, which causes the peppercorn skin to become black and wrinkled. When processed in this way the peppercorns become the strongest and most pungent of the species: they deliver a sharp bite and very aromatic bouquet. Ground, they yield black pepper—the most popular and widely used spice in the world.

◆ White Peppercorns: These peppercorns have been left on the vine a little longer to ripen and turn pink (or red). Then they are soaked in water, rubbed clean, which removes the outer husk, exposing the inner white "kernel." Then, finally, they are dried. White peppercorns are less spicy than black peppercorns, but still have heat but without as much bouquet. White peppercorns are ideal for seasoning white sauces as they do not give the "dusty" appearance ground black peppercorns do.

◆ Pink Peppercorns: At this time there is a good

deal of controversy over these pink berries (which are not related to pepper *(Piper nigrum)* and incorrectly referred to as "pink peppercorns" in the United States. These rose-hued berries are slightly sweet in flavor with just a hint of heat. "Red Berries" is the proper label for these pink berries from the Mountain Ash *(Pyrus Aucuparia)*, which arrive in the United States via France, although most of the supply originates along the east coast of Madagascar.

The conflict began when the Food and Drug Administration (FDA) banned some of the berries that had been incorrectly marketed as "pink peppercorns." Some of these were actually berries of the Brazilian pepper or Florida holly, which belongs to the poison ivy family and has the potential to cause toxic reactions in animals and humans.

As of the spring of 1983, the FDA declared that pink berries with a label that reads Baises Roses which are only exported from the island of *Reunion* (off the east coast of Madagascar), are safe to consume. However, all other "pink peppercorn" products are

cook quickly and make for a nice, simple presentation.

3   whole cloves garlic
1   3-inch-long by 1-inch-wide piece of fresh ginger, peeled and thinly sliced
2   tablespoons *Indian Seasoning Mix* (page 140)
½   teaspoon ground red (cayenne) pepper
¼   cup plain lowfat yogurt
4   split chicken breasts with ribs (about 2¼ pounds), skinned and pricked all over with the tines of a fork
2   teaspoons yellow food coloring mixed together with 1½ teaspoons red food coloring, to brush
8   thin slices of fresh lime, cut in half, to garnish

1. Combine the garlic, ginger, seasoning mix, cayenne and yogurt in the bowl of a food processor fitted with a metal blade or the container of a blender. Process about 1 minute or until it is a well-blended, fairly smooth mixture, scraping down the sides of the bowl as needed.

2. Transfer the pricked chicken to a nonreactive baking dish large enough to accommodate it in a single layer, a 13-inch-by-9-inch-by-2-inch baking dish works well. Using a pastry brush, brush the meaty side of each chicken breast with the food coloring mixture until coated evenly.

3. Dividing evenly, spread the yogurt mixture over the top of each breast until well coated. Cover the baking dish tightly with plastic wrap and allow to marinate in the refrigerator for 8 hours, preferably overnight. Return the chicken to room temperature before broiling.

4. Preheat the broiler.

5. Using the dull edge of a dinner knife, gently scrape off the yogurt marinade and discard. Transfer the chicken breasts, meat side up, to the top half of a broiler pan. Line the bottom half of the broiler pan with aluminum foil. Broil 5 inches from the heat source for 15 minutes, or until the surface is crispy and dappled golden brown, the meat tender and tests done when pierced in the thickest part and the juices run clear. (NOTE: Be careful not to overcook; remember that the chicken will continue to cook slightly even after being removed from the broiler.) Let the chicken stand for 5 minutes before serving,

then slice each on the diagonal into thin slices and garnish each serving with 2 overlapping lime slices. Serve at once as a main course.

Chicken in Spice Gravy

Servings: 4
Preparation Time: About 15 minutes
Cooking Time: About 25 minutes

In America, "curry" refers to a powder, and by inference, any dish with a dash of this powder qualifies as a "curry." Yet, this definition is a Western invention. In India, a "curry" is a stew-like preparation of meat and/or vegetables eaten with hot rice and/or bread. This recipe for "Chicken in Spice Gravy," originally known as Murghi ka Salan, *came to be called Chicken Kari or Chicken Curry because Indians use the Tamil word* Kari *(curry) to mean sauce.*

But, do not expect this recipe to taste as if it were made with a commercial curry blend; I've followed the Indian example in preparing this dish. In India each family has its own recipe for "masala," a mixture of spices, and the combination and quantity of each spice in the masala will vary according to a cook's preference, and the dish to be seasoned. The "masala" I give you is a highly aromatic mixture whose flavors are intensified by the dry-roasting of the spices, prior to grinding, and it serves wonderfully as a point of departure in seasoning all the dishes in this chapter with impressively different results.

3½ tablespoons vegetable oil
2 pounds skinless, boneless chicken breasts, cut into 1-inch cubes
1 medium white onion, finely chopped
3 cloves garlic, crushed
1 tablespoon minced peeled fresh ginger, about a 1-inch-long
　　by 1 inch wide piece
2½ teaspoons *Indian Seasoning Mix* (page 140)
½ teaspoon ground turmeric (available at supermarket)
¼ teaspoon ground red (cayenne) pepper
½ teaspoon salt
3 tablespoons water
2 medium-sized ripe tomatoes, finely chopped

still considered unsafe and are still banned by the FDA.

To make matters more confusing, in Singapore, true pink peppercorns (*Piper nigrum* berries harvested at the pink stage) are now being served in fresh form. At the time of this writing, these are not yet being exported to United States.

TIP: For serving, begin cooking the rice before starting the recipe.

Night's End In India
(*Entertaining Menu for 4*)
Chicken in Spice Gravy
Texmati Rice
Okra with Onion Sauce
　　(page 142)
Gingered Eggplant
　　(page 141)
Puris (Indian deep-fried
　　bread, gourmet store —
　　mix)
Cucumber Raita (page 141)
Mango Chutney
　　(supermarket or
　　gourmet store)
Lime Sorbet (supermarket)
Cardamom Tea

2 tablespoons finely chopped fresh cilantro (coriander)
2 tablespoons fresh lemon juice
Hot cooked white rice, preferably Texmati rice (page 143), to serve

1. Heat 2 tablespoons of the vegetable oil in a deep heavy nonreactive 12-inch skillet over high heat. Add the chicken and sauté about 4 minutes or until it loses its pinkness and turns white, but not browned or cooked through. Transfer to a paper-towel-lined plate to drain, pour off any liquid in skillet and reserve the skillet.

2. Meanwhile, return the skillet to medium heat and add the remaining 1½ tablespoons oil and heat. Add the onion and cook, stirring often for 5 minutes or until the onion is light golden brown. Stir in the garlic, ginger, 2 teaspoons of the seasoning mix, turmeric, cayenne, salt and 3 tablespoons water. Cook, stirring constantly, for 1 minute. Stir in the tomatoes and cook for 2 minutes, stirring.

3. Reduce the heat to low and stir in the fresh cilantro and remaining ½ teaspoon seasoning blend with the reserved chicken and lemon juice. Cook, stirring often for 8 to 10 minutes or until the chicken is tender and cooked throughout. Serve at once as a main course alongside hot cooked rice.

TIP: For serving, start cooking the rice at the beginning of step #3 so that it will be cooked in time.

Lamb Korma

Servings: 4
Preparation Time: About 15 minutes
Cooking Time: 55 to 60 minutes
(can be made up to 2 days ahead)

In India, the most widely — though not exclusively — eaten meat is goat. In America the best substitute for goat is lamb. Beef can also be used, depending on the diners' taste, though I fancy lamb.

Korma is an Indian cooking method analogous to "braising" in Western cuisine, though often the braising liquid in korma is much thicker. Typically it might include yogurt, cream or nut butters, producing thick velvety sauces. Since this technique classically uses a denser milk product like heavy cream, I have suggested half-and-half as a healthier alternative, along with coconut and almonds to help thicken the sauce of this subtly flavored soothing dish.

1 8-ounce container plain lowfat yogurt
1 large white onion, quartered
2 whole cloves garlic
1 2-inch-long by 1-inch-wide piece of fresh ginger,
   peeled and thinly sliced
1 ounce (3 tablespoons) blanched slivered almonds
3 tablespoons shredded unsweetened coconut
   (available at supermarket or health food store)
1½ tablespoons *Indian Seasoning Mix* (page 140)
2 pounds trimmed boneless lamb from shoulder or leg,
   cut into ½-inch cubes
¾ cup half-and-half, at room temperature
½ cup hot water
2 tablespoons finely chopped fresh cilantro (coriander)
Salt and freshly ground pepper to taste

Cooked rice (follow package directions), to serve

1. Combine the yogurt, onion, garlic, ginger, almonds, coconut and seasoning mix in the bowl of a food processor fitted with a metal blade or the container of a blender. Process about 2 minutes or until mixture is well blended and forms a fairly smooth purée.

2. Combine the yogurt mixture with the lamb and half-and-half in a nonreactive heavy 4-quart pot, preferably nonstick, and set over medium-high heat. Bring to a boil, stirring often. Reduce the heat to low and cook, partially covered, for 40 minutes, stirring often.

3. Stir in the ½ cup hot water and continue to cook for 15 minutes more, partially covered, stirring often, or until the meat is tender but not falling apart. Stir in the cilantro, season with salt and pepper and serve hot as a main course alongside rice.

Lentil Dal

Servings: Makes 2¼ cups
Preparation Time: About 10 minutes
Cooking Time: 35 minutes
(can be made up to 2 days ahead)

Dal is the collective Indian name for any member of the legume family—lentils, split peas, chick-peas, and beans. In terms of Indian cooking, dal also refers to any of the puréed spiced cooked dishes made from dried legumes—usually split peas or lentils. Legumes are basic to Indian cooking, especially when the menu is vegetarian. Legumes are high in protein, and in one form or another they are eaten daily in almost every Indian home.

Dal is served thin or thick, hot or mildly spiced. This recipe creates dal that is thick and well spiced but not hot. Dal is always eaten with rice or Indian breads. A meat, chicken or vegetable dish would complete the menu.

1 cup dried brown lentils, rinsed and picked over
1 1-inch by 1-inch piece of fresh ginger, peeled and grated
2 cloves garlic, crushed
½ teaspoon *Indian Seasoning Mix* (page 140)
1 teaspoon salt
2 tablespoons finely chopped fresh cilantro (coriander)

1. Bring 5 cups water to a boil in a 3-quart saucepan over high heat.

Add the lentils and bring to a second boil. Reduce the heat to low and simmer very gently, about 30 minutes, stirring occasionally, until the lentils are soft and creamy.

2. Stir in the ginger, garlic, seasoning mix, salt and cilantro and cook, stirring continuously, for 5 minutes more. Serve hot.

TIP: Stir the canned coconut cream before using to mix well. Gauge the "heat" of this soup by how much additional cayenne you add in step #3.

Mulligatawny Soup

Servings: 4 (1³/4 cups each)
Preparation Time: About 15 minutes
Cooking Time: 20 minutes
(can be made up to 2 days ahead)

The name Mulligatawny is derived from the Tamil words mullaga (pepper) and tanni (water) — mullagatanni — meaning "pepper water." It is believed there was a soup originally made with a black pepper known as Mullaga Rassam (also known as Mullagatanni), but over time, the ingredients of the soup have changed quite a bit, and now there are many versions, both vegetarian and nonvegetarian.

Developed by Southern Indian cooks to suit the tastes of the British, mulligatawny soup is still very Indian in flavor. In addition, it is a very pretty soup: a vivid golden background with green flecks of cilantro. Its aroma combines a hint of the sweetness of coconut contrasted by a bit of cayenne.

1 tablespoon vegetable oil
1 medium white onion, finely chopped
1 tablespoon *Indian Seasoning Mix* (page 140)
1 teaspoon ground turmeric (available at supermarket)
¹/2 to ³/4 teaspoon ground red (cayenne) pepper
1 quart canned low-sodium chicken broth
2 medium boiling potatoes (about ³/4 pound), cut into ¹/2-inch dice
1¹/2 pounds skinless, boneless chicken breasts, cut crosswise into ¹/4-inch-wide strips
¹/3 cup canned coconut cream (available at supermarket)
3 tablespoons finely chopped fresh cilantro (coriander)
Salt and freshly ground pepper to taste

1. Heat the vegetable oil in a heavy 3-quart saucepan over medium-

India's Star Attraction
(Fast One-Dish Menu for 4)
Mulligatawny Soup
Chappatis (Indian
   unleavened bread,
   gourmet store — mix
   or ready-made
   from Indian store)
Plain Lowfat Yogurt
   (supermarket)
Indian Lentil Dal (page 150)
Mango Ice Cream
   (gourmet store or
   Indian grocery)
Indian Beer such as
   Taj-Mahal

high heat. Add the onion and cook about 4 minutes, stirring, or until the onion is soft but not browned. Stir in the seasoning mix, turmeric and cayenne and cook for 1 minute, stirring constantly, being very careful not to let the seasonings burn. Add the chicken broth — *stand back, it may splatter* — and potatoes and bring to a boil.

2. Reduce the heat to medium-low and add the chicken. Cook for 15 minutes, stirring often, or until the chicken is cooked through and the potatoes are tender. Remove the saucepan from the heat.

3. Stir ¼ cup of the hot soup into a small bowl with the coconut cream until well blended. Then stir this mixture back into the pot with the soup until well combined. Stir in the fresh cilantro and season with salt and pepper. (NOTE #1: The soup should be slightly hot; season carefully with more cayenne according to your desired preference.) Serve hot as a main course. (NOTE #2: This soup is at its best made ahead about 4 hours so that the flavors can mingle. Let cool, cover and refrigerate. Reheat gently, stirring often before serving.)

CHAPTER 11

THE CARIBBEAN BEAT

Caribbean Seasoning Mix

Puréed Pumpkin Soup

Pigeon Peas and Rice

Baked Papaya

Jerked Pork

Hearts-of-Palm Salad

Quick Callaloo

Pepperpot

Lobster Salad

Caribbean Red Snapper Kebabs

Fried Plantains

THE ECLECTIC CARIBBEAN diet consists of treasures from the sea, exotic fruits and vegetables and a wonderful blend of spices, all prepared in ways that reflect the diverse culinary heritage of the islands in which the English, African, Chinese and Indian influences can still be noticed.

For example, the recipe for Pigeon Peas and Rice (page 156) may be of African inspiration but it has long been considered typical island fare. It's made all the more delicious by the addition of allspice, ginger, thyme, marjoram, red pepper flakes and black pepper found in the *Caribbean Seasoning Mix.*

Seasoning is the underpinning of this intriguing cuisine, which uses herbs, spices and chile peppers for flavor. Jerked Pork (page 158) is a fine example of a well-spiced dish that draws some of its heat and flavor from the red pepper flakes and black pepper of the seasoning blend. Typically this dish calls for Scotch Bonnet chiles, but they can be hard to find, so I suggest jalapeño peppers instead, offset by fresh lime juice.

Not all dishes are intensely hot and spicy. The smooth, delicate Puréed Pumpkin Soup (page 155) has a characteristic sweetness with added panache from the ginger and allspice of the blend. At times, sweet and hot and spicy are combined as in one of the Caribbean's acclaimed soups, Quick Callaloo (page 160). Callaloo greens, which taste somewhat like spinach, are combined with coconut cream, okra and fresh crabmeat, to make a most unusual soup. Pickapeppa hot pepper sauce, one of the many favorite Caribbean hot pepper condiments, tops off this arrestingly delicious dish.

The cuisine of the Caribbean is as enchanting as its tropic islands. A favorite vacation spot for many, the Caribbean has a beat of its own; its food will inspire you to begin an exciting getaway in your own kitchen.

QUICKIES: EVERYDAY FOODS MADE INTERNATIONAL

Baked Sweet Potato
Cut open a baked sweet potato, drizzle with maple syrup and sprinkle with a little *Caribbean Seasoning Mix.*

Tropical Delight
Mix 2 parts mayonnaise to 1 part mustard and season with some *Caribbean Seasoning Mix.* Brush the mixture evenly over the

top of fish fillets during the final 5 minutes of cooking.

Carrot Slaw

Follow your favorite coleslaw recipe, but substitute shredded raw carrots for some of the cabbage, and season with *Caribbean Seasoning Mix,* salt and pepper for a more "colorful" version.

Spicy Shrimp

Combine 1 cup catsup, ½ teaspoon prepared horseradish and *Caribbean Seasoning Mix* to taste for a quick cocktail sauce to complement chilled cooked shrimp.

Caribbean Seasoning Mix

Makes about ½ cup

2 tablespoons plus 2 teaspoons ground allspice
2 tablespoons ground ginger
1 tablespoon dried thyme leaves
1 tablespoon dried marjoram leaves
1 tablespoon red pepper flakes
    (also called crushed red pepper)
    (available at supermarket)
1 teaspoon freshly ground black pepper

In a small bag or bowl (How-To page 11), combine the allspice, ginger, thyme, marjoram, red pepper flakes and black pepper. Shake or stir until well blended. Transfer to a clean, dry, airtight glass container. Store up to 3 months away from heat, light or moisture. Shake well before using.

Puréed Pumpkin Soup

Servings: 4 (1¾ cups each)
Preparation Time: About 10 minutes
Cooking Time: 5 minutes
(can be made up to 1 day ahead)

The Caribbean pumpkin is unlike the American round, orange "pie" pumpkin variety. The calabaza, *or "West Indian" or "Green Pumpkin," is a large green-skinned squash with a long neck. Its yellowish-orange flesh yields a delicate flavor best replaced by Hubbard or butternut squash. For the sake of convenience, I use frozen "cooked squash" purée. This supermarket product yields fine results with a minimum of fuss. Now you don't have to pre-cook and purée the squash, not to mention having to lug it home from the market!*

2 12-ounce packages frozen squash purée, thawed
1 quart canned low-sodium chicken broth
1 teaspoon *Caribbean Seasoning Mix* (page 154)
½ cup half-and-half, at room temperature
3 tablespoons finely chopped fresh parsley
2 tablespoons unsalted butter or unsalted margarine
Salt and freshly ground pepper to taste

1. Combine the squash purée, chicken broth and seasoning mix in a heavy 4-quart saucepan over medium heat, stir until well blended and bring to a boil, stirring occasionally.

2. Reduce the heat to low, stir ½ cup of the hot soup into a small bowl with the half-and-half and then stir this back into the saucepan until well blended. Simmer for 2 minutes, stirring occasionally. Stir in the butter until melted, then the parsley until well blended. Season with salt and pepper and serve at once as a soup course for 4.

Pigeon Peas and Rice

Servings: 4
Preparation Time: About 10 minutes
Cooking Time: 65 minutes
Bean Soaking Time: 1 hour to overnight
(can be made up to 2 days ahead)

Caribbean Light Summer Supper
(Entertaining Menu for 4)
Cocktails: Piña Coladas
Jerked Pork
Pigeon Peas and Rice
Banana Bread (bakery or mix) with Banana Ice Cream

Pigeon peas, of African origin, are popular in West Indian cooking. They are known by a number of names, including gunga *peas,* gungoo *peas,* congo *peas or* gandules. *Areas of the Caribbean differ in the type of pea used. For example, in Martinique or Guadeloupe, this one-dish meal might be made with black-eyed peas, which are easy to find and resemble pigeon peas.*

3½ ounces (½ cup) pigeon peas (available at health food store of Caribbean or Latin-American market or see Source List page 186) picked over, or black-eyed peas
1 quart canned vegetable broth or 1 quart made from vegetable bouillon cubes (available at supermarket), dissolved in water according to package directions
1 cup long-grain white rice
1 medium onion, finely chopped
½ teaspoon *Caribbean Seasoning Mix* (page 154)
¼ cup canned coconut cream (available at supermarket)
3 tablespoons finely chopped fresh chives
Salt and freshly ground pepper to taste

1. Soak the pigeon peas in cold water to cover by 2 inches overnight, covered, at room temperature. Drain and rinse. Alternatively, place the peas in a heavy 3-quart saucepan over medium-high heat with enough cold water to cover by 2 inches and bring to a boil. Remove the pan from the heat, cover and let stand for 1 hour. Drain the peas and rinse under cold running water.

2. Bring the vegetable broth to a boil in a 4-quart saucepan over high heat. Add the peas, reduce the heat to low and cover. Simmer for 45 minutes, stirring occasionally, or until the peas are tender but not falling apart. Stir in the rice, onion and seasoning mix, cover and simmer for 20 minutes more, stirring once, or until almost all the water has been absorbed and the rice is tender.

3. Stir in the coconut cream and chives until well blended. Season with salt and pepper. Using a fork, fluff the rice and pea mixture and serve at once as a main course for 4 or side dish for 6.

Baked Papaya

Servings: 4
Preparation Time: About 5 minutes
Cooking Time: 35 minutes

¼ cup dry unseasoned bread crumbs
½ teaspoon *Caribbean Seasoning Mix* (page 154)
2 tablespoons unsalted butter or unsalted margarine, cut into small dice
2 medium-sized ripe papayas, cut in half lengthwise and seeded

1. Preheat the oven to 350° F.

2. Combine the bread crumbs and seasoning mix in a small bowl and mix until well blended. Sprinkle each papaya half with 1 tablespoon of the crumb mixture until the surface is coated evenly. Arrange the papaya halves coating-side-up on a baking sheet and dot with the butter. Bake for 35 minutes or until the tops are delicately browned. Serve hot as a side dish.

Jerked Pork

Servings: 4
Preparation: About 10 minutes
Cooking Time: About 20 minutes

There are almost as many different recipes for Jerked Pork as there are cooks. Though piquant, this milder version of the classic Jamaican dish uses jalapeño peppers in place of the hard-to-find Scotch Bonnet chiles. If you desire more heat, add some more jalapeños, preferably fresh.

1 3½-ounce can whole roasted peeled jalapeño peppers, drained and stemmed, or one 4-ounce can peeled chopped hot green chiles, drained (available at supermarket)
3 whole cloves garlic
¼ cup coarsely chopped fresh parsley
¼ cup prepared spicy brown mustard (available at supermarket)
1 teaspoon *Caribbean Seasoning Mix* (page 154)
¼ cup fresh lime juice (2 to 3 small limes)
Salt and freshly ground pepper to taste
4 pork center loin rib chops, about ½ inch thick (4 to 5 ounces each), at room temperature

1. Combine the jalapeño peppers, garlic, parsley, mustard, seasoning mix and lime juice in the bowl of a food processor fitted with a metal blade or the container of a blender. Process the mixture about 2 minutes, scraping down the sides of the bowl as necessary, or until the mixture is finely chopped and well blended. Season with salt and pepper.

2. Preheat the broiler.

3. Arrange the chops in a single layer on top of a broiler pan. Line the bottom pan with aluminum foil. Broil 4 inches from the heat source for 10 to 12 minutes on one side. Remove the broiler pan from the broiler, flip over the chops and spread each "eye" of a chop evenly with a quarter of the jalapeño mixture. Return the chops to the broiler and broil for 4 to 6 minutes more until cooked through and no pink remains, depending on thickness. Be careful not to overcook; remember that the chops will continue to cook slightly even after being removed from the broiler. Serve at once as a main course.

Hearts-of-Palm Salad

Servings: 4
Preparation Time: About 10 minutes
Cooking Time: None
Chilling Time: 2 hours

Palm heart is the inner white heart of a variety of palm tree (the cabbage palmetto) and an unusual delicacy. The hearts are cylindrical, with a delicate flavor and appealing texture, tender yet crunchy. You'll crave them once you've tasted them! They make for an elegant salad tossed with avocado and grapefruit dressing and graced with macadamia nuts. Used fresh in the islands, the canned palm hearts available here are an excellent substitute and are becoming a standard item in American supermarkets.

½ cup pink grapefruit juice (available at supermarket)
¼ teaspoon *Caribbean Seasoning Mix* (page 154)
2 tablespoons vegetable oil
2 14-ounce cans hearts-of-palm (available at supermarket
    or Caribbean food store or see Source List page 186),
    drained, cut in half crosswise, then lengthwise into julienne strips
2 medium-sized ripe but firm avocados
2 ounces (½ cup) unsalted macadamia nuts, finely chopped
    (available at supermarket), to garnish
1 small lime, cut lengthwise into quarters

1. Combine the grapefruit juice, seasoning mix and vegetable oil in a large nonreactive bowl and whisk until well blended. Then gently stir in the julienned hearts-of-palm until well blended. Cover and refrigerate until well chilled, about 2 hours.

2. Cut the avocados in half lengthwise, remove the pits and peel. Cut the avocados into small dice and gently stir into the bowl with the hearts-of-palm. Using a slotted spoon distribute among 4 salad plates, sprinkle each salad with some macadamia nuts and place a lime wedge alongside. Serve at once, suggesting diners squeeze the lime wedges over the salads.

Quick Callaloo

Servings: 4 (1¾ cups each)
Preparation Time: About 15 minutes
Cooking Time: About 30 minutes
(can be made up to 2 days ahead)

The most well-known of the island soups, Callaloo is named for its principal ingredient. "Callaloo" can refer to the leaves of two distinct types of plants: the Malaga or the Amaranth (Chinese spinach). Fresh callaloo is seldom available in the United States. However, canned callaloo greens can be found. Fresh spinach leaves can also be used for they have much the same texture and flavor as callaloo greens.

1 quart canned vegetable broth or 1 quart made from
   vegetable bouillon cubes, dissolved in water according
   to package directions, (available at supermarket)
2 19-ounce cans callaloo greens, drained, rinsed briefly and coarsely
   chopped (available at Caribbean market or see Source List page 186)
   or 2 pounds fresh spinach, washed thoroughly, drained, stemmed
   and coarsely chopped
1 large white onion, finely chopped
1 10-ounce package frozen okra, thawed and cut into ½-inch-thick slices
1½ teaspoons *Caribbean Seasoning Mix* (page 154)
⅓ cup canned coconut cream (available at supermarket)
8 ounces cooked fresh or canned crabmeat, or "sea legs"
   (blend of Alaskan King crab and lobster meat,
   available at supermarket), picked over and cut into bite-size pieces
3 tablespoons fresh lime juice

Pickapeppa hot pepper sauce or Tabasco Sauce, to serve,
   (available at supermarket)

1. Bring the vegetable broth to a boil in a 4-quart saucepan over high heat. Add the callaloo greens and onion, reduce the heat to low and simmer for 10 minutes, stirring once, or until the greens are tender.

2. Stir in the okra and seasoning mix and simmer for 15 minutes more, stirring occasionally or until the okra is tender and the soup has thickened slightly. Stir ½ cup of the hot soup into a small bowl with the coconut cream, then stir this mixture back into the

saucepan until well blended. Stir in the crabmeat and simmer, stirring, for 2 minutes more. Stir in the lime juice and serve at once, with Pickapeppa sauce for guests to help themselves.

Pepperpot

(Spicy Pork Stew)
Servings: 4 (2 cups each)
Preparation Time: About 15 minutes
Cooking Time: About 70 minutes
(can be made up to 2 days ahead)

This soup classically uses the pungent Caribbean peppers "Scotch Bonnets" and cassareep (cassava root juice). Both of these ingredients can be difficult to find. My seasoning mix works very well along with a touch of cayenne in place of the Scotch Bonnets to lend the pepperpot its distinctive "pepperiness," while malt vinegar and coconut cream replace the bittersweet cassareep.

3 cups canned low-sodium beef broth
1 large white onion, coarsely chopped
1½ pounds lean boneless pork, preferably from shoulder, trimmed
     and cut into 1-inch cubes
1 medium green bell pepper, cut into ½-inch-wide strips
1 medium red bell pepper, cut into ½-inch-wide strips
1 tablespoon *Caribbean Seasoning Mix* (page 154)
¼ teaspoon ground red (cayenne) pepper
3 tablespoons quick-cooking tapioca
⅓ cup malt vinegar (available at supermarket or health food store)
     or white vinegar
1 16-ounce can cut yams, packed in light syrup, drained and rinsed briefly
⅛ cup canned coconut cream (available at supermarket or gourmet store)

1. Combine the beef broth, onion, pork, green and red bell peppers, seasoning mix, cayenne, tapioca and malt vinegar in a heavy nonreactive 6-quart pot over high heat. Stir until well blended and bring to a boil.

2. Reduce the heat to low, and simmer, covered, for 1 hour, stirring occasionally, or until the pork is cooked (no pink remains when

tested) until tender, and the stew has thickened. Stir in the cut yams and coconut cream and cook, uncovered, stirring occasionally, for 5 minutes more. Serve hot as a main course.

Lobster Salad

Servings: 4
Preparation Time: About 10 minutes
Cooking Time: None
Assembling Time: 5 minutes

The lobsters of the Caribbean are really saltwater crayfish or spiny or rock lobsters. The Northern lobster available in the United States makes for a fine substitution. To save time, I use precooked fresh lobster meat, usually from Maine, available from the local fishmonger or supermarket. The light green avocado dressing is a lovely complement to the bright red of the lobster salad.

DRESSING: (Makes about 1 cup)
1   medium-sized ripe avocado
½   cup finely chopped onion
⅛   cup cholesterol-free mayonnaise, (available at supermarket)
¼   teaspoon *Caribbean Seasoning Mix* (page 154)
¼   teaspoon salt
⅛   cup vegetable oil

SALAD:
Chilled lettuce leaves, to serve
1   pound cooked lobster meat (available at fishmonger or supermarket),
      cut into bite-size pieces
3   tablespoons finely chopped fresh chives, to garnish (optional)

1. To make the dressing: Cut the avocado in half lengthwise, remove the pit and peel and discard, adding the avocado meat to the bowl of a food processor fitted with a metal blade or the container of a blender. Add the onion, mayonnaise, seasoning mix and salt to the food processor bowl. Process about 1 minute or until well blended and fairly smooth, scraping down the sides of the bowl as necessary. While the machine is running add the vegetable oil through the feed tube until well combined

and the mixture forms a thick mayonnaise-like dressing.

2. To prepare the salad: Line 4 chilled salad plates with the lettuce leaves. Divide the cooked lobster meat evenly among the plates, forming it into a loose "mound." Spoon a large dollop of the dressing over each salad and garnish with chives if desired. Serve at once as a light main course, salad or appetizer.

Caribbean Red Snapper Kebabs

Servings: 4 (2 skewers each)
Preparation Time: About 15 minutes
Cooking Time: 10 minutes
Marinating Time: 30 minutes

1 cup vegetable oil
3 cloves garlic, crushed
2 teaspoons *Caribbean Seasoning Mix* (page 154)
Half 20-ounce can of pineapple chunks, packed in unsweetened pineapple juice, drained but juice reserved
2 pounds red snapper fillets, central bone removed, cut in half lengthwise, then crosswise into 1-inch-wide pieces
1 medium red bell pepper, cut into 1-inch squares
2 scallions, green part only, cut into 1-inch-long pieces

1 small lime, cut lengthwise into quarters, to serve

1. Combine the vegetable oil, garlic, seasoning mix and reserved pineapple juice in a 13-inch-by-9-inch-by-2-inch baking dish and whisk until well blended. Add the red snapper pieces, red bell pepper squares, pineapple chunks and scallion pieces. Cover and refrigerate for 30 minutes.

2. Preheat the broiler.

3. Drain the kebab ingredients and divide the ingredients evenly among eight 12-inch-long metal skewers. Thread the red snapper pieces onto the skewers, alternating them with pieces of bell pepper, pineapple and scallion, in that order.

4. Arrange the kebabs on the top half of a broiler pan. Line the bottom of the pan with aluminum foil. Broil, in two batches, 4 inches

Caribbean Terrace Party
(Fast Entertaining Menu for 4)
Cocktails: Jamaican Planter's Punch
Caribbean Red Snapper Kebabs
Fried Plantains (page 164)
Hearts-of-Palm Salad (page 159)
Coconut Custard Pie (bakery or supermarket — frozen)

Cooks throughout the Caribbean fry up slices of this long, firm member of the banana family and serve it with spicy meat dishes. Plantains are thicker skinned, coarser in texture and far less sweet (they contain more starch and much less sugar) than their banana cousins; they are marketed green and cannot be eaten raw. In America, the plantain is now available in many supermarkets and all Latin-American marketplaces.

Depending on the end result desired, plantains can be cooked when still green or when fully ripe. When a plantain is "ripe" its skin turns dark brown with large black areas, yet its interior remains firm. Its flesh does not become soft as does a banana. The advantage of cooking an unripe plantain is that its flesh holds up well under high temperatures (like frying) and has less of a chance of falling apart; yet a ripe plantain might yield a slightly sweeter result.

from the heat source, for 4 to 5 minutes or until the fish has turned opaque, but springy to the touch. (NOTE: Be careful not to overcook; remember that the fish will continue to cook slightly even after being removed from the broiler.) Drizzle the skewers with any pan drippings and serve with lime wedges for the guests to squeeze over the fish. Serve at once as a main course.

Fried Plantains

Servings: 4
Preparation Time: About 10 minutes
Cooking Time: 5 minutes

½ cup yellow cornmeal
½ teaspoon *Caribbean Seasoning Mix* (page 154)
3 medium-sized ripe plantains (available at supermarket
    or Caribbean or Latin-American market
    or see Source List page 186)
3 cups peanut oil
Salt to taste (optional)

1. Combine the cornmeal and seasoning mix in a large bowl and stir until well combined. Peel each plantain, trim the ends of each fruit and discard the ends and peels. Cut each plantain in half lengthwise and using a small, sharp knife, remove and discard the fiber that runs down the center of each fruit. Cut the plantains crosswise into ¼-inch-thick slices and add to the bowl with the cornmeal mixture. Gently toss together until the plantain slices are evenly coated, shaking off the excess cornmeal mixture, and reserve the plantains until ready to use.

2. Heat the peanut oil in a heavy 6-quart pot over medium-high heat until a deep-fry thermometer reads 375° F.

3. Add the plantain slices to the pot *(be careful — stand back: oil will splatter)*. Deep-fry about 3 minutes, turning, or until the outside is crisp and the edges lightly golden brown. Using a slotted metal spoon, transfer the plantains to a paper-towel-lined plate to drain briefly. Season with salt, if desired, and serve at once as a side dish.

Chinese Seasoning Mix

Sweet and Sour Pork

Beef with Broccoli

Cold Sesame Noodles

Chicken with Shrimp and Cashews

Lemon Chicken

Hot and Sour Soup

Orange Beef

Fried Rice

Stir-Fried Snow Peas with Baby Corn and Water Chestnuts

Chinese Cabbage with Oyster Sauce

CHAPTER 12

China: Harmony in the Kitchen

Chinese cookery is perfect for today's hectic and health-conscious life-styles. The Chinese eat lightly and they eat well. Chinese food is high in nutrients, fairly low in calories and well-balanced with respect to ingredients. Vitamins and minerals are retained by stir-frying in a wok over high heat, or by steaming. Two of my stir-fry favorites are Chinese Cabbage with Oyster Sauce (page 179) and Stir-Fried Snow Peas with Baby Corn and Water Chestnuts (page 178).

Instead of serving a large portion of meat with a small side dish of vegetables as with a standard American meal, the Chinese combine small quantities of meat with lots of vegetables, which is a much healthier alternative. Beef with Broccoli (page 168), is a perennial favorite.

Chinese cooks also base dishes on nutritious staples such as rice or noodles, adding vegetables and other healthy ingredients, rather than excess meat, as sources of protein. A good example is spicy Cold Sesame Noodles (page 169), which is altogether meatless. In these recipes, the seasoning blend containing ginger, white pepper, red pepper flakes, cayenne, cinnamon and cloves is used sparingly — as almost a background flavor to "harmonize" all the ingredients in each dish. I also allow the flavors of condiments such as soy sauce and garlic and fresh ginger to prevail, as Chinese cooks themselves tend to do.

The skillful use of contrasting flavors, textures and ingredients, as noted with Hot and Sour Soup (page 174), for example, results in a remarkably well-balanced dish. In the course of a meal, one dish may be smooth, another crisp; another may be brilliantly green, while still another may feature light- and dark-colored ingredients. Within a single dish, textures may vary, too, such as in Chicken with Shrimp and Cashews (page 171), where tender chicken is served with crunchy cashews, creating a harmonious combination.

QUICKIES: EVERYDAY FOODS MADE INTERNATIONAL

Hog Heaven
Sprinkle cooked ham steak with brown sugar mixed with a pinch of *Chinese Seasoning Mix* just before serving.

Braised Leeks
Heat some chicken stock in a medium skillet over medium heat until it reaches a simmer. Stir in a

few thinly sliced leeks, a pinch of *Chinese Seasoning Mix*, salt and pepper and a dash of Chinese cooking rice wine. Cover and cook until the leeks are tender.

Dinner with a Twist

Combine orange juice and a pinch of *Chinese Seasoning Mix* and salt and pepper until well blended. Use as a baste for skinless chicken breasts or a skinless turkey breast.

Grilled Steak

Before grilling, splash a steak with several dashes of soy sauce and sprinkle lightly with *Chinese Seasoning Mix* and freshly milled pepper.

Chinese Adventure

(One-Dish Menu for 6)
Sweet and Sour Pork
    with Rice
Fortune Cookies
    (supermarket
    or gourmet store)
Chinese Tea such as
    Lapsang Souchong or
    Formosa Oolong
    (supermarket —
    tea bags)

The dishes included in this chapter represent but a small sampling of the world of Chinese cookery. It was very difficult to decide which recipes to include since there are so many magnificent dishes to choose from, but the following are among my favorites.

Chinese Seasoning Mix

Makes about 1/2 cup

1/4 cup ground ginger
3 tablespoons ground white pepper
2 teaspoons red pepper flakes (also called crushed red pepper) (available at supermarket)
1/2 teaspoon ground red (cayenne) pepper
1/4 teaspoon ground cinnamon
1/4 teaspoon ground cloves

In a small bag or bowl (How-To page 11), combine the ginger, pepper, pepper flakes, cayenne, cinnamon and cloves. Shake or stir until well blended. Transfer to a clean, dry, airtight glass container. Store up to 3 months away from heat, light or moisture. Shake well before using.

Sweet and Sour Pork

Servings: 6
Preparation Time: About 25 minutes
Cooking Time: About 35 minutes

SAUCE: (Makes 5 cups)
2 tablespoons cornstarch
1/4 cup cold water
1/2 cup red-wine vinegar
1/2 cup firmly packed light brown sugar
5 tablespoons canned tomato purée
2 teaspoons dark low-sodium soy sauce (page 167, available at supermarket)
2 cloves garlic, crushed

1 large red bell pepper, cut into ½-inch dice
1 large green bell pepper, cut into ½-inch dice
2 carrots, cut into ¹⁄₁₆-inch-thick slices
1 20-ounce can pineapple chunks packed in unsweetened
    pineapple juice, strained with ¾ cup of the juice reserved

BATTER:
2 teaspoons Chinese cooking rice wine (page 178,
    available at supermarket) or dry Sherry
¼ teaspoon *Chinese Seasoning Mix* (page 166)
1 large egg
1 cup cornstarch

PORK:
1½ pounds trimmed boneless pork, preferably
    from the shoulder, cut into 1-inch cubes
2½ cups peanut oil

Hot cooked white rice (follow package directions), to serve

1. To prepare the sauce: Stir the cornstarch and cold water together in a small bowl until the cornstarch is dissolved and the mixture is smooth. Pour into a nonreactive 3-quart saucepan and stir in the vinegar, brown sugar, tomato purée, dark soy sauce, garlic, red bell pepper, green bell pepper, carrots and pineapple with the reserved ¾ cup of its juice. Place the saucepan over medium-high heat and, stirring the mixture occasionally, bring to a boil. Boil for 5 minutes, stirring often, until the bell peppers and carrots are tender and the sauce has thickened. Remove the saucepan from the heat and reserve until ready to use.

2. To prepare the batter: In a medium bowl, stir together the rice wine, seasoning mix and egg until well blended. Place the cornstarch in another medium bowl. Stir the pork into the egg mixture and toss to coat evenly; shake off any excess egg mixture from the pork. Transfer the pork, a handful at a time, to the bowl with the cornstarch and toss the pork until evenly dusted with the cornstarch, shaking off the excess. Using a slotted spoon, transfer the coated pork to a plate and reserve until ready to use.

3. Preheat the oven to 250° F.

THE SOY SAUCE SHUFFLE

Soy Serendipity

Soy sauce, commonly thought of as a condiment for Japanese food, was actually invented in China sometime around the sixth century. Its original form was more of a puréed bean sauce than the liquid we know today. Soy sauce was initially used as a preservative to help store food through the long winter months.

Soy Sauce Secrets: Light or Dark?

Soy sauce is a fermented soybean-meal-based product that is aged anywhere from a few months to two years before being bottled. Dark soy sauce is aged longer than light, and toward the end of its processing is mixed with molasses, which lends its characteristic caramel hue. A good rule of thumb is to use dark soy sauce for heartier foods, such as beef, and light for more delicate foods, such as seafood or vegetables.

Soy Savvy

When buying soy sauce, read the label carefully to find genuine soy sauce. Some brands are not made from soy meal at all, but from hydrolyzed vegetable protein.

4. To cook the pork: Add the peanut oil to a heavy 8- to 10-quart pot over high heat. Heat the oil until it reaches 360° F. on a deep-fat thermometer, or until a small cube of white bread dropped into the oil turns golden in 50 seconds. Using a perforated or slotted metal spatula, lower the pork cubes, a few pieces at a time (a total of 4 batches) into the oil *(be careful — stand back; oil will splatter)*. Using the spatula, separate the pork pieces and deep-fry for 4 to 6 minutes or until the outside is golden brown and crisp. In between batches, transfer the fried pork to an ovenproof dish and keep warm in the oven while you cook the remaining pork.

5. To serve, reheat the sauce over low heat, stirring constantly, until hot, about 4 minutes. Transfer the pork to a heated serving platter, and pour the sauce over it. Serve at once as a main course with rice on the side.

Chinese Delight
(Entertaining Menu for 4)
Chinese Egg Rolls
    (supermarket—frozen)
Beef with Broccoli
Chicken with Shrimp and
    Cashews (page 171)
Hot Cooked Rice for 4
Stir-Fried Snow Peas
    with Baby Corn and
    Water Chestnuts
    (page 178)
Chinese Cabbage with
    Oyster Sauce (page 179)
Lychees with Mandarin
    Oranges (supermarket —
    canned)
Chinese Beer such as
    Tsing-Tao

Beef with Broccoli

Servings: 4
Preparation Time: About 15 minutes
Cooking Time: About 10 minutes

2 tablespoons cornstarch
¼ cup cold water
3 tablespoons peanut oil
3 cloves garlic, minced
1 2-inch-long by 1-inch-wide piece of fresh ginger, peeled and minced
1 1-pound trimmed piece of boneless beef tenderloin, cut in half
    lengthwise, then cut crosswise into ⅛-inch-thick slices
1 cup canned low-sodium beef broth
2 tablespoons dark soy sauce (page 167), preferably low-sodium
    (available at supermarket)
¼ teaspoon *Chinese Seasoning Mix* (page 166)
1 1½-pound head broccoli, cut into small florets

Hot cooked white rice (follow package directions), to serve

1. Stir the cornstarch and cold water together in a small bowl until the cornstarch is completely dissolved and the mixture is well blend-

ed and smooth. Reserve until ready to use.

2. Add the peanut oil to a wok or heavy deep 14-inch skillet with sloping sides, rotating the wok to coat the sides, and heat over high heat until the oil is rippling, about 1 minute.

3. Add the garlic and ginger and stir-fry *(be careful—stand back; oil will splatter)*, tossing quickly, about 1 second, or until aromatic but not browned. Add the beef and stir-fry, tossing quickly, for 2 to 3 minutes or until the beef loses its redness and just turns brown (but only partially cooked). Using a slotted wooden spoon, transfer the beef to a plate and reserve.

4. Add the beef broth, soy sauce and seasoning mix to the wok and bring to a boil. Add the broccoli and cook for 2 minutes, stirring constantly. Reduce the heat to low and cover with a lid or aluminum foil, and simmer, stirring once, for 1 to 2 minutes or until the broccoli is crisp-tender.

5. Raise the heat to high and add the reserved beef to the wok. Stir the reserved cornstarch mixture to recombine. Then gradually stir the cornstarch mixture into the wok, stirring constantly, until the sauce thickens and coats the stir-fry mixture with a glossy coating, about 1 minute, and the beef is fully cooked and tender. Remove the wok from the heat and transfer the stir-fry to a heated serving platter, and pour the sauce over the meat and vegetables. Serve at once as a main course with rice on the side.

Cold Sesame Noodles

Servings: 4
Preparation Time: About 15 minutes
Cooking Time: 10 minutes
(can be made up to 1 day ahead)

NOODLES:
8 ounces fettuccine
1 teaspoon sesame oil (available at supermarket)

TIP: These recipes were tested using a nonstick wok that works beautifully and eliminates the need for excessive amounts of oil.

THE GIFT OF GINGER

Fresh ginger is the rhizome (or underground stem) of *Zingiber officale*, a plant native to tropical Asia. The name "ginger" comes from the Sanskrit *sringavera*, which means "horn-root," as it resembles the horns of an animal.

Ginger Goodies

Ginger is commonly available fresh or ground, but it can also be found candied, pickled or preserved. Ginger is the star of many foods from around the world, from gingerbread to ginger beer, even ginger ice cream! Legend has it that Queen Elizabeth I invented gingerbread men when she had ginger cakes baked in the likeness (rough ones no doubt) of court favorites!

Buying

Look for firm, plump tubers, and avoid the shriveled and dried out pieces. The scent should be fresh and spicy, not musty.

STORING GINGER

◆ **Storage for a few days:** Wrap ginger in plastic and refrigerate.

◆ **Storage for up to 1 month:** Peel, wrap in plastic and freeze. Slice off a portion of the ginger as needed, returning the remainder to the freezer. (Do not thaw and refreeze.)

◆ **Storage for up to 6 months:** Peel and place the ginger in an airtight glass jar, and immerse it in either dry Sherry, or vermouth. Cover tightly and store in the refrigerator.

PREPARATION

Fresh ginger must be peeled before using. For cooking, either slice the peeled ginger thin or grate it. I recommend using a porcelain "ginger grater," because it grates more quickly than a metal grater and is much easier to clean.

**TIP: If you are able to buy Chinese noodles, then use them for this recipe.
However, fettuccine is just as**

SAUCE:

½ cup firmly packed "chunky-style" peanut butter

3 tablespoons sesame oil (available at supermarket)

2 tablespoons light low-sodium soy sauce (page 167, available at supermarket)

2 cloves garlic, crushed

½ teaspoon *Chinese Seasoning Mix* (page 166)

¼ cup hot canned low-sodium chicken broth

1 medium red bell pepper, cut into ½-inch dice

3 scallions, green part only, thinly sliced on the diagonal, to garnish

1. To prepare the noodles: Bring 2 quarts of water to a boil in a large pot over high heat. Stir in the noodles and bring to a second boil. Boil for 6 minutes, stirring occasionally, or until the noodles are *al dente* (slightly firm to the bite). Drain the noodles in a colander under cold running water. Transfer the noodles to a medium bowl and toss with the 1 teaspoon sesame oil to help prevent sticking. Reserve until ready to use.

2. To make the sauce: Combine the peanut butter, the 3 tablespoons sesame oil, soy sauce, garlic, seasoning mix, ¼ cup hot chicken broth and red bell pepper in a medium bowl and stir until well blended. Add the sauce to the bowl with the noodles and gently toss until well blended and the noodles are well coated with sauce. Transfer the noodles to a medium serving platter, sprinkle with the scallions and serve cold or at room temperature as an appetizer or side dish for 6 or main course for 4.

Chicken with Shrimp and Cashews

Servings: 4
Preparation Time: About 20 minutes
Cooking Time: 5 minutes

8 ounces skinless, boneless chicken breasts, cut into ½-inch-dice
12 ounces small shrimp (51 to 60 to the pound), shelled and deveined
   (How-To page 15)
1 tablespoon cornstarch
2 tablespoons light low-sodium soy sauce
   (page 167, available at supermarket)
1 tablespoon Chinese cooking rice wine
   (page 178, available at supermarket) or dry Sherry
¼ teaspoon *Chinese Seasoning Mix* (page 166)
3 scallions, green part only, thinly sliced on the diagonal
3 tablespoons peanut oil
2 cloves garlic, minced
1 1-inch-long by 1-inch-wide piece of fresh ginger, peeled and minced
4 ounces (¾ cup) unsalted cashews, toasted (How-To page 102)

Hot cooked white rice (follow package directions), to serve

2. Position your ring finger against the chopstick, applying just enough pressure to hold the chopstick steady (the chopstick should move only in conjunction with your hand.)

3. Position your hand straight out in front of you, holding the chopstick firm with the base of your thumb and ring finger. Bend the top half of your forefinger and middle finger back toward you.

4. Now, you are ready for the second chopstick. Rest the second chopstick on the pad of your thumb and bend your forefinger and middle finger down onto the chopstick. Make sure that your forefinger is on top of the chopstick and along the length, while your middle finger is supporting the other side of the chopstick—in the same manner as you would hold a pencil.

The secret to using chopsticks is that the bottom chopstick should never move. By applying very slight pressure from your forefinger and middle finger, the chopstick tips will open and close and you can then pick up whatever food you choose.

1. Combine the chicken, shrimp and cornstarch in a medium bowl and toss together until the chicken and shrimp are well coated with the cornstarch. Reserve until ready to use.

2. Combine the soy sauce, rice wine, seasoning mix and scallions in a small bowl, stir until well blended and reserve.

3. Add the peanut oil to a wok or heavy deep 12-inch skillet with sloping sides, rotating the wok to coat the sides, and heat over high heat until the oil is rippling, about 1 minute.

4. Add the garlic and ginger and stir-fry *(be careful — stand back; oil will splatter)*, tossing quickly about 1 second, or until aromatic but not browned. Add the reserved chicken-shrimp mixture and stir-fry, tossing quickly, until the chicken loses its pinkness and turns white and the shrimp turns pink, about 1½ minutes.

5. Stir the reserved soy-sauce mixture to recombine, then gradually stir into the wok, stirring constantly, until the chicken and shrimp are cooked through and the sauce thickens and coats the shrimp and chicken with a glossy coating, about 1 minute. Remove the wok from the heat and transfer the stir-fry to a heated serving platter. Pour the sauce over all, then sprinkle with the toasted cashews. Serve at once as a main course with rice on the side.

Lemon Chicken

Servings: 4
Preparation Time: About 15 minutes
Cooking Time: About 30 minutes

SAUCE: (Makes 2 cups)

2 tablespoons cornstarch
¼ cup cold water
½ cup canned low-sodium chicken broth
¼ cup Chinese cooking rice wine (page 178,
    available at super market)or dry Sherry
1 cup fresh lemon juice (8 to 10 small lemons)
½ cup sugar

BATTER:

1 large egg
½ teaspoon *Chinese Seasoning Mix* (page 166)
1 cup cornstarch

CHICKEN:

1 pound skinless, boneless chicken breasts, cut crosswise
    into ¼-inch-wide strips
2½ cups peanut oil
2 scallions, white and green parts, thinly sliced on the diagonal

2 large lemons, cut into thin slices, to serve
Hot cooked white rice (follow package directions), to serve

1. To make the sauce: Stir the cornstarch and cold water together in a small bowl until the cornstarch is dissolved and the mixture is well blended and smooth. Add to a nonreactive 2-quart saucepan along with the chicken broth, cooking rice wine, lemon juice and sugar. Place the saucepan over medium-high heat and stirring the mixture constantly, bring to a boil. Boil for 2 minutes, stirring constantly, until the sauce has thickened and is no longer cloudy, but a clear pale yellow. Remove the saucepan from the heat and reserve until ready to use.

2. To make the batter: In a large bowl, stir together the egg and seasoning mix until well blended. Place the cornstarch in another large

bowl. Stir the chicken into the egg mixture and toss to evenly coat, shaking off any excess egg mixture from the chicken. Transfer the chicken, a handful at a time, to the bowl with the cornstarch and toss the chicken until evenly dusted with the cornstarch, shaking off the excess. Using a slotted spoon, transfer the coated chicken to a plate and reserve.

3. Preheat the oven to 250° F.

4. To cook the chicken: Add the peanut oil to a heavy 8- to 10-quart pot over high heat. Heat the oil until it reaches 360° F. on a deep-fat thermometer, or until a small cube of bread dropped into the oil turns golden in 50 seconds. Using a perforated or slotted metal spatula, lower the chicken, a few pieces at a time, (a total of 4 batches) into the oil *(be careful — stand back; oil will splatter)*. Using the spatula, separate the chicken pieces and deep-fry for 3 to 5 minutes or until the outside is golden brown and crisp. In between batches, transfer the fried chicken to an ovenproof dish and keep warm in the oven while you cook the remaining chicken.

5. To serve, reheat the sauce over low heat, stirring constantly, until hot, about 4 minutes. Transfer the chicken to a heated serving platter, pour the sauce over all and sprinkle evenly with the scallions. Arrange the lemon slices around the chicken and serve at once as a main course with rice on the side.

Hot and Sour Soup

Servings: 4 (1¼ cups each)
Preparation Time: About 15 minutes
Cooking Time: 5 minutes

TIP: Fresh Tofu (bean curd) is available in different sizes and textures, from "soft" to "firm." Firm works best for this soup; however, medium-firm will be fine, too.

Hot and sour soup is often served as a "banquet" dish, part of an elaborate Chinese feast. It can contain such exotic ingredients as cloud ears, tiger lily buds, and dried black winter mushrooms. Unfortunately these foods are not only hard-to-find, but most are available dried only, and require pre-soaking, a time-consuming step. Therefore, I have simplified matters by eliminating the exotica and employing easily obtainable foodstuffs such as straw mushrooms that still produce a delectable result.

¼ cup cornstarch

½ cup cold water

1 quart canned low-sodium beef broth

⅓ cup white-wine vinegar

2 tablespoons light soy sauce (page 167), preferably low-sodium
(available at supermarket)

¼ teaspoon Chinese chili sauce (available at supermarket
or Chinese grocery) or Tabasco sauce

½ teaspoon *Chinese Seasoning Mix* (page 166)

1 large egg

1 15-ounce can whole, peeled straw mushrooms, drained
and rinsed (available at supermarket or Chinese grocery)

8 ounces fresh *tofu* (bean curd), cut into ¼-inch dice,
preferably "firm" (available at supermarket or Chinese grocery)

2 scallions, green part only, thinly sliced, to garnish

1. Stir the cornstarch and cold water together in a small bowl until the cornstarch is dissolved and the mixture is well blended and smooth. Reserve until ready to use.

2. Bring the beef broth to a boil in a nonreactive 3-quart saucepan over high heat. Stir in the vinegar, soy sauce, chili sauce and seasoning mix. Cook, stirring, for 1 minute.

3. Stir in the reserved cornstarch mixture to recombine, then gradually stir it into the saucepan, stirring constantly, until the soup thickens, about 1 minute.

4. Reduce the heat to medium. In a small bowl, lightly beat the egg. Using a fork, begin to rapidly stir the soup. As the soup is swirling around in the saucepan, pour the beaten egg in a slow, steady stream toward the edge of the saucepan, and continue to "swirl" the soup with the fork, so that the egg separates into threads. (This is called an "egg flower.") As soon as the egg has set, about 30 seconds, stir in the mushrooms and *tofu* until well blended. Divide the soup among 4 soup bowls, sprinkle with the scallions and serve at once as an appetizer, soup course or light supper.

Orange Beef

Servings: 4
Preparation Time: About 15 minutes
Cooking Time: 5 minutes

TIP: This Chinese dish is universally cooked with dried mandarin orange peel, which can be difficult to obtain. In fact, I prefer the flavor of fresh orange peel, as it is a much "cleaner," lighter flavor and the aroma is superb!

SAUCE:

1 tablespoon dark soy sauce (page 167),
     preferably low-sodium (available at supermarket)
1 tablespoon sugar
2 teaspoons sesame oil (available at supermarket)
2 tablespoons rice vinegar (available at supermarket)
½ cup canned low-sodium beef broth or beef bouillon cubes, dissolved
     in water according to package directions (available at supermarket)
⅛ teaspoon *Chinese Seasoning Mix* (page 166)
½ teaspoon red pepper flakes
¼ cup loosely packed, very finely julienned fresh orange zest
2 tablespoons cornstarch

BEEF:

3 tablespoons peanut oil
3 cloves garlic, minced
1 1-inch-long by 1-inch-wide piece of fresh ginger, peeled and minced
1 1-pound beef top round steak, trimmed, cut in half lengthwise,
     then crosswise into ⅛-inch-thick strips

1 medium orange, thinly sliced and cut in half crosswise, to garnish
Hot cooked white rice (follow package directions), to serve

1. To prepare the sauce: Combine the soy sauce, sugar, sesame oil, rice vinegar, beef broth, seasoning mix, red pepper flakes, orange zest and cornstarch in a small bowl. Stir well until the cornstarch is completely dissolved and the mixture is well blended and smooth. Reserve until ready to use.

2. To cook the beef: Add the peanut oil to a wok or a heavy deep 12-inch skillet with sloping sides, rotating the wok to coat the sides, and heat over high heat until the oil is rippling, about 1 minute.

3. Add the garlic and ginger to the wok and stir-fry *(be careful — stand back; oil will splatter)*, tossing quickly about 1 second, or until

aromatic but not browned. Add the beef and stir-fry, tossing quickly for 2 to 3 minutes or until the beef loses its redness and just turns brown (but is only partially cooked).

4. Stir the reserved sauce to recombine. Then gradually stir the sauce into the wok, stirring constantly, until the sauce thickens and coats the beef with a glossy coating, about 1 minute, and the beef is fully cooked and tender. Remove the wok from the heat and transfer the stir-fry to a heated serving patter. Pour the sauce over the meat. Arrange the orange slices around the beef to garnish. Serve at once as a main course with rice on the side.

Fried Rice

Servings: 4
Preparation Time: About 10 minutes
Cooking Time: 5 minutes

3   tablespoons peanut oil
1   small white onion, finely chopped
3   cloves garlic, minced
1½ cups cooked long-grain white rice
2½ tablespoons light soy sauce (page 167),
     preferably low-sodium (available at supermarket)
¾   teaspoon *Chinese Seasoning Mix* (page 166)
2   scallions, white and green parts, thinly sliced on the diagonal
3   large eggs, well beaten
1   cup cooked fresh green peas (1 pound in pods)
     or frozen green peas, thawed

1. Add the peanut oil to a wok or heavy deep 12-inch skillet with sloping sides, rotating the wok to coat the sides, and heat over high heat until the oil is rippling, about 1 minute.

2. Add the onion and garlic and stir-fry *(be careful — stand back; oil will splatter)*, tossing quickly about 1 second or until the onion and garlic are aromatic but not browned.

3. Add the rice and stir-fry, tossing quickly for 2 minutes, breaking up any lumps to separate the grains and coat them with the oil. Stir

HINT: When pressed for time, prepare the rice up to 1 day ahead. Follow the package directions to make 1½ cups cooked long-grain white rice. Let cool to room temperature, cover and refrigerate. Bring back to room temperature before beginning the recipe.

TIP: Precook fresh green peas for 1 minute in lightly salted boiling water and drain in a colander under cold running water.

in the soy sauce, seasoning mix and scallions and stir-fry, tossing quickly but gently for 10 seconds.

4. Pour the beaten eggs into the center of the wok, and immediately stir to combine, tossing the eggs with the rice until they have scrambled lightly and are broken up into small pieces, about 1 minute. Stir in the peas just until well mixed. Remove the wok from the heat to prevent the eggs from getting dry, transfer to a warm serving platter and serve immediately as a side dish.

TIP: "Chinese cooking rice wine" is available at the supermarket; Ka-Me makes a good one. Or, you can use sake (Japanese rice wine), but, if you do use sake purchase a dry, not sweet variety.

Stir-Fried Snow Peas with Baby Corn and Water Chestnuts

Servings: 4
Preparation Time: About 15 minutes
Cooking Time: 5 minutes

SAUCE:

2 tablespoons light soy sauce (page 167),
    preferably low-sodium, (available at supermarket)
1 tablespoon Chinese cooking rice wine or dry Sherry
2 teaspoons sesame oil (available at supermarket or Chinese grocery)
½ teaspoon sugar
¼ teaspoon *Chinese Seasoning Mix* (page 166)
2 tablespoons cornstarch
¼ cup cold water

STIR-FRY:

3 tablespoons peanut oil
2 cloves garlic, minced
3 scallions, white and green parts,
    cut on the diagonal into 1-inch-long pieces
8 ounces fresh snow peas, stems and strings removed
1 14-ounce can baby corn, drained and cut crosswise
    into thirds (available at supermarket)
1 8-ounce can sliced water chestnuts, drained (available at supermarket)

1. To prepare the sauce: Combine the soy sauce, rice wine, sesame oil, sugar, seasoning mix, cornstarch and cold water in a small bowl.

Stir well until the sugar and the cornstarch are completely dissolved and the mixture is well blended and smooth. Reserve until ready to use.

2. To make the stir-fry: Add the peanut oil to a wok or heavy deep 14-inch skillet with sloping sides, rotating the wok to coat the sides, and heat over high heat until the oil is rippling, about 1 minute.

3. Add the garlic and scallions and stir-fry *(be careful — stand back; oil will splatter),* tossing quickly about 1 second, or until aromatic but not browned. Add the snow peas and baby corn and stir-fry, tossing quickly but gently, about 2 minutes, or until the snow peas are crisp-tender. Add the water chestnuts and stir-fry, tossing quickly but gently for 1 second. Stir the reserved sauce to recombine. Then gradually stir into the wok, stirring constantly until the sauce thickens and coats the vegetables with a glossy coating, about 1 minute. Remove the wok from the heat and serve the stir-fry at once as a side dish.

Chinese Cabbage with Oyster Sauce

Servings: 4
Preparation Time: About 15 minutes
Cooking Time: About 8 minutes

1 tablespoon plus 1 teaspoon oyster sauce
  (available at supermarket or Chinese grocery)
2 teaspoons light soy sauce, (page 167),
  preferably low-sodium (available at supermarket
  or Chinese grocery)
¼ teaspoon *Chinese Seasoning Mix* (page 166)
2 teaspoons Chinese cooking rice wine
  (page 178, available at supermarket) or dry Sherry
¾ teaspoon sugar
2 tablespoons cornstarch
¼ cup cold water
2 1-pound heads *bok choy* (Chinese cabbage), tough outer leaves
  removed and discarded (available at supermarket or Chinese grocery)
3½ tablespoons peanut oil

TIP: You will find that using two flat wooden spoons makes it more manageable to stir-fry the cabbage and cooks it more evenly, preventing it from burning.

1. Combine the oyster sauce, soy sauce, seasoning mix, rice wine, sugar, cornstarch and cold water in a small bowl. Stir well until the cornstarch is completely dissolved and the mixture is well blended and smooth. Reserve until ready to use.

2. Separate the leaves of the Chinese cabbage, wash thoroughly, drain and pat dry with paper towels. Cut each cabbage leaf in half lengthwise, then cut each piece crosswise into 1-inch-long pieces.

3. Add the peanut oil to a wok or heavy deep 14-inch skillet with sloping sides, rotating the wok to coat the sides, and heat over medium-high heat until the oil is rippling, about 1½ minutes.

4. Add the Chinese cabbage and stir-fry *(be careful — stand back; oil will splatter)*, tossing quickly, for 4 to 5 minutes or until crisp-tender. Stir the reserved sauce to recombine, then gradually stir it into the wok, stirring constantly until the sauce thickens and coats the cabbage with a glossy coating, about 1 minute. Remove the wok from the heat, transfer the Chinese cabbage to a heated serving platter and serve at once as a side dish.

Glossary of International Ingredients, Herbs and Spices

Allspice: Allspice is the berry of a myrtle tree native to the Caribbean region, but now grown elsewhere commercially. Jamaica remains the leader of production, responsible for more than half the world's supply. Whole seeds are generally used in savory foods, ground seeds in sweet ones. Allspice tastes like a combination of nutmeg, cinnamon and cloves.

Baby corn: Baby corn is a miniature ear of corn less than two inches long. The Chinese use it in stir-fry dishes and as a condiment. Available in cans and jars, baby corn should be added to the wok last, as it only needs to be warmed, not cooked.

Bacon, Hungarian: There are several varieties of Hungarian bacon to choose from, among them single-smoked, double-smoked, with or without paprika; the list goes on.

Basil: Basil is an aromatic member of the mint family. Italians associate it with love. The basil most commonly found in supermarkets is also known as sweet basil, common basil, Genovese basil and the tomato herb. Bush or Greek basil has smaller leaves; purple basil isn't as flavorful.

Bok choy: *Bok choy* is a Chinese cabbage that the Chinese refer to as *"white vegetable."* It is sold fresh in supermarkets and Chinese markets. Its tall white stems and dark green leaves impart a delicate flavor and texture to stir-fry dishes and soups.

Callaloo: *Callaloo* is the name of a tropical stew made from crabmeat and Caribbean greens that are known as *"callaloo."* The greens are available canned, very rarely fresh. Spinach is a good substitute.

Capers, vinegar-packed: Capers are the small, round, green unopened flowers of the *Capparis spinosa* bush. They are grown in Spain, France and Africa, and pickled and packed in vinegar, brine or salt.

Caraway seed: Caraway seeds derive from the caraway plant, a member of the parsley family. The seeds may have been man's first herb, used in Mesolithic times 5,000 years ago. Caraway flavors rye bread, cheese and Aquavit.

Cardamom seeds: The cardamom plant is related to ginger. Called the Queen's Spice and priced to fit its name, cardamom has an illustrious reputation: Saudi Arabians consider it an aphrodisiac; other Middle Easterners brew it with coffee, sugar and cloves as a welcome to visitors; ancient Greeks and Romans added it to perfumes; the Finnish bake it into breads for spring celebrations; and many people the world over chew the seeds as a stomach settler and breath freshener. Used with dishes both sweet and savory, cardamom is found in the cuisines of East India, Scandinavia, the Middle East and Central Africa.

Celery seed: The dried seeds of the wild celery plant known as *smallage,* celery seeds were used by ancient Greeks and Romans and are imported today from India and China. Whole and ground seeds flavor foods alone, and ground seeds are mixed with table salt to make celery salt.

Chili powder: Chili powder is a blend of dried ground chile pepper, cumin, garlic, sometimes paprika, red pepper, cayenne, oregano, salt, cloves, allspice, powdered onion and/or marjoram. This combination was first marketed a century ago in the American Southwest to flavor Tex-Mex foods, specifically for the stew-like dish called chili.

Chili sauce: A fiery sauce used in Chinese cuisine, chili sauce is made of red chile peppers flavored with garlic, lemon and apricot.

Chorizo sausage: Spain's most popular sausage, chorizo is deep red in color and made from pork, fat, paprika, garlic and salt, and usually ground coriander, red pepper, and cumin. Dried *chorizo* is eaten like cold cuts, while the fresh variety is cooked alone or with other foods.

Cilantro (fresh coriander, Chinese parsley): Cilantro is a sharply flavored cousin of parsley commonly used in the cuisines of China, Mexico, India and the Middle East. Originally from the Middle East some 3,000 years ago, cilantro has been said to make humans lustful, even immortal. Both its leaves and seeds are used for flavoring.

Cinnamon: Cinnamon is the dried bark of an evergreen tree. The Chinese knew of it nearly 5,000 years ago. Ground cinnamon is used widely in baking, and, in India, for cooking.

Cloves: Cloves are the unripened flowers of the clove tree, native to the Moluccas Islands in Indonesia. Cloves are available sun-dried whole or ground and are used in cooking and baking.

Coconut cream: The cream derived from coconut milk, coconut cream is used in the cuisines of Asia and Latin America. Coconut cream can be made at home by steeping coconut meat in boiling water. Squeeze out the extract and let the milk stand until the cream rises to the top. Coconut cream is also available canned.

Cognac: Cognac is a French brandy made from white wine in the areas of Charente and Charente-Maritime.

Conchigliette: *Conchigliette* are pasta in the shapes of little shells, which are frequently added to soups and broths.

Coriander seeds: Coriander seeds are the fruit of a member of the parsley family, whose leaves are also called Chinese parsley and cilantro. The seeds are sweeter than the leaves and are used in curries, pickling spices, sausages (including hot dogs) and baked goods. Cooks in Southern Asia, the Middle East, Europe and Morocco all use the seeds.

Creole mustard: A pungent pale-brown mustard made from spicy brown mustard seeds.

Cumin seeds: Cumin comes from a member of the parsley family. Its flavorful seeds, native to Egypt, have been used as flavoring since biblical times. Cumin seeds have been associated with happy marriages and stinginess. Most frequently used in Latin American and Indian cooking, cumin seeds are available whole and ground.

Dillweed: The leaves of the dill plant, whose seeds (dill seed) are also used whole and crushed in cooking, dill is native to southern Russia and the Mediterranean and is used extensively in northern Europe. Dill was believed to work as a charm against witches, and the "evil eye" could be warded off by carrying a bag of dried dill over the heart. Ancient Greek and Roman war heroes wore garlands of dill on their return march home. Fragrant wreaths of the dried yellow flowers hung in Roman banquet halls.

Ditalini: *Ditalini* is a tiny, tubular pasta, the name of which means "little thimbles."

Fennel: Fennel is a licorice-flavored member of the parsley family. The feathery, sweet variety of leaves are added to salads in France. Fresh Florence fennel root has the texture of celery and is used raw or is braised. Dried fennel seeds are used to flavor sweet and savory dishes. Chewing the seeds was once said to curb appetites.

Garbanzos: Also known as chickpeas and, in Italy, *ceci,* garbanzos are round yellowish peas used as beans in cooking throughout the world. North Africans and Middle Easterners cultivated them around 5000 B.C. Garbanzos are available dried and ready-to-use in cans.

Ginger: The irregularly shaped creeping rhizomes of a tropical plant, these knobby roots are dried and ground into powder and used to spice baked goods; or are used fresh in cooking and baking. Crystallized ginger is often eaten as candy.

Grits (quick-cooking): When whole dried hominy is ground, the particles are called "grits." Grits are sold in coarse, medium or fine grinds, which are interchangeable in recipes. The quick-cooking variety is prepared by lightly steaming and compressing the grits. Grits are integral to Southern cooking, especially as a breakfast staple.

Guacamole, prepared: Guacamole is a Mexican dip or sauce made from avocados mashed with onion, hot peppers (usually *serrano*), cilantro, salt and tomato. The word comes from the Nahuatl language, with *ahuacatl,* meaning avocado, and *molli,* meaning mixture.

Hearts-of-palm: The tasty centers of a variety of palm tree (the cabbage palmetto) native to Florida, these thin-stalked ivory, silky vegetables have a flavor akin to that of artichokes. Usually sold in cans.

Hominy: Hominy, a native American food introduced by the American Indians to the early colonists, consists of whole kernels of dried corn that have been treated and soaked to remove the germs and hulls. White or golden hominy is sold in cans.

Jalapeño pepper: Jalapeños are fiery peppers frequently used in Mexican cooking. They are about 2 inches long, 1 inch in diameter, cylindrical and green, and measure 5 on the heat scale. Fresh jalapeños are sold green but quickly turn red. Jalapeños canned in water can be substituted; pickled varieties are also available. Dried and smoked jalapeños are called by their ancient name *chipotle.*

Kefalotíri cheese: A hard sheep's milk cheese from Greece, *kefalotíri* is pale yellow in color with a strong, salty flavor.

Kohlrabi: Kohlrabi is a light green or purplish round root vegetable, a member of the cabbage family that looks like a turnip. Fresh kohlrabi has a crisp texture with a mild broccoli-like taste. The bulb, if young — smaller than a lime — and very tender, can be eaten raw, or it can be peeled and cooked.

Kosher salt: Kosher salt is used in cooking like table salt, but has larger, coarser granules. Kosher salt has no additives and is easy to handle because it doesn't stick to the hand as table salt does. The flavor of kosher salt is less intense than that of table salt. I find it has a cleaner taste.

Lasagna noodles: Lasagna noodles are thick, wide flat pieces of pasta with curly or straight edges. They are generally boiled first, then used in baked dishes.

Lavender flowers, dried French: Lavender is a fragrant herb often used for its scented oil. Native to the Mediterranean, it was thought of as an aphrodisiac in the Middle Ages.

The French variety enhances jellies, vinegars, salads and other foods. When purchasing for cooking, make sure to buy dried French lavender flowers that are edible — organic — completely pesticide-free, *not* the type meant for potpourri or room scent.

Lingonberry preserves: From the wild lingonberry these preserves have a tart slight pine-like flavor. Lingonberries are the fruit of the mountain cranberry and grow wild in Scandinavia, Russia, Canada and Maine.

Mace: Mace is the scarlet lace-like coating of the nutmeg kernel. This aril turns red-orange or orange-yellow by the time the mace blades reach the marketplace and is usually sold ground. Mace was discovered in the Moluccas Islands in Indonesia in 600 A.D. and brought to Europe during Mohammed's time. Its mild, sweet, warm flavor enhances many foods.

Malt vinegar: Vinegar is an acidic liquid made from fermented grains or fruits. Malt vinegar, derived from malted barley, is amber colored, with a slight bitter quality. Used on English fish and chips and for pickling.

Manicotti: *Manicotti* is a pasta noodle. The name means "small muff" because, in Italy, it refers to large flat squares of fresh pasta rolled around a stuffing. In the United States, *manicotti* is a commercial form of pasta that has come to refer to a large, ridged tube with the ends cut on a diagonal. Most often stuffed with ricotta cheese and topped with tomato sauce and mozzarella.

Marjoram: Marjoram, like its similar-tasting cousin oregano, is a member of the mint family. It is native to Southwest Asia and North Africa and was a symbol of romantic love to ancient Greeks.

Marsala: Marsala is a sweet dessert wine made near the Italian town of Marsala. Invented in the 18th century, it is made with several grapes grown in sandy to pale chalky soil. Marsala Corrente has been aged at least six months; Marsala Superiore three years and Marsala Virgine five years. Marsala all'uovo is blended with egg yolk. The wine is also available in almond, coffee, chocolate and fruit flavors.

Mint: Mint flavor comes from the leaves of spearmint, peppermint and other mint plants. It was named after a Greek nymph who was turned into a plant and then was made sweet-smelling by her lover Pluto. Mint was once a symbol for hospitality. The leaves are sold dried whole and as flakes, usually of spearmint. Mint's clean, fresh taste is most often used in sweets, salads, vegetables and lamb dishes.

Nutmeg: Nutmeg is the kernel of the seed of a pale fruit that resembles an apricot. Mace is the scarlet lacy growth known as the aril, which surrounds the seed. Almost a third of the world's nutmeg produced today is grown in Grenada in the West Indies. Nutmeg can be purchased whole (grate it with a metal nutmeg grater) or ground. It is always used ground in cooking and baking and adds a sweet, warm flavor.

Okra: Okra is a small firm green vegetable, the length of a green bean but thicker, with a tapered end. A member of the Hibiscus family, okra is prevalent in the cuisine of the South. Okra turns gelatinous when cooked and will thicken soups and stews. To use, cut off stems and scrape off surface fuzz with a small, sharp knife. Frozen okra makes an excellent substitute for fresh.

Olives, calabrese: Calabrese olives are cracked Italian olives with a bronze-green hue.

Olives, Greek Kalamata: Greek Kalamatas are oblong, purple-black, vinegar-cured olives with pointy ends. Their strong, salty flavor is further encouraged when processors slit one side to allow the brine to penetrate.

Olives, Nyons: Nyons olives are mildly bitter-tasting French olives with a reddish-brown color.

Olives, picholine: Picholine olives are firm, green olives from France.

Olives, Spanish green, pimiento-stuffed: The fruit of a tree, green olives from Spain are hand-picked unripe, then treated in sodium hydroxide and preserved in brine or dry salt. The Spanish think of olives as lucky. Spanish green olives are available with a variety of stuffings, including pimientos, almonds and anchovies.

Oregano: Oregano is a mild member of the mint family whose leaves are used for flavoring savory dishes. Oregano means "joy of the mountain."

Oregano (Mexican): Mexican oregano is not really oregano at all but a related herb that is used in Mexican dishes, with a taste similar to but stronger than that of oregano. Compared to Mediterranean oregano, Mexican oregano is much stronger and more robustly flavored. Its leaves are a somewhat darker shade of green.

Oregano (Greek): Greek oregano is a purer version of oregano sold here, with a slightly different, sweeter, milder flavor than the Italian type.

Oyster sauce: Oyster sauce, a dark brown flavoring used in Chinese cooking, is made from oysters, soy sauce and brine. The product enhances seafood, poultry and meat dishes and is good for dipping; it thickens sauces. Available bottled.

Paprika: Brought to Hungary from the Western hemisphere in the 16th century, paprika is the ground red powder of a mild red pepper used extensively in Hungarian cooking. Authentic Hungarian paprika is available in six strengths varying in color and hotness from very mild to hot.

Parmesan cheese: Parmesan is a hard, sharp grating cheese that has been aged at least one year. The authentic variety, called Parmigiano-Reggiano, is from Parma, Italy. Many domestic and imported substitutes are available.

Parsley, fresh: Parsley is a mild herb and its vitamin-packed leaves are often used to enhance other flavors in Western cooking. Originally from the Mediterranean, parsley has been credited with making people serene and hungry. Flat-leaf Italian parsley is best for cooking, but the popular curly-leaf variety is a fine substitute. I do not recommend using dried parsley.

Peppercorns: Peppercorns are berries from a climbing vine native to India and grown today in Brazil, Indonesia and Malaysia. Popular black peppercorns — often purchased ground — are sun-dried and the strongest variety; white peppercorns are more mature and milder in flavor; green peppercorns, picked before ripening, then dried or pickled, are fruitier. Pink peppercorns sold in the U.S. are not related to the others; these slightly sweet berries can be poisonous if not originating from Reunion, an island off of Madagascar.

Pigeon peas: Pigeon peas, a type of field pea, are small peas, native to Africa and common in the cuisines of the Caribbean, Africa and India. They can be purchased fresh and eaten raw but are more commonly allowed to mature and dry, after which they turn yellow or grayish in color.

Pita bread, plain (white), whole wheat: Pita bread is a flat, round bread from the Middle East. It is often stuffed like a pocket with fillings. Available in white and whole-wheat varieties, sometimes with sesame seeds.

Plantain: Plantains are large, banana-like fruits that must be cooked before eating. Popular in Caribbean cuisine, plantains can be cooked when the skin is still green, or when it turns nearly black, indicating ripeness. To remove the skin, cut it away or soak slices of plantains in lightly salted water for 30 minutes, then push the flesh through.

Polenta: *Polenta* is the Italian word for a type of cornmeal that is a staple starch in Northern Italy. It is sold in Italian markets in fine and coarse grinds; in America, it is also available labeled "quick-cooking." The primary dish made with polenta is a type of mush that goes by the same name.

Poppy seed: Tiny poppy seeds with their nut-like flavor range in color from dark blue-gray to white. They are the mature seed of the *poppy* flower. The plant, which has been used for at least 5,000 years, also produces opium. However, poppy seeds cannot form until after the plant has matured to the point where it has lost all of its opium potential. Used mainly on breads or crushed for pastry fillings, most poppy seeds consumed are black, with the similar-tasting white ones preferred in East India.

Prawns: Prawns are small, lobster-like crustaceans that resemble large shrimp in appearance and taste.

Prosciutto: *Prosciutto* is a dark red, flavorful ham from the Parma area of Italy. A pig's hind thigh that has been aged, cured, salted and covered with a mix of pork fat, salt and flour, *prosciutto* is generally sliced paper-thin and served alone or with melon or fresh figs as an appetizer.

Red (cayenne) pepper: Red and cayenne pepper are similar, often interchanged, dried hot peppers originally from Asia, available ground or crushed. Columbus discovered them in the Caribbean. Also known as "red bird pepper," "goat's pepper," "cockspur pepper" and "Africa pepper," this fiery hot spice is a relative of paprika.

Red pepper flakes (crushed red pepper): Red pepper flakes are made of crushed red pepper, or *capsicum*. "Cayenne," "Thai" and "Serrano" are the red pepper varieties most commonly used.

Refried beans, prepared: Refried beans of Mexican-American origin usually made from pinto beans, that have been cooked, mashed and fried with lard.

Rice wine: Frequently used in Chinese cooking, this wine is made from glutinous rice that has been fermented with yeast. The best of these yellowish-in-color wines is from Shaosing. If necessary, substitute dry Sherry.

Rosemary: Rosemary, a member of the mint family, grows on an evergreen shrub. It has been credited with encouraging fidelity and warding off evil. Its fragrant smell has made it popular over the years as incense and as a bath scent. Dried, the leaves are pine-needle shaped.

Rotini: A pasta, the name of which translates to "tiny wheels."

Saffron: Saffron is the dried thread of a crocus that is grown primarily in Spain. It has been cultivated since ancient times; Homer referred to a "saffron-robed" morning and Romans used it to improve the smell of homes and public spaces. Saffron threads add flavor and a yellowish color to Paella, Bouillabaisse and other dishes. The most expensive spice in the world, saffron is best purchased in threads, not ground.

Sage: Sage is a member of the mint family that comes from an evergreen shrub. Native to the Northern Mediterranean, sage was once credited with providing one with a long memory, even immortality. The leaves are available dried whole, dried crushed, ground and rubbed.

Sauerkraut: Made from fermented cabbage, sauerkraut is a German staple today, but is said to have originated in China. In Germany, sauerkraut is typically eaten out of the jar; mixed raw with pineapple or apples; cooked, flavored with caraway seeds or juniper berries or served with smoked meats.

Sausage, German bratwürst: *Bratwürst* refers to a plump fresh German pork or occasionally part veal sausage, sold either fresh or precooked. *Bratwürst* may be fine or coarse in texture and is often flavored with mace or nutmeg, coriander or caraway, sage and lemon juice. *Bratwürst* is whitish in color; a red variety is made without milk. Smoked *Bratwürst,* larger than the fresh variety, can be steamed and is served cold or hot.

Sausage, fresh Hungarian: There are many varieties of Hungarian sausage: fresh or dried, mild or hot, single-smoked, double-smoked, and the list goes on.

Sausage, fresh Italian hot: Pork sausages flavored with red pepper, garlic, fennel seeds and wine, these also come in a sweet variety — made without the red pepper, just a bit of freshly ground black pepper. Often crumbled and used in sauces, these sausages must be cooked before eating.

Savory: Savory is an herb of the mint family. "Summer savory" is most often used in cooking, though slightly stronger, sharper "winter savory" is sometimes substituted. Their names have no relation to the time of year they are grown. Both are from the Mediterranean area. Long ago, winter savory was said to decrease sex drive, summer savory to increase it. Dried savory leaves are available whole and ground.

Sesame oil, Chinese: Made from toasted white sesame seeds, this fragrant oil adds strong flavor to the foods of northern China, among others. Buy the amber-colored oil available in specialty stores, not the paler version, which is cold pressed, found in supermarkets.

Soy sauce, Chinese: The Chinese variety is made from steamed, kneaded soybeans and wheat, yeast and salt. Light soy sauce is pale and thin and adds flavor to clear soups; dark soy sauce, black and heavy and made with the addition of caramel, adds flavor and color to meat, seafood and vegetables; the heaviest is black soy, made thick with molasses, which adds color to beef and pork dishes. Black soy and heavy soy can be used interchangeably.

Spaghetti: Spaghetti is a long, thin, round strand of Italian pasta, the name of which means "length of cord or string."

Straw mushrooms, Chinese: Subtly flavored but aromatic, these mushrooms are yellowish in color with pointy caps. Also called "grass mushrooms," they are available peeled (and have a finer texture) and unpeeled, where the cap completely surrounds the stem.

Swedish mustard: Prepared mustards — from the yellow kind we slather on hot dogs to the sharper French Dijon styles — are all made from mustard seeds, vinegar or wine and flavorings. The Swedish varieties are smooth and relatively sweet.

Thyme: Fragrant thyme leaves are mild members of the mint family, commonly mixed with other herbs in Mediterranean cooking. Thyme signified elegance to the ancient Greeks and chivalry in the Middle Ages.

Tofu (bean curd), Chinese: *Tofu* is the spongy white result of soybeans that have been soaked, puréed, strained and cooked. Vinegar, salt or other solidifiers help give *tofu* its custard-like texture. *Tofu,* used as a protein substitute in Oriental cooking, is such a good source of nutrients that the Chinese often refer to it as "meat without bones." Tofu is sold in blocks — soft, medium and firm textures — and should be stored in fresh water. Choose the firm variety for Chinese dishes. NOTE: There are other kinds of bean curd products such as dried, fermented, fried and pressed. However, these are not interchangeable with fresh *tofu* in recipes.

Tomatillos: Tomatillos, or Mexican green tomatoes, are used as a base for Mexico's flavorful *salsa verde,* or green sauce. They look like small, firm green tomatoes and have split parchment-like light brown husks and yellow-green skins with a slightly tart apple-like flavor. They can be eaten raw or cooked and are available fresh or canned.

Tortillas, corn: The corn *tortilla* is the "bread" of central and southern Mexico. It is a thin cake made of corn flour that is quickly baked on a *comal* (griddle). Available in packages in the refrigeration sections of most supermarkets.

Tortillas, white flour: In northern Mexico, the traditional "bread" is the flour *tortilla,* made of flour, salt, lard and warm water. Unlike corn

tortillas, they are rolled with a rolling pin rather than being patted, and are cooked quickly on a griddle.
Turmeric: Bright yellow-orange turmeric is a spice used in Southern Asian cuisine. A member of the ginger family, the musky-flavored rhizome is grown mostly in India, dried in the sun for several weeks and ground by spice manufacturers before selling. Indonesians serve turmeric-colored rice during weddings, Indian women use turmeric as a cosmetic and Pacific Islanders wear it as protection from evil spirits.
Water chestnuts: The tuber of a "sedge," an aquatic plant grown in East Asian marshes, water chestnuts have a slightly sweet taste and crisp texture and are available in cans, whole or sliced.

Source List

In case your supermarket or grocer is out of an ingredient that you might need, I have provided this list of mostly mail-order sources. You may also want to explore other international foods not called for in this book.

ETHNIC FOOD SHOPS

CARIBBEAN

Casa Lucas Market
2934 24th Street
San Francisco, CA 94110
415-826-4334
Carries ingredients used in Caribbean cooking, such as canned calalloo leaves, pigeon peas and hearts-of-palm.

CREOLE

Community Kitchens
P.O. Box 2311
Baton Rouge, LA 70821-2311
504-381-3900
800-535-9901
Catalog available
Louisiana's best ingredients for indigenous gumbos, jambalayas, preserves, Creole mustard and more.

Luzianna Blue Plate Foods
Box 60296
New Orleans, LA 70160
800-692-7895
Catalog available
Cajun and Creole prepared meals and a strong selection of local coffees, including some with chicory.

Poche's Meat Market & Restaurant
Route 2, Box 415
Breaux Bridge, LA 70517
318-332-2108
Catalog available
Tasso (a Louisiana-style seasoned, dried, heavily smoked pork) most often used as a seasoning ingredient in vegetables and soups), *andouille* sausage and more.

Vieux Carre Foods, Inc.
P.O. Box 50277
New Orleans, LA 70150
504-822-6065
Catalog available
Such standards of New Orleans as shrimp and crab boil, *remoulade* sauce and pralines.

CHINESE

Chinese American Trading Co.
91 Mulberry Street
New York, NY 10013
212-267-5224
A wealth of bottled, canned and dried Chinese foods.

Kam Man Food Products
200 Canal Street
New York, NY 10013
212-571-0171
Extensive assortment of Chinese ingredients, including dried seafood, noodles and teas.

Oriental Food Market and Cooking School
2801 West Howard Street
Chicago, IL 60645
312-274-2826

Catalog available
From preserved jellyfish to boiled gingko nuts, this source will mail every Oriental dried vegetable, herb, spice, tea, seasoning or serviceware you need.

Spice Merchant
P.O. Box 524
Jackson Hole, WY 83001
307-733-7811
800-551-5999
Catalog available
Oriental condiments, spices, cookbooks and equipment from China, Japan, Indonesia and Thailand. The catalog is an education in and of itself.

PROVENCE

Pierre Deux
870 Madison Avenue
New York, NY 10021
212-570-9343
800-874-3773
Catalog available
This chain of French furniture shops now has a line of foods from Provence. Stores are in Atlanta; Boston; Carmel, Newport Beach, Beverly Hills and San Francisco, CA; Philadelphia; Houston; New York; Palm Beach; Washington, D.C.; Winnetka, IL; and Toronto. Honeys, coffees, chocolates, oils, vinegars, mustards and spices are available.

GERMANY

Schaller & Weber
1654 Second Avenue
New York, NY 10028
(212) 879-3047
Catalog available
German specialty shop of sausages, hams and bacons. Stocks fresh and smoked *bratwürst* and Hungarian paprika.

GREEK

The Greek Store
612 Boulevard
Kenilworth, NJ 07033
908-272-2550
Greek cheeses, olives, oils, herbs and spices.

International Grocery Store and Meat Market
529 Ninth Avenue
New York, NY 10018
212-279-5514
International specialty shop loaded with grains, spices and more from Greece, the Middle East, India, the Caribbean and West Africa. Carries savory, Greek oregano and *kefalotíri* cheese.

Ninth Avenue International Foods
543 Ninth Avenue
New York, NY 10018
212-279-1000
Greek superstore specializing in prepared meals, olives, dried fruits, nuts and coffees.

HUNGARIAN

Hungarian Rigo Bakery
318 East 78th Street
New York, NY 10021
212-988-0052
A feast for sweet lovers. Specialties include babka, pecan cookies and poppy-seed strudel.

Paprikas Weiss
1572 Second Avenue
New York, NY 10028
212-288-6117
FAX 212-734-5120
Catalog available
Emporium of Hungarian and international foods, including sweet, half-sweet and hot paprika, lavender flowers, nine Hungarian sausages, dried fruits and much more.

Tibor Meat Products
1508 Second Avenue
New York, NY 10021
(212) 744-8292
Catalog available
Tiny specialty store but stocked to the brim with many types of homemade sausages and salamis. Carries *bratwürst*, fresh Hungarian sausage, Hungarian bacon and Hungarian paprika.

INDIA

Foods of India Sinha Trading Co.
121 Lexington Avenue
New York, NY 10016
(212) 683-4419
Catalog available
Curry spices, pickles and more.

House of Spices
76-17 Broadway
Jackson Heights, NY 11373
718-476-1577
Catalog available
Indian bazaar with full stock of beans, flours, syrups, teas and spices.

Kalustyan's
123 Lexington Avenue
New York, NY 10016

212-685-3451
Indian and Middle Eastern specialties such as chutneys, curry pastes, cardamom seeds and hard-to-find items like roasted green peas.

ITALY

E. Alleva
188 Grand Street
New York, NY 10013
212-226-7990
Wide selection of Italian cheeses, including homemade fresh ricotta and mozzarella.

Fretta Brothers
117 Mott Street
New York, NY 10013
212-226-0232
A remarkable selection of Italian sausages.

Morisi's Pasta
647 Fifth Avenue
Brooklyn, NY 11215
718-499-0146
Catalog available
More than 200 homemade pastas, from old favorites to the extremely inventive — such as black fig and goat-cheese walnut.

Todaro Brothers
555 Second Avenue
New York, NY 10016
212-532-0633
Italian emporium of olives, salamis, *soppressatas,* meats and breads.

MEXICO

Casa America
102-08 Roosevelt Avenue
Corona, NY 11368
718-426-5920
A Mexican *bodega* of south-of-the-border produce and dried goods.

El Galindo Inc.
1601 East Sixth Street
Austin, TX 78702
800-447-8905
Catalog available
Manufacturer of Mexican ingredients like corn and flour *tortillas,* 13 varieties of

tortilla chips and four salsas.

SCANDINAVIA

Old Denmark
133 East 65 Street
New York, NY 10021
212-744-2533
Scandinavian delights, such as herring, mackerel, pickles and cheeses, plus lingonberry preserves and Swedish mustard.

SPAIN

Espanol Specialties
41-01 Broadway
Queens, NY 11103
718-932-9335
Large selection of Spanish canned goods, sweets, cheeses and other miscellany.

BEANS

The Bean Bag Bulk Foods
818 Jefferson Street
Oakland, CA 94607
510-839-8988
Catalog available
More than 85 beans and associated seasonings. Seasoned mixes for chilis, soups and more.

BEVERAGES

Gillies Coffee Company
160 Bleecker Street
New York, NY 10012
212-614-0900
Catalog available
Coffees and teas for every taste from every nation.

Madame Chung's Finest Teas
P.O. Box 597871
Chicago, IL 60659
312-743-5545
Catalog available
Special teas from China such as Lichee Black are available, along with information and serving pieces.

CHEESE

Cheese of All Nations
153 Chambers Street
New York, NY 10007

212-732-0752
Catalog available
Over 1,000 international cheeses available by mail order.

Ideal Cheese Shop
1205 Second Avenue
New York, NY 10021
212-688-7579
800-382-0109
Catalog available
An interesting cheese shop stocked with 150 international varieties, with extensive selections from Italy, Switzerland, Holland, Spain and France.

HERBS AND SPICES

Adrianna's Bazaar
2152 Broadway
New York, NY 10023
212-877-5757
More than 200 hard-to-find herbs and spices, as well as ingredients and condiments from Thailand, Vietnam, Japan, India, Italy, the Southwest, etc. Soy sauces galore.

American Spice Trade Association, Inc.
580 Sylvan Avenue
Englewood Cliffs, NJ 07632
201-568-2163
Write for catalog of informative publications.

Aphrodisia Products
282 Bleecker Street
New York, NY 10014
212-989-6440
800 herbs and spices, including 300 for cooking, edible (organic and pesticide-free) French lavender flowers (for cooking), dried mushrooms and 7 kinds of peppercorns.

Fox Hill Farm
440 West Michigan Avenue
Box 9
Parma, MI 49269-0009
Catalog available
Fresh and dried herbs by mail or phone. Herb-seasoned foods, too.

The Kobos Company

5620 S.W. Kelly Avenue
Portland, OR 97201
503-222-5226
Catalog available
Chain of specialty stores
stocked with coffees, teas,
herbs and spices. Stocks
French lavender,
Hungarian paprika,
summer savory, Spanish
saffron.

Pete's Spice

174 First Avenue
New York, NY 10009
212-254-8773
Catalog available
An abundance of
macrobiotic products and
legumes, grains, spices,
coffees and nuts.

San Francisco Herb Co.

250 14th Street
San Francisco, CA 94103
415-861-7174
U.S.: 800-227-4530
Calif: 800-622-0768
Catalog available
Extensive selection of
herbs, spices, botanicals and
more. Stocks cut Greek
oregano; cut, whole and
ground Mexican oregano;
savory; and imported
paprika.

S.E. Rykoff & Company

P.O. Box 21467
Market Street Station
Los Angeles, CA 90021
800-421-9873 (orders)
213-624-6094 (information)
Spices, herbs and blends
by the dozen. Exotic oils
and vinegar, too.

The Spice House

P.O. Box 1633
Milwaukee, WI 53201
414-768-8799
Catalog available
More than 400 common
and obscure herbs and
spices. Best known for
high-quality cinnamon,
black pepper and vanilla.

HOT SAUCE

Hot Stuff

227 Sullivan Street
New York, NY 10012
212-254-6120
Catalog available
More than 80 hot sauces, plus
spicy snacks, dried chiles, salsas, hot mustards, barbecue
sauces and spices.

MEATS AND SAUSAGES

Aidells Sausage Company

1575 Minnesota Street
San Francisco, CA 94107
415-285-6660
Catalog available
Sausages for the new genera-
tion. Try Creole hot,
whiskey-fennel or chicken-
apple for starters.

Amana Meat Shop and Smokehouse

One Smokehouse Lane
Amana, LA 52203
319-622-3113
800-373-MEAT
Catalog available
Smoked German specialties
from pork chops to hickory-
smoked ham.

Cavanaugh Lakeview Farms, Ltd.

P.O. Box 580
Chelsea, MI 48118-0580
313-475-9391
800-475-9391
FAX 313-475-1133
Catalog available
Venison, honey-cured
smoked turkey, buffalo burgers and more. Ready-to-heat
entrees and cheeses, too.

Organic Beef, Inc.

P.O. Box 642
Mena, AR 71953
501-387-7111
800-3634-3058
Catalog available
The name says it: beef
from cattle raised with caution and care. Many cuts and
preservative-free breakfast
sausage.

Salumeria Biellese

378 Eighth Avenue
New York, NY 10001
212-736-7376
Manufacturer of sausages
from many nations,
especially Italy.

OILS AND VINEGARS

The Chef's Pantry

P.O. Box 3
Post Mills, VT 05058
802-333-4141
800-666-9940
Catalog available
Fine oils and vinegars — from
Provence, Italy and Spain.

Santa Barbara Olive Company

1661 Mission Drive
Solvang, CA 93463-2631
800-624-4896
800-521-0475
Catalog available
Other worldly oils and vinegars like grapeseed oil and
mango vinegar. Uncountable
variety of olives, too.

PICKLES

Essex Street Pickles

35 Essex Street
New York, NY 10002
212-254-4477
800-252-GUSS
Catalog available
Pickle heaven — chock full of
delicious sour vegetables.

SPECIALTY FOOD STORES

Balducci's

424 Avenue of the Americas
New York, NY 10011
212-673-2600
800-822-1444
Catalog available
Gourmet specialty store,
stocking packaged gourmet
items; sausages like *chorizo,*
cured meats, cheeses and
ready-to-cook dinners.

Dean & Deluca

560 Broadway
New York, NY 10012
212-431-1691
800-221-7714

Catalog available
Epicurean specialty shop fea-
turing dried pastas, many
grains, dried beans, oils and
vinegars and much more.

Food of All Nations

2121 Ivy Road
Charlottesville, VA 22903
804-296-6131
Catalog available
Foods, gift baskets and wines
from around the world. Try
Dresden *stollen,* wild huckle-
berry mountain candies or
gift baskets from the country
of your choice.

G.B. Ratto & Company

821 Washington Street
Oakland, CA 94607
800-325-3483
800-228-3515 (in
California)
FAX 415-836-2250
Catalog available
International grocery store,
selling everything from garlic
jelly to Basmati rice to instant
lasagna noodles that don't
need to be boiled before baking and an unusual variety of
oils and vinegars.

Haig's Delicacies

642 Clement Street
San Francisco, CA 94118
415-752-6283
Catalog available
Packaged foods from India,
Southeast Asia, Europe, the
Middle East and elsewhere.

Natura

615 Ninth Avenue
New York, NY 10036
212-397-4700
Multinational emporium
stocking everything Mediterranean and Middle Eastern
from Turkish dried okra to
Thai jasmine rice.

Zabar's

2245 Broadway
New York, NY 10024
212-787-2000
Catalog available
Megastore with a vast array

of smoked fishes, cheeses, prepared dishes, coffees, breads, oils, vinegars, pastas and cooking equipment.

SOUTHWESTERN:

Casados Farms
Box 1269
San Juan Pueblo, NM 87566
Catalog available
Cornucopia of chiles, including *pequin, molido* and *caribe.* Other Southwestern ingredients, too, such as spices, taco sauce and blue cornmeal.

The Chili Shop
109 East Water Street
Santa Fe, NM 87501
505-983-6080
Catalog available
Chile pepper heaven, with New Mexico red chiles, several Mexican chiles and a wealth of service items with pepper themes. Salsas, *moles* and other foods of the Southwest.

The El Paso Chili Company
909 Texas Street
El Paso, TX 79901
915-544-3434
Catalog available
Southwestern specialty shop that features six different salsas, chili spices, chips and condiments.

Los Chileros De Nuevo Mexico
P.O. Box 6215
Santa Fe, NM 87502
505-471-6967
Catalog available
Chiles, house-ground spices and one of the country's largest selections of blue and white corn products.

Pesos Valley Spice Company
1450 Heggen Street
Hudson, WI 54016
715-386-8832
FAX 715-386-6731
Catalog available
Fiesta of Southwestern fare, including *sopaipilla,* corn husks, spices, herbs and ground chiles.

Santa Cruz Chili and Spice Company
P.O. Box 177
Tumacacori, AZ 85640
602-398-2591
Catalog available
Vast selection of chiles and spices, salsas, jellies and mustards.

KITCHEN EQUIPMENT

Bridge Kitchenware
214 East 52 Street
att.: Catalog Sales
New York, NY 10022
212-688-4220
Catalog available
1,800 best-sellers from this store's 30,000 hard-to-find cookware items for home and professional kitchens. Most imported from Europe.

J.B. Prince Company
29 West 38th Street
New York, NY 10018
212-302-8611
Catalog available
Hard-to-find kitchenware

from Germany, Italy, France, Japan and other nations. Everything from knives to ice-carving tools.

Pottery Barn
Mail-Order Department
P.O Box 7044
San Francisco, CA 94120-7044
415-421-3400
Catalog available
Ever-changing selection of earthenware cookware, serving ware and glassware.

Williams-Sonoma
Mail-Order Department
P.O. Box 7456
San Francisco, CA 94120-7456
415-421-4242
Catalog available
Plethora of cookery items: pots and pans, baking equipment, knives, clay cookers, fondue pots and casseroles.

The Kitchen Bookshelf: A Select Bibliography

A partial bibliography of the many books researched that I recommend for further reading.

Autumn, Violeta. *Flavors of Northern Italy.* Berkeley, California: 101 Productions, 1989.

Casas, Penelope. *The Food & Wines of Spain.* New York: Alfred A. Knopf, Inc., 1982.

Escudier, Jean Noël, and Peta J. Fuller. *The Wonderful Food of Provence.* Boston: Houghton Mifflin Company, 1968.

Folse, John D. *The Evolution of Cajun & Creole Cuisine.* Donaldsonville, Louisiana: Chef John Folse and Company, Inc., 1991.

Grigson, Jane. *The World Atlas of Food.* New York: Simon & Schuster, 1974

Hazelton, Nika. *Classic Scandinavian Cooking.* New York: Charles Scribner's Sons, 1965.

Jaffrey, Madhur. *Madhur Jaffrey's Indian Cooking.* New York: Barron's Educational Series, Inc., 1983.

Kennedy, Diana. *The Cuisines of Mexico.* New York: Harper & Row Publishers, Inc., 1972.

Kowalchik, Claire, *et al. Rodale's Illustrated Encyclopedia of Herbs.* Emmaus, Pennsylvania: Rodale Press, Inc., 1987.

Lang, George. *The Cuisine of Hungary.* New York: Bonanza Books, distributed by Crown Publishers, Inc., 1971.

Middione, Carlo. *The Food of Southern Italy.* New York: William Morrow and Company, Inc., 1987.

Miller, Gloria Bley. *The Thousand Recipe Chinese Cookbook.* New York: G.P. Putnam's Sons, 1983.

Norman, Jill. *The Complete Book of Spices.* London:

Dorling Kindersley Limited, 1990.

Ortiz, Elizabeth Lambert. *The Complete Book of Caribbean Cooking.* New York: Ballantine Books, 1973.

Scharfenberg, Horst. *The Cuisines of Germany.* New York: Poseidon Press, a division of Simon & Schuster, Inc., 1989.

Skoura, Sophia. *The Greek Cook Book.* New York: Crown Publishers, Inc., 1967.

Williams, Richard L., ed. *Foods of The World.* (series) New York: Time-Life Books Inc., 1971.

Index

A

aïoli, bourride flavored
  with 79
apples, calves' liver with
  onions and 48
arroz con pollo 114
arroz verde.......................105
artichoke(s):
  omelette 70
  plantation-style seafood-
    stuffed 23
avocado:
  quesadillas with
    guacamole..................106
  sauce, salad or dip,
    Mexican 99

B

bacon:
  and egg sauce, spaghetti
    with 89
  sweet and sour cabbage
    with 33
  yellow pea soup with.....128
basil, Provençal vegetable
  bean soup with garlic
  and..................................72
bean(s):
  green, and tomato
    with Creole mustard
    dressing........................17
  lima, with ham................122
  minestrone.......................85
  red, and rice with ham,
    Louisiana's 18
  refried 109
  Spanish-style green........120
  vegetable soup with
    basil and garlic,
    Provençal......................72
beef:
  Black Forest hunter's
    stew 42
  with broccoli 168
  Hungarian goulash 34
  keftéthes 63
  krautwickel 46
  lasagne.............................90
  meat loaf wrapped in
    sour-cream pastry.......136
  orange 176

pastítsio.............................64
picadillo 102
rolls, Hungarian pork
  and onion-stuffed 35
sauerbraten 43
Southern dirty rice...........15
in spinach sauce,
  fragrant 143
Swedish meatballs..........126
and wine stew,
  Provençal......................75
beet-horseradish salad 29
Black Forest hunter's
  stew 42
bourride flavored with
  aïoli 79
bratwürst, Oktoberfest 45
briami 60
broccoli, beef with 168
burritos with chilorio 107

C

cabbage:
  rolls, German stuffed.......46
  sweet and sour, with
    bacon 33
cabbage, Chinese, with
  oyster sauce 179
callaloo, quick 160
calves' liver with apples
  and onions 48
caraway soup with
  noodles 31
Caribbean seasoning
  mix 154
cashews, chicken with
  shrimp and...................171
casserole, Greek
  vegetable 60
cauliflower:
  with dilled egg 134
  spiced and breaded..........31
cheese:
  kefalotíri, stuffed
    peppers with rice
    and..............................57
  manicotti, baked 87
  quesadillas
    with guacamole..........106
  zucchini with
    Parmesan 88

chicken:
  cacciatore with black
    and green olives............86
  enchiladas with mole 101
  gumbo 21
  lemon 173
  mulligatawny soup 151
  paprikás 28
  with rice 114
  with Romesco-style
    sauce............................123
  savory............................144
  with shrimp and
    cashews 171
  in spice gravy 147
  Swedish-style 129
  Tandoori-style 145
  with walnut sauce 65
chick-pea and sausage
  stew 116
chile sauce, Mexican...........110
chilorio, burritos with 107
Chinese seasoning mix 166
cold sesame noodles..........169
corn:
  baby, stir-fried snow
    peas with water
    chestnuts and..............178
  pudding, Creole 19
  soup, fresh, with
    pimientos 103
crab(meat):
  quick callaloo 160
  stuffed whole..................20
Creole seasoning mix..........14
crispy potato cakes 49
csipetke 38
cucumber:
  raita 141
  salad 128

D

dal, lentil 150
daube de boeuf
  provençale 75
dill(ed):
  egg, cauliflower with 134
  sauce, lamb with 135
  dip, Mexican avocado 99
  dumplings, pinched 38

E

egg(s):
  artichoke omelette 70
  and bacon sauce,
    spaghetti with...............89
  dilled, cauliflower
    with 134
  and lemon-based soup,
    Greek 55
  poached, garlic soup
    with 112
  Spanish-style colorful
    baked 117
  tortilla española..............115
eggplant:
  gingered 141
  mousse, Provençal 81
  Parma style 94
  ratatouille 69
  salad, Greek roasted 56
empanada de lomo 118
enchiladas, chicken, with
  mole 101

F

fish and shellfish:
  baked fish with tomato
    sauce............................61
  bourride flavored
    with aïoli 79
  Caribbean red snapper
    kebabs 163
  chicken with shrimp
    and cashews.................171
  gravlax...........................132
  lobster salad....................162
  plantation-style
    seafood-stuffed
    artichokes 23
  poached salmon steaks
    with mustard sauce 130
  prawns in red sauce..........91
  quick callaloo 160
  red snapper Veracruz.....100
  seafood paella 121
  shrimp Creole 14
  stuffed whole crab 20
fresh corn soup with
  pimientos.....................103
fried plantains 164
fried rice..........................177

G

garlic:
mayonnaise, Provençal fish stew with 79
Provençal vegetable bean soup with basil and.....................................72
sauce, Greek, lamb chops with 62
soup with poached eggs 112
German seasoning mix 40
gingered eggplant..............141
goulash, Hungarian 34
gravlax.................................132
Greek seasoning mix 54
green beans:
Spanish-style 120
and tomato with Creole mustard dressing....................17
grits, veal grillades with 26
guacamole.............................99
quesadillas with..............106
gumbo, chicken...................21
gypsies' sausage with peppers 36

H

ham:
lima beans with 122
Louisiana's red beans and rice with 18
hearts-of-palm salad 159
hominy, stewed okra with 16
horseradish-beet salad........29
hot and sour soup 174
huevos a la flamenca 117
Hungarian seasoning mix 28

I

Indian seasoning mix 140
Italian seasoning mix 84

J

jerked pork 158

K

kefalotíri cheese, stuffed peppers with rice and 57
keftéthes..............................63
kohlrabi, stuffed..................32
krautwickel..........................46

L

lamb:
chops with mint, Provençal shepherds'...................78
chops with skorthaliá 62
with dill sauce................135
keftéthes 63
korma..............................148
Swedish meatballs..........126
lasagne.................................90
lemon:
chicken............................173
and egg-based soup, Greek 55
lentil(s):
dal..................................150
stewed 44
lihamurekepiiras 136
lima beans with ham 122
liver, calves', with apples and onions 48
lobster salad.......................162
Louisiana's red beans and rice with ham..........18

M

macaroni:
gratin...............................77
with meat, baked.............64
minestrone.......................85
mancha manteles..............104
manicotti, baked cheese.....87
marhatekercs 35
Marsala, veal scaloppine with 95
meatballs:
Greek 63
Swedish..........................126
meat loaf wrapped in sour-cream pastry.......136
meats:
Black Forest hunter's stew 42
calves' liver with apples and onions 48
chick-pea and sausage stew 116
gypsies' sausage with peppers 36
Oktoberfest bratwürst 45
see also beef; lamb; pork; veal
melanzane alla parmigiana .94
melitzanosaláta....................56
Mexican seasoning mix.......98

minestrone..........................85
mint, Provençal shepherds' lamb chops with 78
mole 110
chicken enchiladas with 101
mulligatawny soup 151
mustard:
dressing, Creole, green beans and tomato with....................17
sauce, poached salmon steaks with 130

N

noodles:
caraway soup with 31
cold sesame.....................169
see also pasta

O

okra:
with onion sauce 142
stewed, with hominy 16
Oktoberfest bratwürst 45
olive(s):
black, pissaladière with....74
black and green, chicken cacciatore with 86
Greek summer salad 58
spread, Provençal.............71
omelettes:
artichoke..........................70
Spanish...........................115
onion(s):
calves' liver with apples and................................48
and pork-stuffed beef rolls, Hungarian............35
sauce, okra with 142
tart, Provençal 74
orange beef 176
oyster sauce, Chinese cabbage with 179

P

paella, seafood 121
papaya, baked...................157
papeton d'aubergines 81
paprika:
chicken, Hungarian 28
potatoes 30
pasta:
baked cheese manicotti....87
caraway soup with noodles 31

cold sesame noodles.......169
lasagne...............................90
macaroni gratin 77
minestrone.......................85
pastítsio............................64
spaghetti alla carbonara ...89
pastítsio................................64
pastry:
empanada de lomo 118
pissaladière with black olives............................74
sour-cream, meat loaf wrapped in.................136
pea(s):
fried rice.........................177
mancha manteles............104
pigeon, and rice 156
stir-fried snow, with baby corn and water chestnuts........................178
yellow, soup with bacon 128
pepperpot 161
peppers:
gypsies' sausage with 36
stuffed, with rice and kefalotíri cheese 57
picadillo 102
pie, Spanish pork-filled 118
pigeon peas and rice 156
pimientos, fresh corn soup with.....................103
pissaladière with black olives 74
pizza alla Napoletana 92
plantains, fried..................164
plantation-style seafood-stuffed artichokes 23
poached salmon steaks with mustard sauce...........130
polenta 84
pork:
-filled pie, Spanish..........118
filling, Mexican shredded, burritos with 107
jerked 158
krautwickel......................46
mancha manteles............104
and onion-stuffed beef rolls, Hungarian............35
picadillo 102
with sauerkraut 50
Southern dirty rice..........15
stew, spicy 161

stuffed kohlrabi................32
sweet and sour................166
potato(es):
   cakes, crispy 49
   paprika.............................30
   salad, German warm........41
   Swedish creamed............133
poultry, see chicken
prawns in red sauce.............91
Provençal seasoning mix.......68
pumpkin soup, puréed 155
puréed pumpkin soup 155

Q

quesadillas with
   guacamole...................106
quick callaloo 160

R

raita, cucumber 141
ratatouille 69
red beans and rice with
   ham, Louisiana's 18
red snapper:
   baked, with tomato
     sauce.........................61
   kebabs, Caribbean 163
   Veracruz.......................100
refried beans 109
rice:
   chicken gumbo.................21
   chicken with 114
   fried...............................177
   Louisiana's red beans
     and, with ham.............18
   Mexican green 105
   pigeon peas and 156
   seafood paella 121
   shrimp Creole 14
   Southern dirty 15
   stuffed peppers with
     kefalotíri cheese and 57
Romesco-style sauce,
   chicken with 123

S

salads:
   beet-horseradish 29
   cucumber.......................128
   German warm potato 41
   Greek roasted eggplant ...56
   Greek summer 58
   green beans and tomato
     with Creole mustard
     dressing,......................17
   hearts-of-palm 159

lobster 162
Mexican avocado 99
salmon:
   marinated.......................132
   steaks, poached, with
     mustard sauce.............130
salsa fresca 109
sauces and condiments:
   cucumber raita 141
   Mexican avocado 99
   Mexican chile 110
   Mexican fresh tomato....109
sauerbraten 43
sauerkraut, pork with 50
sausage:
   and chick-pea stew.........116
   gypsies', with peppers 36
   Oktoberfest bratwürst 45
   savory chicken 144
Scandinavian seasoning
   mix 126
seafood, see fish and shellfish
seasoning mixes:
   Caribbean 154
   Chinese 166
   Creole 14
   German..........................40
   Greek.............................54
   Hungarian 28
   Indian...........................140
   Italian............................84
   Mexican 98
   Provençal.......................68
   Scandinavian 126
   Spanish..........................112
sesame noodles, cold.........169
shellfish, see fish and shellfish
shrimp:
   chicken with cashews
     and.............................171
   Creole 14
   plantation-style seafood-
     stuffed artichokes 23
   seafood paella 121
skorthaliá, lamb chops
   with 62
snapper, see red snapper
snow peas, stir-fried, with
   baby corn and water
   chestnuts.......................178
sopa de ajo con huevos 112
sopa de tortilla...................99
soúpa avgolémono 55

soupe au pistou 72
soups:
   caraway, with noodles.....31
   fresh corn, with
     pimientos....................103
   garlic, with poached
     eggs 112
   Greek egg and lemon-
     based 55
   hot and sour.................174
   Mexican tortilla.............99
   minestrone....................85
   mulligatawny 151
   Provençal vegetable
     bean, with basil
     and garlic 72
   puréed pumpkin 155
   quick callaloo 160
   yellow pea, with bacon..128
sour-cream pastry,
   meat loaf
   wrapped in...................136
Southern dirty rice............15
spaghetti alla carbonara.....89
Spanish seasoning mix 112
spiced and breaded
   cauliflower....................31
spinach sauce, beef in
   fragrant 143
stewed lentils 44
stewed okra with hominy ..16
stews:
   Black Forest hunter's.......42
   chicken gumbo...............21
   chick-pea and sausage....116
   Hungarian goulash 34
   Provençal beef
     and wine 75
   Provençal fish, with
     garlic-mayonnaise 79
   spicy pork 161
stir-fried snow peas with
   baby corn and water
   chestnuts.......................178
stuffed:
   cabbage rolls, German.....46
   kohlrabi 32
   peppers with rice and
     kefalotíri cheese 57
   whole crab 20
Swedish creamed
   potatoes 126
Swedish meatballs............126
Swedish-style chicken 129

sweet and sour:
   cabbage with bacon 33
   pork...............................166

T

Tandoori-style chicken 145
tapenade.............................71
tart, Provençal onion 74
tomato(es):
   gratin.............................73
   Greek summer salad 58
   and green beans with Cre-
     ole mustard dressing.....17
   sauce, baked fish with......61
   sauce, Mexican fresh 109
tortilla(s):
   chicken enchiladas with
     mole 101
   quesadillas with
     guacamole...................106
   soup, Mexican 99
tortilla española...............115

V

veal:
   cutlets, German-style 51
   grillades with grits............26
   lasagne............................90
   scaloppine with Marsala..95
   stuffed kohlrabi................32
   Swedish meatballs..........126
vegetable(s):
   bean soup with basil and
     garlic, Provençal............72
   casserole, Greek 60
   ratatouille 69
   see also specific vegetables

W

walnut sauce, chicken
   with 65
water chestnuts, stir-fried
   snow peas with baby
   corn and.......................178
wiener schnitzel 51

Y

yellow pea soup with
   bacon 128
yogurt:
   cucumber raita 141
   cucumber salad 128
   lamb korma 148

Z

zucchini with Parmesan 88